Mirror for Humanity

A CONCISE INTRODUCTION
TO CULTURAL ANTHROPOLOGY

Conrad Phillip Kottak

University of Michigan

Overture Books

McGraw-Hill, Inc.

New York St. Louis San Francisco Auckland Bogotá Caracas
Lisbon London Madrid Mexico City Milan Montreal New Delhi
San Juan Singapore Sydney Tokyo Toronto

To My Daughter
Juliet Kottak Mavromatis

MIRROR FOR HUMANITY
A Concise Introduction to Cultural Anthropology

Copyright ©1996 by McGraw-Hill, Inc. All rights reserved. Adapted from *Cultural Anthropology*, Sixth Edition. Copyright ©1994, 1991, 1987, 1982, 1979, 1978, 1975, 1974 by McGraw-Hill, Inc. All rights reserved. Printed in the United States of America. Except as permitted under the United States Copyright Act of 1976, no part of this publication may be reproduced or distributed in any form or by any means, or stored in a data base or retrieval system, without the prior written permission of the publisher.

Photo Credits appear on pages 297–299, and on this page by reference.

This book is printed on acid-free paper.

5 6 7 8 9 0   DOC   DOC   9 0 9 8 7

ISBN 0-07-035783-8

This book was set in Janson by Ruttle, Shaw & Wetherill, Inc.
R. R. Donnelley & Sons Company was printer and binder.

Sponsoring Editor: Jill S. Gordon
Editing Supervisor: Linda Richmond
Designer: Wanda Siedlecka
Photo Editor: Barbara Salz
Production Supervisor: Kathryn Porzio
Cover Photo: Hiroji Kubota/Magnum

Library of Congress Cataloging-in-Publication Data

Kottak, Conrad Phillip.
    Mirror for humanity: a concise introduction to cultural
  anthropology / Conrad Phillip Kottak.
       p.   cm.
    Includes bibliographical references and index.
    ISBN 0-07-035783-8
    1. Ethnology.   I. Title.
  GN316.K66   1996
  306—dc20   95-15382

About the Author

Conrad Phillip Kottak (A.B. Columbia, 1963; Ph.D. Columbia, 1966) is Professor and Chair of Anthropology at the University of Michigan, where he has taught since 1968. In 1991 he was honored for his teaching by the University and the state of Michigan. In 1992 he received an excellence in teaching award from the College of Literature, Sciences, and the Arts of the University of Michigan.

Professor Kottak has done field work in cultural anthropology in Brazil (since 1962), Madagascar (since 1966), and the United States. His general interests are in the processes by which local cultures are incorporated into larger systems. This interest links his earlier work on ecology and state formation in Africa and Madagascar to his more recent research on global change, national and international culture, and the mass media.

The second edition of Kottak's case study *Assault on Paradise: Social Change in a Brazilian Village,* based on his field work in Arembepe, Bahia, Brazil, from 1962 through 1992, was published in 1992 by McGraw-Hill. In a project during the 1980s, collaborating with Brazilian and North American researchers, Kottak blended ethnography and survey research in studying "Television's Behavioral Effects in Brazil." That research is the basis of Kottak's book *Prime-Time Society: An Anthropological Analysis of Television and Culture* (Wadsworth 1990)—a comparative study of the nature and impact of television in Brazil and the United States.

Kottak's other books include *The Past in the Present: History, Ecology and Cultural Variation in Highland Madagascar* (1980), *Researching American Culture: A Guide for Student Anthropologists* (1982) (both University of Michigan Press) and *Madagascar: Society and History* (1986) (Carolina Academic Press). Six editions of Kottak's texts *Anthropology: The Exploration of Human Diversity* and *Cultural Anthropology* were published by McGraw-Hill in 1994.

Conrad Kottak's articles have appeared in academic journals including *American Anthropologist, Journal of Anthropological Research, American Ethnologist, Ethnology, Human Organization,* and *Luso-Brazilian Review.* He has also written for more popular journals, including *Transaction/SOCIETY, Natural History, Psychology Today,* and *General Anthropology.*

In current and recent research projects, Kottak and his colleagues have investigated the emergence of ecological awareness in Brazil, the social context of deforestation in Madagascar, and popular participation in economic development planning in northeastern Brazil.

Conrad Kottak appreciates comments about his textbook from professors and students. He can be readily reached by e-mail at the following internet address:

ckottak@umich.edu

Ordinarily we are unaware of the special lens through which we look at life. It would hardly be fish who discovered the existence of water. Students who had not yet gone beyond the horizon of their own society could not be expected to perceive custom which was the stuff of their own thinking. *Anthropology holds up a great mirror to man and lets him look at himself in his infinite variety.*

(Kluckhohn 1944, p. 16—his emphasis)

Contents in Brief

Contents

CHAPTER ELEVEN: The World System, Industrialism, and Stratification — 206

CHAPTER TWELVE: Applied Anthropology — 223

CHAPTER THIRTEEN: Development and Innovation — 237

MFH has four important chapters not consistently found in cultural anthropology texts: Ethnicity and Ethnic Relations (3), The Cultural Construction of Race (4), Gender (10), and Cultural Exchange and Survival (14). These and other chapters explore the nature, role, and preservation of human diversity in the face of globalization. I recognize and try to show how linkages in the modern world system have both enlarged and erased old boundaries and distinctions as described in standard anthropology textbooks. People travel more than ever, but migrants maintain their ties with home, so that they live multilocally. With so many people "in motion," the unit of anthropological study expands from the local community to the transnational diaspora.

In considering ethnic and national cultural identities, Chapter 3 examines multiculturalism in North America and the revival of ethnic expression and conflict in eastern Europe and the former Soviet Union. Chapter 14 focuses on issues of cultural exchange and survival in a global culture driven by flows of people, technology, finance, images, information, and ideology. Different degrees of destruction, domination, resistance, survival, adaptation, and modification of native cultures have followed contact between cultures and ethnic groups. Indigenous peoples have devised various strategies to resist attacks on their autonomy, identity, and livelihood. New forms of political mobilization and cultural expression have emerged from the interplay of local, regional, national, and international cultural forces.

I am pleased to have been one of the textbook authors chosen to participate in the **Gender in the Curriculum** Project of the American Anthropological Association. In that project I was paired with Yolanda Moses, who commented extensively on, and met with me to discuss, the treatment of gender issues in my texts *Anthropology: The Exploration of Human Diversity* and *Cultural Anthropology*. The lessons I learned have also been incorporated in MFH, in which gender issues are the focus of a separate chapter (10) but are also considered throughout the text.

*****

Pedagogy: MFH incorporates suggestions made by users of my other texts and pre-publication reviewers of this one. The result, I hope, is a sound, well-organized, interesting, and "user-friendly" introduction to cultural anthropology.

MFH contains several **issues boxes**, intended to give students a chance to consider anthropology's relevance to today's multicultural world and to their own lives. Some boxes examine current events or debates. Others are personal accounts of field experiences, which add human feeling to the presentation of cultural anthropology's subject matter. Many boxes illustrate a point by bringing in an example familiar to students from their enculturation or everyday experience.

A **glossary** defining terms boldfaced in each chapter is found at the end of the book, along with a **bibliography** of references cited.

Available for use with MFH is an **ethnographic case studies** book *Culture*

Sketches by Holly Peters-Golden. This supplement profiles several of the cultures discussed in MFH. Dr. Peters-Golden has taught introductory anthropology at the University of Michigan, using my textbook, for several years.

ACKNOWLEDGMENTS

I am grateful to many present and past colleagues at McGraw-Hill. I thank Jill Gordon, McGraw-Hill's anthropology editor, for her support and input. Sylvia Shepard, my former developmental editor, will also recognize her contribution, especially in helping me conceptualize Chapters 3 and 14. Lori Pearson, a previous anthropology editor at McGraw-Hill, helped me develop the idea of this book; I appreciate her enthusiasm. I continue to enjoy working with Phil Butcher, McGraw-Hill's social science publisher.

I thank Linda Richmond for her efficient work as editing supervisor and for keeping everything moving on schedule. It's been a pleasure to work again with Barbara Salz, photo researcher, and Kathy Bendo, photo manager. I also thank Mary Louise Byrd, for her copyediting; Joan O'Connor, for conceiving and executing the design; Kathryn Porzio, for shepherding the manuscript through production; and Lesley Denton, marketing project manager.

I am grateful to the following pre-publication reviewers: Alice James, Penn State University; Terry L. Reuther, Anoka-Ramsey Community College; Charles F. Urbanowicz, California State University–Chico; and Norman Whitten, University of Illinois–Urbana. I was delighted by the enthusiasm expressed in their reviews.

I thank all the colleagues and students who have used my other texts and who have sent me their comments, corrections, and suggestions—personally, through McGraw-Hill sales representatives, and via e-mail. Anyone—student or instructor—with access to e-mail (internet) can send me messages and suggestions at the following address: **ckottak@umich.edu**

As usual, my family has offered me understanding, support, and inspiration during the preparation of *Mirror for Humanity*. I dedicate this book to my daughter, Juliet Kottak Mavromatis, M.D., who continues our family tradition of exploring human diversity and diagnosing and treating the human condition.

After 27 years of teaching, I have benefitted from the knowledge, help, and advice of so many friends, colleagues, teaching assistants, and students that I can no longer fit their names into a short preface. I hope they know who they are and accept my thanks.

Annually since 1968 I've taught Anthropology 101 (Introduction to Anthropology) to a class of 500-600 students, with the help of 7-12 teaching assistants each time. Feedback from students and teaching assistants keeps me up-to-date on the interests, needs, and views of the people for whom MFH is written. I continue to believe that effective textbooks have to be based in enthusiasm and in practice—in the enjoyment of one's own teaching experience. I hope that this product of my experience will be helpful to others.

Conrad Phillip Kottak

CHAPTER ONE

The Exploration of Cultural Diversity

HUMAN DIVERSITY

GENERAL ANTHROPOLOGY

RESEARCH METHODS

ETHNOGRAPHY: ANTHROPOLOGY'S DISTINCTIVE STRATEGY

ETHNOGRAPHIC TECHNIQUES
Observation ~ Participant Observation ~ Conversation, Interviewing,
and Interview Schedules ~ The Genealogical Method ~ Well-Informed
Informants ~ BOX: The Evolution of Ethnography ~ Life Histories ~ Emic
and Etic Research Strategies ~ Problem-Oriented Ethnography ~
Longitudinal Research

SURVEY RESEARCH

ANTHROPOLOGICAL RESEARCH IN COMPLEX SOCIETIES
Research Methods for Complex Societies

hat's just human nature." "People are pretty much the same all over the world." Such opinions, which we hear in conversations, in the mass media, and in a hundred scenes in daily life, promote the erroneous idea that people in other countries have the same desires, feelings, values, and aspirations that we do. Such statements proclaim that because people are essentially the same, they are eager to receive the ideas, beliefs, institutions, practices, and products of an expansive North American culture. Often this assumption turns out to be wrong.

Anthropology offers a broader view—a distinctive comparative, cross-cultural perspective. Most people think that anthropologists study nonindustrial cultures, and they do. My research has taken me to remote villages in Brazil and Madagascar, a large island off the southeast coast of Africa. In Brazil I sailed with fishermen in simple sailboats on Atlantic waters. Among Madagascar's Betsileo people I worked in rice fields and took part in ceremonies in which I entered tombs to rewrap the corpses of decaying ancestors.

However, anthropology is much more than the study of nonindustrial peoples.

1

It is a comparative science that examines all societies, ancient and modern, simple and complex. Most of the other social sciences tend to focus on a single society, usually an industrial nation such as the United States or Canada. Anthropology, however, offers a unique cross-cultural perspective, constantly comparing the customs of one society with those of others.

To become a cultural anthropologist, one normally does **ethnography** (the firsthand, personal study of local settings). Ethnographic fieldwork usually entails spending a year or more in another culture, living with the local people and learning about their customs. No matter how much the ethnographer discovers about that culture, he or she remains an alien there. That experience of alienation has a profound impact. Having learned to respect other customs and beliefs, anthropologists can never forget that there is a wider world. There are normal ways of thinking and acting other than our own.

HUMAN DIVERSITY

Humans are the most adaptable animals in the world. In the Andes of South America, people awaken in villages 17,500 feet above sea level and then trek 1,500 feet higher to work in tin mines. Tribes in the Australian desert worship animals and discuss philosophy. People survive malaria in the tropics. Men have walked on the moon. The model of the *Starship Enterprise* in Washington's Smithsonian Institution symbolizes the desire to seek out new life and civilizations, to boldly go where no one has gone before. Wishes to know the unknown, control the uncontrollable, and bring order to chaos find expression among all peoples. Flexibility and adaptability are basic human attributes, and human diversity is the subject matter of anthropology.

Students are often surprised by the breadth of anthropology, which is a uniquely **holistic** science. It studies the whole of the human condition: past, present, and future; biology, society, language, and culture. People share **society**—organized life in groups—with other animals. Culture, however, is distinctly human. **Cultures** are traditions and customs, transmitted through learning, that govern the beliefs and behavior of the people exposed to them. Children *learn* these traditions by growing up in a particular society.

Cultural traditions include customs and opinions, developed over the generations, about proper and improper behavior. Cultural traditions answer such questions as: How should we do things? How do we interpret the world? How do we tell right from wrong? A culture produces consistencies in behavior and thought in a given society.

The most critical element of cultural traditions is their transmission through learning rather than biological inheritance. Culture is not itself biological, but it rests on hominid biology. (**Hominids** are members of the zoological family that includes fossil and living humans.) Human **adaptation** (the process by which organisms cope with environmental stresses) involves an interplay between culture and biology; and for more than a million years, hominids have had at least some of the biological capacities on which culture depends. These abilities are to learn, to think symbolically, to use language, and to employ tools and other cultural features in organizing their lives and adapting to their environments.

GENERAL ANTHROPOLOGY

The academic discipline of anthropology, also known as **general anthropology,** includes four main subdisciplines: sociocultural, archeological, biological, and linguistic anthropology. (From here on, I will use the shorter term *cultural anthropology* as a synonym for "sociocultural anthropology," the subject of this book.) Most American anthropologists, myself included, specialize in cultural anthropology. However, most are also familiar with the basics of the other subdisciplines. Major departments of anthropology usually include representatives of each.

There are historical reasons for the inclusion of four subdisciplines in a single field. American anthropology arose a century ago out of concern for the history and cultures of the native populations of North America ("American Indians"). Interest in the origins and diversity of Native Americans brought together studies of customs, social life, language, and physical traits. Such a unified anthropology did not develop in Europe, where the subdisciplines tend to exist separately.

There are also logical reasons for the unity of American anthropology. Each subdiscipline considers variations in time and space (that is, in different geographic areas). Cultural and archeological anthropologists study (among many other topics) changes in social life and customs. Biological anthropologists examine changes in physical characteristics. Linguistic anthropologists may reconstruct the basics of ancient languages by studying modern ones.

The subdisciplines influence each other as anthropologists talk, read professional books and journals, and associate in professional organizations. General anthropology explores the basics of human biology, psychology, society, and culture and considers their interrelationships. Anthropologists share certain key assumptions. One is that sound conclusions about "human nature" can't be drawn from a single cultural tradition.

We often hear "nature-nurture" and "genetics-environment" questions. For example, consider gender differences. Do male and female capacities, attitudes, and behavior reflect biological or cultural variation? Are there universal emotional and intellectual contrasts between the sexes? Are females less aggressive than males? Is male dominance a human universal? By examining diverse cultures, anthropology shows that many contrasts between men and women arise from cultural learning rather than from biology.

Anthropology is not a science of the exotic carried on by scholars in ivory towers but a discipline with a lot to tell the public. One of its contributions is its broad-

Cross-cultural comparison shows that many differences between the
sexes arise from cultural learning rather than biology. Here men in
Kenya do the laundry in the river.

ening, liberating role in a college education. Anthropology's foremost professional
organization, the American Anthropological Association, has formally acknowl-
edged a public service role by recognizing a fifth subdiscipline, **applied anthropology**—the application of anthropological data, perspectives, theory, and methods to
identify, assess, and solve contemporary social problems. More and more anthropologists from the four main subdisciplines now work in such "applied" areas as public
health, family planning, and economic development.

RESEARCH METHODS

Cultural anthropology and sociology share an interest in social relations, organization, and behavior. However, important differences between these disciplines arose
from the kinds of societies each traditionally studied. Initially sociologists focused
on the industrial West; anthropologists, on nonindustrial societies. Different methods of data collection and analysis emerged to deal with those different kinds of societies. To study large-scale, complex nations, sociologists came to rely on questionnaires and other means of gathering masses of quantifiable data. For many years
sampling and statistical techniques have been basic to sociology, whereas statistical
training has been less common in anthropology (although this is changing as anthropologists increasingly work in modern nations).

Traditional ethnographers studied small, nonliterate (without writing) populations and relied on ethnographic methods appropriate to that context. "Ethnography is a research process in which the anthropologist closely observes, records, and engages in the daily life of another culture—an experience labeled as the fieldwork method—and then writes accounts of this culture, emphasizing descriptive detail" (Marcus and Fischer 1986, p. 18). One key method described in this quote is **participant observation**—taking part in the events one is observing, describing, and analyzing.

Anthropology started to separate from sociology around the turn of the twentieth century. Early students of society, such as the French scholar Émile Durkheim, were among the founders of both sociology and anthropology. Comparing the organization of simple and complex societies, Durkheim studied the religions of Native Australians (Durkheim 1912/1961), as well as mass phenomena (such as suicide rates) in modern nations (Durkheim 1897/1951). Eventually anthropology would specialize in the former, sociology in the latter.

ETHNOGRAPHY: ANTHROPOLOGY'S DISTINCTIVE STRATEGY

Anthropology developed into a separate field as early scholars worked on Indian (Native American) reservations and traveled to distant lands to study small groups of foragers (hunters and gatherers) and cultivators. Traditionally, the process of becoming a cultural anthropologist has required a field experience in another society. Early ethnographers lived in small-scale, relatively isolated societies, with simple technologies and economies.

Ethnography thus emerged as a research strategy in societies with greater cultural uniformity and less social differentiation than are found in large, modern, industrial nations. In such nonindustrial settings, ethnographers have needed to consider fewer paths of enculturation to understand social life. Traditionally, ethnographers have tried to understand the whole of an alien culture (or, more realistically, as much as they can, given limitations of time and perception). To pursue this holistic goal, ethnographers adopt a free-ranging strategy for gathering information. They move from setting to setting, place to place, and subject to subject to discover the totality and interconnectedness of social life.

Ethnography provides an "ethnopicture" of a particular group, society, or culture. During ethnographic fieldwork, the ethnographer gathers data, which he or she organizes, describes, analyzes, and interprets to build and present the *ethnopicture* (e.g., a book, an article, or a film). Ethnography, by expanding our knowledge of the range of human diversity, provides a foundation for generalizations about human behavior and social life. Ethnographers draw on varied techniques to piece together a picture of otherwise alien lifestyles. Anthropologists usually employ several (but rarely all) of the techniques discussed here.

ETHNOGRAPHIC TECHNIQUES

The characteristic *field techniques* of the ethnographer include the following:

1. Direct, firsthand observation of daily behavior, including *participant observation*
2. Conversation with varying degrees of formality, from the daily chitchat that helps maintain rapport and provides knowledge about what is going on to prolonged *interviews*, which can be unstructured or structured
3. *Interview schedules* to ensure that complete, comparable information is available for everyone of interest to the study
4. The *genealogical method*
5. Detailed work with *well-informed informants* about particular areas of community life
6. In-depth interviewing, often leading to the collection of *life histories* of particular people
7. *Emic* (actor-oriented) research strategies that focus on local (native) beliefs and perceptions and *etic* (observer-oriented) approaches that give priority to the ethnographer's perceptions and conclusions
8. Problem-oriented research of many sorts
9. Longitudinal research—the continuous long-term study of an area or a site

Observation

Ethnographers must pay attention to hundreds of details of daily life, seasonal events, and unusual happenings. They must observe individual and collective behavior in varied settings. They should record what they see as they see it. Things will never seem quite as strange as they do during the first few days and weeks in the field. The ethnographer eventually gets used to, and accepts as normal, cultural patterns that were initially alien.

Many ethnographers record their impressions in a personal *diary*, which is kept separate from more formal *field notes*. Later, this record of early impressions will help point out some of the most basic aspects of cultural diversity. Such aspects include distinctive smells, noises people make, how they cover their mouths when they eat, and how they gaze at others. These patterns, which are so basic as to seem almost trivial, are part of what Bronislaw Malinowski called "the imponderabilia of native life and of typical behavior" (Malinowski 1922/1961, p. 20). These features of culture are so fundamental that natives take them for granted. They are too basic even to talk about, but the unaccustomed eye of the fledgling anthropologist perceives them. Thereafter they are submerged in familiarity and fade to the periphery of consciousness. This is why initial impressions are valuable and should be recorded. First and foremost, ethnographers should be accurate observers, recorders, and reporters of what they see in the field.

Participant Observation

Ethnographers don't study animals in laboratory cages. The experiments that psychologists do with pigeons, chickens, guinea pigs, and rats are very different from ethnographic procedure. Anthropologists don't systematically control subjects' rewards and punishments or their exposure to certain stimuli. Our subjects are not speechless animals but human beings. It is not part of ethnographic procedure to manipulate them, control their environments, or experimentally induce certain behaviors.

One of ethnography's characteristic procedures is *participant observation*, which means that we take part in community life as we study it. As human beings living among others, we cannot be totally impartial and detached observers. We must also take part in many of the events and processes we are observing and trying to comprehend.

In Arembepe, Bahia state, Brazil, I sailed on the Atlantic in simple boats with

Ethnographers strive to establish rapport—a good, friendly relationship based on personal contact—with informants. These women in Guatemala are pleased with this anthropologist's gift—photos of themselves.

Brazilian fishermen. I gave Jeep rides into the capital to malnourished babies, to pregnant mothers, and once to a teenage girl possessed by a spirit. All those people needed to consult specialists outside the village. I danced on Arembepe's festive occasions, drank foul-tasting libations commemorating new births, and became a godfather to a village girl. Most anthropologists have similar field experiences. The common humanity of the student and the studied, the ethnographer and the researched community, makes participant observation inevitable.

Conversation, Interviewing, and Interview Schedules

Participating in local life means that ethnographers constantly talk to people and ask questions about what they observe. As their knowledge of the native language increases, they understand more. There are several stages in learning a field language. First is the naming phase—asking name after name of the objects around us. Later we are able to pose more complex questions and understand the replies. We begin to understand simple conversations between two villagers, and if our language expertise proceeds far enough, we eventually become able to comprehend rapid-fire public discussions and group conversations.

One data-gathering technique I have used in both Arembepe and Madagascar involves an ethnographic survey that includes an interview schedule. In 1964, my fellow fieldworkers and I attempted to complete an interview schedule in each of Arembepe's 160 households. We entered almost every household (fewer than 5 percent refused to participate) to ask a set of questions on a printed form.

Our results provided us with a census and basic information about the village. We wrote down the name, age, and sex of each household member. We gathered data on family type, political party, religion, present and previous jobs, income, expenditures, diet, possessions, and many other items on our eight-page form.

Although we were doing a survey, our approach differed from the survey research design (see below) routinely used by sociologists and other social scientists working in large, populous, industrial nations. That survey research involves sampling (choosing a small, manageable study group from a larger population) and impersonal data collection. We did not select a partial sample from the total population. Instead, we tried to interview in all households in the community we were studying (that is, to have a total sample). We used an interview schedule rather than a questionnaire. With the **interview schedule**, the ethnographer talks face to face with informants, asks the questions, and writes down the answers. **Questionnaire** procedures tend to be more indirect and impersonal; the respondent often fills in the form.

Our goal of getting a total sample allowed us to meet almost everyone in the village and helped us establish rapport. Arembepeiros still talk warmly about how, three decades ago, we were interested enough in them to visit their homes and ask them questions. We stood in sharp contrast to the other outsiders the Arembepeiros had known who considered them too poor and backward to be taken seriously.

Like other survey research, however, our interview-schedule survey did gather comparable quantifiable information. It gave us a basis for assessing patterns and exceptions in village life. Our home visits also provided opportunities to do informal and follow-up interviewing. Our schedules included a core set of questions that were posed to everyone. However, some interesting side issues often came up during the interview.

We would pursue these leads into many dimensions of village life. One woman, for instance, a mid-wife, became the "well-informed informant" we consulted later, when we wanted detailed information about local childbirth. Another woman had done an internship at an Afro-Brazilian cult (*candomblé*) house in the city. She still went there regularly to study, dance, and get possessed. She became our *candomblé* expert.

Thus, our interview-schedule survey provided a structure that *directed but did not confine* us as researchers. It enabled our ethnography to be both quantitative and qualitative. The quantitative part consisted of the basic information we gathered and later analyzed statistically. The qualitative dimension came from our follow-up questions, open-ended discussions, pauses for gossip, and work with well-informed informants.

The Genealogical Method

Another ethnographic technique is the **genealogical method.** Early ethnographers developed genealogical notation to deal with principles of kinship, descent, and marriage, which are the social building blocks of nonindustrial cultures. In contemporary North America most of our contacts outside the home are with nonrelatives. However, people in nonindustrial cultures spend their lives almost exclusively with relatives. Anthropologists must record genealogical data to reconstruct history and understand current relationships. In societies without a central government, these links have been basic to social life and to political organization. Anthropologists even classify such societies as **kin-based.** Everyone is related to, and spends most of his or her time with, everyone else, and rules of behavior attached to particular kin relationships are basic to everyday life. Marriage is also crucial in organizing nonindustrial societies because strategic marriages between villages, tribes, and clans create political alliances.

Well-Informed Informants

Every community has people who by accident, experience, talent, or training can provide the most complete or useful information about particular aspects of life. These people are **well-informed informants.** In Ivato, Madagascar, the Betsileo village where I spent most of my time, a man named Rakoto was a particularly good informant about village history. However, when I asked him to work with me on a genealogy of the fifty to sixty people buried in the village tomb, he called in his

The Evolution of Ethnography

The Polish anthropologist Bronislaw Malinowski (1884–1942), who spent most of his professional life in England, is generally considered the father of ethnography. Like most anthropologists of his time, Malinowski did *salvage ethnography*, in the belief that the ethnographer's job is to study and record cultural diversity threatened by westernization. Early ethnographic accounts (*ethnographies*), including Malinowski's classic *Argonauts of the Western Pacific* (1922/1961), were similar to earlier traveler and explorer accounts in describing the writer's discovery of unknown people and places. However, the *scientific* aims of ethnographies set them apart from books by explorers and amateurs.

The style that dominated "classic" ethnographies was *ethnographic realism*. The writer's goal was to present an accurate, objective, scientific account of a different way of life, written by someone who knew it firsthand. This knowledge came from an "ethnographic adventure" involving immersion in an alien language and culture. Ethnographers derived their authority—both as scientists and as voices of "the native" or "the other"—from this personal research experience.

Malinowski wrote *functionalist* ethnographies, guided by the assumption that all aspects of culture are linked (functions of each other). A functionalist ethnography begins with *any* aspect of a culture, such as a Trobriand Islands sailing expedition. The ethnographer then follows the links between that entry point and other areas of the culture, such as magic, religion, myths, kinship, and trade. Contemporary ethnographies tend to be less inclusive, focusing on particular topics, such as kinship or religion.

According to Malinowski, a primary task of the ethnographer is "to grasp the native's point of view, his relation to life, to realize *his* vision of *his* world (1922/1961, p. 25—Malinowski's italics). Since the 1970s, *interpretive anthropology* has considered the task of describing and interpreting that which is meaningful to natives. Interpretivists such as Clifford Geertz (1973) view cultures as meaningful texts which natives constantly "read" and which ethnographers must decipher. According to Geertz, anthropologists may choose anything in a culture that interests them, fill in details, and elaborate to inform their readers about meanings in that culture. Meanings are carried by public symbolic forms, including words, rituals, and customs. In the interpretive view, cross-cultural understanding emerges through "dialogues" between natives, anthropologist, and reader, who are all parties to a conversation.

A current trend in ethnographic writing is to question traditional goals, methods, and styles, including salvage ethnography and ethnographic realism (Marcus and Cushman 1982; Clifford 1982, 1988). Marcus and Fischer argue that anthropology has reached "an experimental moment." Experimentation is needed because all people and cultures have already been "discovered" and must now be "*re*discovered . . . in changing historical circumstances" (1986, p. 24).

These experimental anthropologists recognize that ethnographies are works of art as well as works of science. Ethnographic texts are literary creations in which the ethnographer, as mediator, communicates information from the "natives" to readers. Some recent experimental ethnographies are "dialogic," presenting ethnography as a dialogue between the anthropologist and one or more native informants (e.g., Dwyer 1982). These works draw attention to ways in which ethnographers, and by extension their readers, communicate with other cultures.

Ethnographers interpret and mediate between cultures in two ways. During fieldwork they must interpret from native categories to their own, and in writing they must interpret for their readers. However, some dialogic ethnographies have been criticized as being too confessional, spending too much time on the anthropologist and too little on the natives and their culture.

The dialogic ethnography is one genre within a larger experimental category—*reflexive ethnography*. Here the ethnographer-writer puts his of her personal feelings and reactions to the field situation right in the text. An experimental writing strategy is prominent in reflexive accounts. The ethnographer may adopt some of the conventions of the novel, including first-person narration, conversations, dialogues, and humor.

Marcus and Fischer (1986) caution that the desire to be personal can be overplayed to the point of exhibitionism. Nevertheless, experimental ethnographies, using new ways of showing what it means to be a Samoan or a Brazilian, may convey to the reader a richer and more complex understanding of human experience. The result may be to convince readers that culture matters more than they might otherwise have thought.

Recent ethnographic writers have also attempted to correct the deficiency of *romanticized timelessness*, which is obvious in the classics. Linked to salvage ethnography was the idea of the *ethnographic present*—the period before westernization, when the "true" native culture flourished. This notion gives classic ethnographies an eternal, timeless quality. The cultures they describe seem frozen in the ethnographic present. Providing the only jarring note in this idealized picture are occasional comments by the author about traders or missionaries, suggesting that in actuality the natives were already part of the world system.

Anthropologists now recognize that the ethnographic present is a rather unrealistic and romantic construct. Cultures have been in contact—and have been changing—throughout history. Most native cultures had at least one major foreign encounter before any anthropologist ever came their way. Most of them had already been incorporated in some fashion into nation-states or colonial systems.

The classic ethnographies neglected history, politics, and the world system, but contemporary ethnographies usually recognize that cultures constantly change and that an ethnographic account applies to a particular moment. A current trend in ethnography is to focus on the ways in which cultural ideas serve political and economic interests. Another trend is to describe how particular "natives" participate in broader historical, political, and economic processes (Shostak 1981).

cousin Tuesdaysfather, who knew more about this subject. Tuesdaysfather had survived an epidemic of Spanish influenza that ravaged Madagascar, along with much of the world, around 1919. Immune to the disease himself, Tuesdaysfather had the grim job of burying his kin as they died. He kept track of everyone buried in the tomb. Tuesdaysfather helped me with the tomb genealogy. Rakoto joined him in telling me personal details about the deceased villagers.

Life Histories

In nonindustrial societies as in our own, individual personalities, interests, and abilities vary. Some villagers prove to be more interested in the ethnographer's work and are more helpful, interesting, and pleasant than others. Anthropologists develop likes and dislikes in the field as we do at home. Often, when we find someone unusually interesting, we collect his or her **life history.** This recollection of a lifetime of experiences provides a more intimate and personal cultural portrait than would be possible otherwise. Life histories reveal how specific people perceive, react to, and contribute to changes that affect their lives. Such accounts can illustrate diversity, which exists within any community, since the focus is on how different people interpret and deal with some of the same problems.

All communities have well-informed informants, natives
who can provide the best information about particular
areas of life. Here the researcher (right) collects folklore
from a well-informed informant.

Emic and Etic Research Strategies

To study cultures, anthropologists have used two approaches, emic (actor-oriented)
and etic (observer-oriented). An **emic** approach investigates how natives (or one native, in the case of a life history) think. How do they perceive and categorize the
world? What are their rules for behavior and thought? What has meaning for them?
How do they imagine and explain things? The anthropologist seeks the "native
viewpoint" and relies on the culture bearers—the actors in a culture—to determine
whether something they do, say, or think is significant.

However, natives aren't scientists. They may think that spirits cause illnesses
that come from germs. They may believe political leaders who tell them that mis-
siles are peacemakers. The **etic** (observer-oriented) approach shifts the focus of research from native categories, expressions, explanations, and interpretations to those

of the anthropologist. The etic approach realizes that culture bearers are often too involved in what they are doing to interpret their cultures impartially. The etic ethnographer gives more weight to what he or she (the observer) notices and considers important. As a trained scientist, the anthropologist should try to bring an objective and comprehensive viewpoint to the study of other cultures. Of course, the anthropologist, like any other scientist, is also a human being with cultural blinders that prevent complete objectivity. As in other sciences, proper training can reduce but not totally eliminate the observer's bias. But anthropologists do have special training to compare behavior among different societies.

In practice, most anthropologists combine emic and etic strategies in their fieldwork. Native statements, perceptions, and opinions help ethnographers understand how cultures work. Native beliefs are also interesting and valuable in themselves and broaden the anthropologist's view of the world. However, natives often fail to admit, or even recognize, certain causes and consequences of their behavior. This is as true of North Americans as it is of people in any other society. To describe and interpret culture, ethnographers should recognize the biases that come from their own culture as well as those of the people being studied.

Problem-Oriented Ethnography

Although anthropologists are interested in the whole context of human behavior, it is impossible to study everything, and field research usually addresses specific questions. Most ethnographers enter the field with a specific problem to investigate, and they collect data about variables deemed relevant to that problem. And informants' answers to questions are not the only data source. Anthropologists also gather information on factors like population density, environmental quality, climate, physical geography, diet, and land use. Sometimes this involves direct measurement—of rainfall, temperature, fields, yields, dietary quantities, or time allocation (Bailey 1990; Johnson 1978). Often it means that we consult government records or archives.

The information of interest to ethnographers is not limited to what informants can and do tell us. For much that is significant we can rely neither on participant observation nor intensive local interviews. In an increasingly interconnected world, local informants lack knowledge about many factors (regional, national, and international) that affect their lives.

Longitudinal Research

Geography limits anthropologists less now than in the past, when it could take months to reach a field site, and return visits were rare. New systems of transportation allow anthropologists to widen the area of their research and to return repeatedly. Ethnographic reports now routinely include data from two or more field stays.

Longitudinal research is the long-term study of a community, region, society, culture, or other unit, usually based on repeated visits.

One example of such research is the longitudinal study of the interplay of social and economic forces in Gwembe District, Zambia. This study, planned in 1956 as a longitudinal project by Elizabeth Colson and Thayer Scudder, continues with Colson, Scudder, and their associates of various nationalities. The Gwembe research project is both longitudinal (multitime) and multisite (considering several local field sites), because no single village or neighborhood could adequately represent Gwembe's diversity (Colson and Scudder 1975; Scudder and Colson 1980). Four villages, in different areas, have been followed for four decades. Periodic village censuses (1956–57, 1962–63, 1965, 1972–73, 1981–82, and 1987–88) provide basic data on population, economy, and other variables chosen to monitor changes in kinship and religious behavior. Censused people who have moved are traced and interviewed (if possible) to see how their lives compare with those of people who have stayed in the village. Information on labor migration, visits between town and country, and other linkages show the extent to which rural and urban belong to a single system.

Successively different questions have come to the fore, while basic data on communities and individuals continue to be collected. The first focus of study was the impact of a large hydroelectric dam, which flooded much of the Zambezi River plain and subjected the Gwembe people to forced resettlement. By the late 1960s, education had become a major concern at Gwembe and was playing an important role in changes then taking place. Accordingly, Scudder and Colson (1980) designed research to examine the role of education in providing access to new opportunities and in increasing social differentiation within the district and nation.

SURVEY RESEARCH

As anthropologists work increasingly in large-scale societies, they have developed innovative ways of blending ethnography and survey research (Fricke 1994). Before considering such combinations of field methods, I must describe survey research and the main differences between survey research and ethnography as traditionally practiced. Working mainly in large, populous nations, sociologists, social psychologists, political scientists, and economists have developed and refined the **survey research** design, which involves sampling, impersonal data collection, and statistical analysis. Survey research usually draws a **sample** (a manageable study group) from a much larger population. By studying a properly selected and representative sample, social scientists can make accurate inferences about the larger population.

In smaller-scale societies, ethnographers get to know most of the people, but given the greater size and complexity of nations, survey research cannot help being more impersonal. Survey researchers call the people they study **respondents.**

For research in large, populous nations, sociologists, social psychologists, and political scientists have developed and refined survey research, which is indispensable for the scientific study of such societies. A typical social survey relies on sampling, questionnaires, and statistical analysis. Survey research is also used in political polling and market research, as in this photo.

(Ethnographers work with **informants.**) Respondents are people who respond to questions during a survey. Sometimes survey researchers personally interview them. Sometimes, after an initial meeting, they ask respondents to fill out a questionnaire. In other cases researchers mail printed questionnaires to randomly selected sample members or have graduate students interview or telephone them. (In a **random sample,** all members of the population have an equal statistical chance of being chosen for inclusion. A random sample is selected by randomizing procedures, such as tables of random numbers, which are found in many statistics textbooks.)

Anyone who has grown up recently in the United States or Canada has heard of sampling. Probably the most familiar example is the polling used to predict political races. The media hire agencies to estimate outcomes and do exit polls to find out what kinds of people voted for which candidates. During sampling, researchers gather information about age, gender, religion, occupation, income, and political party preference. These characteristics (**variables**—attributes that vary among members of a sample or population) are known to influence political decisions.

Many more variables affect social identities, experiences, and activities in a modern nation than is the case in the small communities and local settings where ethnography grew up. In the contemporary United States or Canada hundreds of factors influence social behavior and attitudes. These social predictors include our religion; the region of the country we grew up in; whether we come from a town, a suburb, or an inner city; and our parents' professions, ethnic origins, and income levels.

ANTHROPOLOGICAL RESEARCH IN COMPLEX SOCIETIES

During World War I the anthropologist Bronislaw Malinowski spent several years studying the Trobriand Islanders. In his classic ethnographic **monograph** (a report based on ethnographic fieldwork) *Argonauts of the Western Pacific*, Malinowski describes how an ethnographer "sets up shop" in another society. Like Malinowski's research in the Trobriands, my fieldwork in Arembepe focused on a single community as the object of intensive study. I could get to know everyone in Arembepe because its population was small and its social system was uncomplicated. However, unlike the Trobriands, Arembepe was not a tribal society but part of a large, populous, and diverse nation. The Trobriand Islands are small enough for an ethnographer to visit every village. Malinowski might well have managed to talk with every Trobriander. I could never hope to visit every Brazilian community or meet every Brazilian.

Malinowski used his field site as a basis for describing Trobriand society as a whole. Anthropologists have been criticized for generalizing about an entire culture on the basis of research in just one community, a practice which is somewhat more defensible for small-scale, homogeneous societies than for complex nations. My study of Arembepe, a rural community in a particular region of an urbanized nation, could never encapsulate Brazil as a whole. Thus I viewed my Arembepe field study as part of a larger research program. I was just one ethnographer among many, each working separately in different Brazilian communities. Eventual comparison of those studies would help reveal the range of diversity in Brazil.

One way of using ethnography in modern nations is to do such a series of **community studies.** Field sites in different regions can be used to sample different economic adaptations, degrees of participation in the modern world, and historical trends. However, even a thousand rural communities cannot constitute an adequate sample of national diversity—especially given the extent of contemporary urbanization and globalization. City, nation, and world increasingly invade local communities in the guise of tourists, development agents, government and religious officials, and political candidates. Such **linkages,** or interconnections, are prominent components of regional, national, and international systems of politics, economics, and information. These larger systems increasingly affect the people and places that anthropology has traditionally studied.

Anthropologists recognize that cultures are not isolated. As Franz Boas (1940/1966) noted many years ago, contact between neighboring tribes has always existed and has extended over enormous areas. A **world-system perspective** recognizes that many local cultural features reflect the economic and political position that a society occupies in a larger system. "Human populations construct their cultures in interaction with one another, and not in isolation" (Wolf 1982, p. ix). The study of such linkages and systems is a prominent part of the subject matter of modern anthropology.

A series of community studies in a nation reveals variation in its small-town and rural life. However, there is much more to national life than small communities. One response to this problem has been **urban anthropology**—the anthropological study of cities. Particularly since the 1950s, anthropologists have systematically investigated urban problems and lifestyles in the United States, Canada, and abroad. A common illustration of urban anthropology is the practice of having students do local fieldwork for an anthropology course (assuming that the college is in an urban setting). Anthropologists have been studying their own culture for decades, and anthropological research is booming today in the United States and Canada.

With increasing interdisciplinary communication, anthropology and sociology are converging. As the modern world system grows, sociologists pursue research topics in Third World countries and in places that were once almost exclusively within the anthropological orbit. As industrialization spreads, many anthropologists work in industrial societies, where they study diverse topics, including rural decline, inner-city life, and the role of the mass media in creating national culture patterns. Anthropologists and sociologists also share an interest in race, ethnicity, social class, gender, and popular or mass culture in modern nations.

Research Methods for Complex Societies

Anthropologists can use field techniques such as participant observation and first-hand data collection in any social setting. However, for contemporary societies, anthropologists increasingly supplement traditional techniques with new procedures, many borrowed from survey research. During studies of urban life, modern anthropologists routinely gather statistical data. In any **complex society** (a large and populous society with cities, social stratification, extensive economic specialization, and a central government), many predictor variables (*social indicators*) influence behavior and opinions. Because we must be able to detect, measure, and compare the influence of social indicators, many contemporary anthropological studies have a statistical foundation. Even in rural fieldwork, more anthropologists now draw samples, gather quantitative data, and use statistics to interpret them (see Bernard 1994).

Quantifiable information may permit a more precise assessment of similarities and differences between communities. Statistical analysis can support and round out an ethnographic account of local social life.

However, in the best studies, the hallmark of ethnography remains: Anthropologists enter the community and get to know the people. They participate in local activities, networks, and associations, in the city or in the countryside. They observe and experience social conditions and problems. They watch the effects of national policies and programs on local life. I believe that the ethnographic method and the emphasis on personal relationships in social research are valuable gifts that anthropology brings to the study of a complex society.

SUMMARY

Anthropology, a uniquely holistic discipline, studies human biological and cultural diversity. It attempts to explain similarities and differences in time and space. Culture, which is passed on through learning rather than through biological inheritance, is a major reason for human adaptability.

Anthropology is characterized by an interest in the origins of and changes in biology and culture. The four subdisciplines of general anthropology—(socio)cultural, archeological, biological, and linguistic anthropology—share an interest in variation in time and space and in adaptation, the process by which organisms cope with environmental stresses.

Cultural anthropology examines the cultural diversity of the present and the recent past. Applied anthropology uses anthropological knowledge and methods to identify and solve social problems in North America and abroad.

Ethnography has several characteristic field procedures, including observation, establishing rapport, participant observation, conversation, listening to native accounts, formal and informal interviewing, the genealogical method, work with well-informed informants, life histories, emic and etic research strategies, problem-oriented ethnography, and longitudinal research. Recording the imponderabilia of daily life is particularly useful early in fieldwork. That is when the most basic, distinctive, and alien features of another culture are most noticeable. Ethnographers do not systematically manipulate their subjects or conduct experiments. Rather, they work in natural communities and form personal relationships with informants as they study their lives.

Interview schedules are forms that ethnographers fill in by visiting many households. The schedules guide formal interviews, ensuring that the ethnographer collects comparable information from everyone. Ethnographers work closely with well-informed informants to learn about particular areas of native life. Life histories dramatize the fact that culture bearers are also individuals and document personal experiences with culture and culture change. The collection and analysis of genealogical information is particularly important in societies in which principles of kinship, descent, and marriage organize and integrate social and political life. Emic approaches focus on native perceptions and explanations of behavior. Etic approaches give priority to the ethnographer's own observations and conclusions. Anthropologists do many kinds of problem-oriented ethnography, and people are not their only data source. Measurements are made as well. Longitudinal research is the systematic study of an area or a site over time.

Traditionally, anthropologists worked in small-scale societies; sociologists, in modern nations. Different field techniques emerged for the study of different types of societies. Sociologists and other social scientists who work in complex societies use survey research to sample variation. There are several contrasts between survey research and ethnography. With more literate respondents, sociologists employ questionnaires, which the research subjects fill out. Anthropologists are more likely to use interview schedules, which the ethnographer fills in during a personal interview. Anthropologists do their fieldwork in communities and study the totality of social life. Sociologists study samples to make inferences about a larger population. Sociologists are often interested in relationships among a limited number of variables. Anthropologists are more typically concerned with the interconnectedness of all aspects of social life.

Anthropologists use modified ethnographic techniques to study complex societies. The diversity of social life and subcultural variation in modern nations and cities requires social survey procedures. However, anthropologists add the intimacy and firsthand investigation characteristic of ethnography. Community studies in regions of modern nations provide firsthand, in-depth accounts of cultural variation and of regional historical and economic forces and trends. Anthropologists may use ethnographic procedures to study urban life, but they also make greater use of statistical techniques and analysis of the mass media in their research in complex societies.

CHAPTER TWO

Culture

WHAT IS CULTURE?
Culture Is Learned ~ BOX: Touching, Affection, Love, and Sex ~ Culture
Is Symbolic ~ Culture Seizes Nature ~ Culture Is General and
Specific ~ Culture Is All-Encompassing ~ Culture Is Shared ~ Cultured
Is Patterned ~ People Use Culture Creatively ~ Culture Is Adaptive and
Maladaptive ~ Levels of Culture ~ Ethnocentrism and Cultural Relativism

UNIVERSALITY, PARTICULARITY, AND GENERALITY
Universality ~ Particularity ~ Generality

MECHANISMS OF CULTURAL CHANGE

he idea of culture has long been basic to anthropology. More than a century ago, in his classic book *Primitive Culture*, British anthropologist Edward Tylor proposed that systems of human behavior and thought are not random. Rather, they obey natural laws and therefore can be studied scientifically. Tylor's definition of culture still offers a good overview of the subject matter of anthropology and is widely quoted.

"Culture . . . is that complex whole which includes knowledge, belief, arts, morals, law, custom, and any other capabilities and habits acquired by man as a member of society" (Tylor 1871/1958, p. 1). The crucial phrase here is "acquired by man as a member of society." Tylor's definition focuses on beliefs and behavior that people acquire not through biological heredity but by growing up in a particular society where they are exposed to a specific cultural tradition. **Enculturation** is the process by which a child *learns* his or her culture.

WHAT IS CULTURE?

Culture Is Learned

The ease with which children absorb any cultural tradition reflects the uniquely elaborated hominid capacity to learn. There are different kinds of learning, some of which we share with other animals. One kind is **individual situational learning,**

Touching, Affection, Love, and Sex

C omparing the United States with Brazil—or virtually any Latin na-tion—we can see a striking cultural contrast between a culture that discourages physical contact and demonstrations of affection and one in which the contrary is true. We can also see rampant confusion in American culture about love, sex, and affection. This stands in sharp contrast to the more realistic Brazilian separation of the three.

"Don't touch me." "Take your hands off me." These are normal statements in American culture that are virtually never heard in Brazil, the Western Hemi-sphere's second most populous country. Americans don't like to be touched. The world's cultures have strikingly different opinions about matters of personal space. When Americans talk, walk, and dance, they maintain a certain distance from others—their personal space. Brazilians, who maintain less physical dis-tance, interpret this as a sign of coldness. When conversing with an American, the Brazilian characteristically moves in as the American "instinctively" retreats. In these body movements, neither Brazilian nor American is trying consciously to be especially friendly or unfriendly. Each is merely executing a program writ-ten on the self by years of exposure to a particular cultural tradition. Because of different ideas about proper social space, cocktail parties in international meet-ing places such as the United Nations can resemble an elaborate insect mating ritual as diplomats from different cultures advance, withdraw, and sidestep.

One of the most obvious differences between Brazil and the United States involves kissing, hugging, and touching. Middle-class Brazilians teach their chil-dren—both boys and girls—to kiss (on the cheek, two or three times, coming and going) every adult relative they ever see. Given the size of Brazilian ex-tended families, this can mean hundreds of people. Females continue kissing throughout their lives. They kiss male and female kin, friends, relatives of friends, friends of relatives, friends of friends, and, when it seems appropriate, more casual acquaintances. Males go on kissing their female relatives and friends. Until they are adolescents, boys also kiss adult male relatives. There-after, Brazilian men greet each other with hearty handshakes and a traditional male hug (*abraço*). The closer the relationship, the tighter and longer-lasting the embrace. These comments apply to brothers, cousins, uncles, and friends. Many Brazilian men keep on kissing their fathers and uncles throughout their lives.

Like other Americans who spend time in a Latin culture, I miss these kisses and handshakes when I get back to the United States. After several months in

The world's cultures have strikingly different opinions about personal space—how far apart people should be in normal encounters and interactions. Contrast the gap between the two American men with the closeness of the Egyptian Bedouins.

Brazil, I find North Americans rather cold and impersonal. Many Brazilians share this opinion. I have heard similar feelings expressed by Italian Americans describing Americans of different ethnic backgrounds.

Many Americans fear physical contact and confuse love and affection with sex. According to clinical psychologist David E. Klimek, who has written about intimacy and marriage, "in American society, if we go much beyond simple touching, our behavior takes on a minor sexual twist" (Slade 1984). Americans define demonstrations of affection with reference to marriage. Love and affection are supposed to unite the married pair, and they blend into sex. When a wife asks her husband for "a little affection," she may mean, or he may think she means, sex. As Americans discuss love and sex on talk shows and in other public forums, it becomes obvious that American culture confuses these needs and feelings.

This confusion between love, affection, and sex is clear on Valentine's Day, which used to be just for lovers. Valentines used to be sent to wives, husbands, girlfriends, and boyfriends. Now, after years of promotion by the greeting card industry, they also go to mothers, fathers, sons, daughters, aunts, and uncles. Valentine's Day "personals" in the local newspaper also illustrate this blurring of sexual and nonsexual affection, which is a source of so much confusion in contemporary American culture. In Brazil, Lovers' Day retains its autonomy. Mother, father, and children have their own separate days.

It is true, of course, that in a good marriage love and affection exist alongside sex. Nevertheless, affection does not imply sex. Brazilian culture shows that there can be rampant kissing, hugging, and touching without sex—or fears of improper sexuality. In Brazilian culture, physical demonstrations help cement several kinds of close personal relationships that have no sexual component.

which occurs when an animal learns from, and bases its future behavior on, its own experience—for example, avoiding fire after discovering that it hurts. Animals also exhibit **social situational learning,** in which they learn from other members of the social group, not necessarily through language. Wolves, for example, learn hunting strategies from other pack members. Social situational learning is particularly important among monkeys and apes, our closest relatives. Finally there is **cultural learning.** This depends on the uniquely developed human capacity to use *symbols*, signs that have no necessary or natural connection with the things for which they stand.

A critical feature in hominid evolution is dependence on cultural learning. Through culture people create, remember, and deal with ideas. They grasp and apply specific systems of symbolic meaning. Anthropologist Clifford Geertz defines culture as ideas based on cultural learning and symbols. Cultures have been characterized as sets of "control mechanisms—plans, recipes, rules, constructions, what computer engineers call programs for the governing of behavior" (Geertz 1973, p. 44). These programs are absorbed by people through enculturation in particular traditions. People gradually internalize a previously established system of meanings and symbols which they use to define their world, express their feelings, and make their judgments. Thereafter, this system helps guide their behavior and perceptions throughout their lives.

Every person begins immediately, through a process of conscious and unconscious learning and interaction with others, to internalize, or incorporate, a cultural tradition through the process of enculturation. Sometimes culture is taught directly, as when parents tell their children to say "thank you" when someone gives them something or does them a favor.

Culture is also transmitted through observation. Children pay attention to the things that go on around them. They modify their behavior not just because other people tell them to but as a result of their own observations and growing awareness of what their culture considers right and wrong. Culture is also absorbed unconsciously. North Americans acquire their culture's notions about how far apart people should stand when they talk not by being told to maintain a certain distance but through a gradual process of observation, experience, and conscious and unconscious behavior modification. No one tells Latins to stand closer together than North Americans do, but they learn to do so anyway as part of their cultural tradition.

Culture Is Symbolic

Symbolic thought is unique and crucial to humans and to culture. Anthropologist Leslie White defined culture as

> an extrasomatic (nongenetic, nonbodily), temporal continuum of things and events dependent upon symbolling. . . . Culture consists of tools, implements, utensils, clothing, ornaments, customs, institutions, beliefs, rituals, games, works of art, language, etc. (White 1959, p. 3)

For White, culture originated when our ancestors acquired the ability to symbol, or

> freely and arbitrarily to originate and bestow meaning upon a thing or event, and, correspondingly, . . . to grasp and appreciate such meaning. (White 1959, p. 3)

A **symbol** is something verbal or nonverbal, within a particular language or culture, that comes to stand for something else. There is no obvious, natural, or necessary connection between the symbol and what it symbolizes. A pet that barks is no more naturally a *dog* than a *chien*, *Hund*, or *mbwa*, to use the words for the animal we call "dog" in French, German, and Swahili. Language is one of the distinctive possessions of *Homo sapiens*. No other animal has developed anything approaching the complexity of language.

Symbols are usually linguistic. However, there are also nonverbal symbols, such as flags, which stand for countries, as arches do for hamburger chains. Holy water is a potent symbol in Roman Catholicism. As is true of all symbols, the association between a symbol (water) and what is symbolized (holiness) is arbitrary and conventional. Water is not intrinsically holier than milk, blood, or other liquids. Holy water is not chemically different from ordinary water. Holy water is a symbol within Roman Catholicism, which is part of an international cultural system. A natural thing has been arbitrarily associated with a particular meaning for Catholics, who share common beliefs and experiences that are based on learning and are transmitted across the generations.

For hundreds of thousands of years, people have shared the abilities on which culture rests. These abilities are to learn, to think symbolically, to manipulate language, and to use tools and other cultural products in organizing their lives and coping with their environments. Every contemporary human population has the ability to symbol and thus to create and maintain culture. Our nearest relatives—chimpanzees and gorillas—have rudimentary cultural abilities. However, no other animal has elaborated cultural abilities—to learn, to communicate, and to store, process, and use information—to the same extent as *Homo*.

Culture Seizes Nature

Culture imposes itself on nature. I once arrived at a summer camp at 5 P.M. I was hot and wanted to swim in the lake. However, I read the camp rules and learned that no swimming was permitted after five. A cultural system had seized the lake, which is part of nature. Natural lakes don't close at five, but cultural lakes do.

Culture takes the natural biological urges we share with other animals and teaches us how to express them in particular ways. People have to eat, but culture teaches us what, when, and how. In many cultures people have their main meal at noon, but Americans prefer a large dinner. English people eat fish for breakfast, but Americans prefer hotcakes and cold cereals. Brazilians put hot milk into strong coffee, whereas Americans pour cold milk into a weaker brew. Midwesterners dine at five or six, Spaniards at ten.

Like the lake at summer camp, human nature is appropriated by cultural systems and molded in hundreds of directions. All people must eliminate wastes from their bodies. However, some cultures teach people to defecate standing up, while others tell them to do it sitting down. Frenchmen aren't embarrassed to urinate in public, routinely stepping into barely shielded *pissoirs* in Paris streets. Peasant women in the Andean highlands squat in the streets and urinate into gutters. They get all the privacy they need from their massive skirts. All these habits are parts of cultural traditions that have converted natural acts into cultural customs.

Culture Is General and Specific

All human populations have culture, which is therefore a generalized possession of the genus *Homo*. This is **Culture** (capital C) in the **general** sense, a capacity and possession shared by hominids. However, anthropologists also use the word *culture* to describe the different and varied cultural traditions of specific societies. This is **culture** in the **specific** sense (small c). Humanity shares a capacity for Culture, but people live in particular cultures, where they are enculturated along different lines. All people grow up in the presence of a particular set of cultural rules transmitted over the generations. These are the specific cultures or cultural traditions that anthropologists study.

Culture Is All-Encompassing

For anthropologists, Culture includes much more than refinement, taste, sophistication, education, and appreciation of the fine arts. Not only college graduates but all people are "cultured." The most interesting and significant cultural forces are those which affect people every day of their lives, particularly those which influence children during enculturation. *Culture*, as defined anthropologically, encompasses features that are sometimes regarded as trivial or unworthy of serious study, such as "popular" culture. To understand contemporary North American culture, we must consider television, fast-food restaurants, sports, and games. As a cultural manifestation, a rock star may be as interesting as a symphony conductor, a comic book as significant as a book-award winner.

Culture Is Shared

Culture is an attribute not of individuals per se but of individuals as members of *groups*. Culture is transmitted in society. We learn our culture by observing, listening, talking, and interacting with other people. Shared cultural beliefs, values, memories, expectations, and ways of thinking and acting override differences between people. Enculturation unifies people by providing us with common experiences.

People in the United States sometimes have trouble understanding the power of Culture because of the value that American culture places on the idea of the individual. Americans are fond of saying that everyone is unique and special in some way. However, in American culture individualism itself is a distinctive shared value that is transmitted through hundreds of statements and settings in our daily lives. From daytime TV's Mr. Rogers to real-life parents, grandparents, and teachers, our enculturative agents insist that we are all "someone special."

Today's parents were yesterday's children. If they grew up in American culture, they absorbed certain values and beliefs transmitted over the generations. People become agents in the enculturation of their children, just as their parents were for them. Although a culture constantly changes, certain fundamental beliefs, values, worldviews, and child-rearing practices endure. Consider a simple American example of enduring shared enculturation. As children, when we didn't finish a meal, our parents reminded us of starving children in some foreign country, just as our grandparents had done a generation earlier. The specific country changes (China, India,

Bangladesh, Ethiopia, Somalia, Rwanda). Still, American culture goes on transmitting the idea that by eating all our brussels sprouts or broccoli, we can justify our own good fortune, compared with a hungry Third World child.

Culture Is Patterned

Cultures are not haphazard collections of customs and beliefs but integrated, patterned systems. Customs, institutions, beliefs, and values are interrelated; if one changes, others change as well. During the 1950s, for example, most American women expected to have domestic careers as homemakers and mothers. Most of today's college women expect to get jobs when they graduate.

As women enter the workforce in increasing numbers, attitudes toward marriage, family, and children change. Outside work places strains on marriage and the family. Late marriage, "living together," and divorce become more common. Economic changes have produced changes in attitudes and behavior in regard to work, gender roles, marriage, and the family.

Cultures are integrated not simply by their dominant economic activities and social patterns but also by sets of values, ideas, and judgments. Cultures train their individual members to share certain personality traits. Separate elements of a culture can be integrated by key symbols, such as fertility or militarism. A set of characteristic **core values** (key, basic, or central values) integrates each culture and helps distinguish it from others. For instance, the work ethic, individualism, achievement, and self-reliance are core values that have integrated American culture for generations. Different sets of values pattern other cultures.

People Use Culture Creatively

Although cultural rules tell us what to do and how to do it, we don't always do what the rules dictate. People can learn, interpret, and manipulate the same rule in different ways. People use their culture creatively, rather than blindly following its dictates. Even if they agree about what should and shouldn't be done, people don't always do as their culture directs or as other people expect. Many rules are violated, some very often (for example, automobile speed limits). Some anthropologists find it useful to distinguish between ideal and real culture. The *ideal culture* consists of what people say they should do and what they say they do. *Real culture* refers to their actual behavior as observed by the anthropologist. This contrast is like the emic-etic contrast discussion in the previous chapter.

Culture is both public and individual, both in the world and in people's minds. Anthropologists are interested not only in public and collective behavior but also in how *individuals* think, feel, and act. The individual and culture are linked because human social life is a process in which individuals internalize the meanings of *public* (i.e., cultural) messages. Then, alone and in groups, people influence culture by converting their private understandings into public expressions (D'Andrade 1984). We

Cultures are integrated, patterned systems: When one custom, belief, or value changes, others change as well. During the 1950s, most American women expected to have domestic careers. With women entering the workforce in increasing numbers over the past three decades, attitudes toward work and family have changed. Most of today's college graduates plan to balance jobs and family responsibilities. Contrast the "fifties Mom" with three modern career women: Senators Carol Moseley Braun (Illinois) and Dianne Feinstein (California) greet Supreme Court Justice Ruth Bader Ginsburg on the first day of her confirmation hearing (July 20, 1993).

may study this process by focusing on shared, public aspects of culture or by focusing on individuals. Anthropology and psychology intersect in *psychological anthropology*, the ethnographic and cross-cultural study of differences and similarities in human psychology. Focusing on the individual, psychological anthropology exists because a complete account of cultural process requires both perspectives—private and public.

Culture Is Adaptive and Maladaptive

To cope with or adapt to environmental stresses, humans can draw on both biological traits and learned, symbol-based behavior patterns. Besides biological means of adaptation, human groups also employ "cultural adaptive kits" containing customary patterns, activities, and tools. Although humans continue to adapt biologically as well as culturally, reliance on social and cultural means of adaptation has increased during hominid evolution.

Sometimes, adaptive behavior that offers short-term benefits to particular individuals may also harm the environment and threaten the group's long-term survival. Creative manipulation of culture and the environment by men and women can foster a more secure economy, but it can also deplete strategic resources (Bennett 1969, p. 19). Thus, despite the crucial role of cultural adaptation in human evolution, cultural traits and patterns can also be **maladaptive,** threatening the group's continued existence (survival and reproduction). Many modern cultural patterns, such as policies that encourage overpopulation, inadequate food distribution systems, overconsumption, and pollution, appear to be maladaptive in the long run.

Levels of Culture

Of increasing importance in today's world is the distinction among different levels of culture: national, international, and subcultural. **National culture** refers to the experiences, beliefs, learned behavior patterns, and values shared by citizens of the same nation. **International culture** is the term for cultural traditions that extend beyond national boundaries. Because culture is transmitted through learning rather than genetically, cultural traits can spread through borrowing or *diffusion* from one group to another.

Through diffusion, migration, and multinational organizations, many culture traits and patterns have international scope. Roman Catholics in different countries share experiences, symbols, beliefs, and values transmitted by their church. Contemporary United States, Canada, Great Britain, and Australia share cultural traits they have inherited from their common linguistic and cultural ancestors in Great Britain.

Cultures can also be smaller than nations. Although people in the same society or nation share a cultural tradition, all cultures also contain diversity. Individuals, families, villages, regions, classes, and other subgroups within a culture have different learning experiences as well as shared ones. **Subcultures** are different symbol-based patterns and traditions associated with subgroups in the same complex society. In a complex nation such as the contemporary United States or Canada, subcultures originate in ethnicity, class, region, and religion. The religious backgrounds of Jews, Baptists, and Roman Catholics create subcultural differences between them. Although they share the same national culture, northerners and southerners exhibit differences in beliefs and customary behavior as a result of regional subcultural variation. French-speaking Canadians contrast on the subcultural level with English speakers in the same country. Italian Americans have ethnic traditions different from those of Irish, Polish, and African Americans.

Despite characteristic American notions that people should "make up their own minds" and "have a right to their opinion," little of what we think is original or unique. We share our opinions and beliefs with many other people. Illustrating the power of shared cultural background, we are most likely to agree with and feel comfortable with people who are socially, economically, and culturally similar to ourselves. This is one reason why Americans abroad tend to socialize with each other, just as French and British colonials did in their overseas empires. Birds of a feather flock together, but for people the familiar plumage is culture.

Ethnocentrism and Cultural Relativism

One of anthropology's main goals is to combat **ethnocentrism,** the tendency to view one's own culture as superior and to apply one's own cultural values in judging the behavior and beliefs of people raised in other cultures. Ethnocentrism is a cultural universal. People everywhere think that familiar explanations, opinions, and customs are true, right, proper, and moral. They regard different behavior as strange or savage. The tribal names that appear in anthropology books often come from the native word for *people*. "What are you called?" asks the anthropologist. "Mugmug," reply informants. *Mugmug* may turn out to be synonymous with *people*, but it also may be the only word the natives have for themselves. Other tribes are not considered fully human. The not-quite-people in neighboring groups are not classified as *Mugmug*. They are given different names that symbolize their inferior humanity.

The opposite of ethnocentrism is **cultural relativism,** the argument that behavior in a particular culture should not be judged by the standards of another. This position can also present problems. At its most extreme, cultural relativism argues that there is no superior, international, or universal morality, that the moral and ethical rules of all cultures deserve equal respect. In the extreme relativist view, Nazi Germany is evaluated as nonjudgmentally as Athenian Greece.

How should anthropologists deal with ethnocentrism and cultural relativism? I believe that anthropology's main job is to present accurate accounts and explanations of cultural phenomena. The anthropologist doesn't have to approve customs such as infanticide, cannibalism, and torture to record their existence and determine their causes. However, each anthropologist has a choice about where to do fieldwork. Some anthropologists choose not to study a particular culture because they discover in advance or early in fieldwork that behavior they consider morally repugnant is practiced there. Anthropologists respect human diversity. Most ethnographers try to be objective, accurate, and sensitive in their accounts of other cultures.

However, objectivity, sensitivity, and a cross-cultural perspective don't mean that anthropologists have to ignore international standards of justice and morality.

UNIVERSALITY, PARTICULARITY, AND GENERALITY

Anthropologists agree that cultural learning is uniquely elaborated among hominids, that Culture is the major reason for human adaptability, and that the capacity for Culture is shared by all humans. Anthropologists also unanimously accept a doctrine originally proposed in the nineteenth century: "the psychic unity of man." Anthropology assumes **biopsychological equality** among human groups. This means that although *individuals* differ in emotional and intellectual tendencies and capacities, all human *populations* have equivalent capacities for culture. Regardless of physical appearance and genetic composition, humans can learn *any* cultural tradition.

To understand this point, consider that contemporary Americans and Canadians are the genetically mixed descendants of people from all over the world. Our ancestors were biologically varied, lived in different countries and continents, and participated in hundreds of cultural traditions. However, the earliest colonists, later immigrants, and their descendants have all become active participants in American and Canadian life. All now share a common national culture.

To recognize biopsychological equality is not to deny differences between populations. In studying human diversity in time and space, anthropologists distinguish between the universal, the generalized, and the particular. Certain biological, psychological, social, and cultural features are **universal**, shared by all human populations in every culture. Others are merely **generalities**, common to several but not all human groups. Still other traits are **particularities**, unique to certain cultural traditions.

Cultural anthropologists study society and culture, describing and explaining social and cultural similarities and differences. Cultural anthropology has two aspects: ethnography (based on fieldwork) and ethnology (based on cross-cultural comparison). **Ethnology** examines and compares the results of ethnography—the data gathered in different societies. Ethnologists try to identify and explain cultural differences and similarities, to distinguish between universality, generality, and particularity.

Universality

Universal traits are the ones that more or less distinguish *Homo sapiens* from other species (see Brown 1991). Biologically based universals include a long period of infant dependency, year-round (rather than seasonal) sexuality, and a complex brain that enables us to use symbols, languages, and tools. Psychological universals arise from human biology and from experiences common to human development in all cases. These include growth in the womb, birth itself, and interaction with parents and parent substitutes.

Among the social universals is life in groups and in some kind of family. In all human societies culture organizes social life and depends on social interactions for its expression and continuation. Family living and food sharing are universals. Among the most significant cultural universals are **exogamy** and the **incest taboo** (prohibition against marrying or mating with a close relative). Humans everywhere consider some people (various cultures differ about *which* people) too closely related to mate or marry. The violation of this taboo is *incest*, which is discouraged and punished in a variety of ways in different cultures. If incest is prohibited, exogamy—marriage outside one's group—is inevitable. Because it links human groups together into larger networks, exogamy has been crucial in hominid evolution. Exogamy elaborates on tendencies observed among other primates. Recent studies of monkeys and apes show that these animals also avoid mating with close kin and often mate outside their native groups.

Particularity

Many cultural traits are widely shared because of diffusion and independent invention and as cultural universals. Nevertheless, different cultures emphasize different things. Cultures are patterned and integrated differently and display tremendous variation and diversity. Uniqueness and particularity stand at the opposite extreme from universality.

Unusual and exotic beliefs and practices lend distinctiveness to particular cultural traditions. Many cultures ritually observe such universal life-cycle events as birth, puberty, marriage, parenthood, and death. However, cultures vary in just which event merits special celebration. Americans regard expensive weddings as more socially appropriate than lavish funerals. However, the Betsileo of Madagascar take the opposite view. The marriage ceremony is a minor event that brings together just the couple and a few close relatives. However, a funeral is a measure of the deceased person's social position and lifetime achievement, and it may attract a thousand people. Why use money on a house, the Betsileo say, when one can use it on the tomb where one will spend eternity in the company of dead relatives? How different from contemporary Americans' growing preference for quick and inexpensive funerals and cremation, which would horrify the Betsileo, whose ancestral bones and relics are important ritual objects.

Cultures vary tremendously in their beliefs and practices. By focusing on and trying to explain alternative customs, anthropology forces us to reappraise our familiar ways of thinking. In a world full of cultural diversity, contemporary American culture is just one cultural variant, no more natural than the others.

Generality

Between universals and uniqueness is a middle ground that consists of cultural generalities: regularities that occur in different times and places but not in all cultures. One reason for generalities is diffusion. Societies can share the same beliefs and customs because of borrowing or through (cultural) inheritance from a common cultural ancestor. Other generalities originate in independent invention of the same culture trait or pattern in two or more different cultures. Similar needs and circumstances have led people in different lands to innovate in parallel ways. They have independently come up with the same cultural solution or arrangement.

One cultural generality that is present in many but not all societies is the **nuclear family,** a kinship group consisting of parents and children. Although many middle-class Americans ethnocentrically view the nuclear family as a proper and "natural" group, it is not universal. It is totally absent, for example, among the Nayars, who live on the Malabar Coast of India. The Nayars live in female-headed households, and husbands and wives do not co-reside. In many other societies, the nuclear family is submerged in larger kin groups, such as extended families, lineages, and clans. However, the nuclear family is prominent in many of the technologically simple societies that live by hunting and gathering. It is also a significant kin group among contemporary middle-class North Americans and Western Europeans. Later, an explanation of the nuclear family as a basic kinship unit in specific types of society will be given.

MECHANISMS OF CULTURAL CHANGE

In biology, different species cannot share their genes, but cultures in contact can get traits from each other through borrowing or **diffusion.** Diffusion, an important mechanism of cultural change, has gone on throughout human history, because cultures have never been truly isolated. As the anthropologist Franz Boas (1940/1966) noted many years ago, contact between neighboring tribes has always existed and has extended over enormous areas. Diffusion is direct when two cultures trade, intermarry, or wage war on one another. Diffusion is forced when one culture subjugates another and imposes its customs on the dominated group. Diffusion is indirect when products and patterns move from group A to group C via group B without any firsthand contact between A and C. In the modern world much international diffusion is due to the spread of the mass media.

Acculturation, another mechanism of cultural change, is the exchange of cultural features that results when groups come into continuous firsthand contact. The original cultural patterns of either or both groups may be changed by this contact (Redfield, Linton, and Herskovits 1936). We usually speak of acculturation when the contact is *between* nations or cultures. Parts of the cultures change, but each group remains distinct. One example of acculturation is a **pidgin**—a mixed language that develops to ease communication between members of different cultures in contact. This usually happens in situations of trade or colonialism. Pidgin English, for example, is a simplified form of English. It blends English grammar with the grammar of a native language. Pidgin English was first used in commerce in Chinese ports. Similar pidgins developed later in Papua-New Guinea and West Africa. In situations of continuous contact, cultures have also exchanged and blended foods and recipes, music and dance, clothing, tools, and techniques.

Independent invention—the process by which humans innovate, creatively finding new solutions to old and new problems—is another important mechanism of cultural change. Faced with comparable problems and challenges, people in different cultures have innovated in similar or parallel ways, which is one reason that cultural generalities exist. One example is the independent invention of agriculture in the Middle East and Mexico. In both areas people who faced food scarcity began to domesticate crops. Over the course of human history, major innovations have spread at the expense of earlier ones. Often a major invention, such as agriculture, triggers a series of subsequent interrelated changes. Economic revolutions have social and cultural repercussions. Thus, in both Mexico and the Middle East, agriculture led to many social, political, and legal changes, including notions of property and distinctions in wealth, class, and power.

Cultural convergence or **convergent cultural evolution** refers to the development of similar traits, institutions, and behavior patterns by separate groups as a result of adaptation to similar environments. Given long-term adaptation by different cultures to similar environments, the same institutions tend to develop, in the same order. Julian Steward (1955), an influential advocate of the position that scientific laws govern human behavior and cultural change, sought to explain convergent cultural evolution. He showed that parallel cultural changes have occurred repeatedly and independently in different places, mainly for economic or environmental reasons.

Another reason for cultural change is **globalization**—the process that links modern nations and people economically and politically and through modern media and transportation. Local people must increasingly cope with forces generated by progressively larger systems—region, nation, and world. Different degrees of destruction, domination, resistance, survival, adaptation, and modification of native cultures have followed contact between cultures and ethnic groups. Indigenous peoples and traditional cultures have devised various strategies to resist attacks on their autonomy, identity, and livelihood. New forms of political mobilization and cultural expression are emerging from the interplay of local, regional, national, and international cultural forces.

SUMMARY

Culture, a distinctive possession of humanity, is acquired by all humans through enculturation. Culture encompasses rule-governed, shared, symbol-based learned behavior and beliefs transmitted across the generations. Culture rests on the hominid capacity for cultural learning. *Culture* refers to customary beliefs and behavior and to the rules for conduct internalized in human beings through enculturation. These rules lead people to think and act in certain consistent, distinctive, and characteristic ways.

Other animals learn, but only humans have cultural learning, which depends on symbols. Cultural learning rests on the universal human capacity to think symbolically, arbitrarily bestowing meaning on a thing or an event. By convention, a symbol, which may be linguistic or nonverbal, stands for something else with which it has no necessary or natural relation. Symbols have a particular meaning and value for people in the same culture. People share experiences, memories, values, and beliefs as a result of common enculturation. People absorb cultural lessons consciously and unconsciously.

Cultural traditions seize natural phenomena, including biologically based desires and needs, and channel them in particular directions. Everyone is cultured, not just people with elite educations. The genus *Homo* has the capacity for Culture (in a general sense), but people live in specific cultures where they are raised according to different traditions. Cultures are patterned and integrated through their dominant economic forces, social patterns, key symbols, and core values. Cultural rules do not always dictate behavior. There is room for creativity, flexibility, and diversity within cultures. Anthropologists distinguish between what people say they do and what they actually do. Cultural means of adaptation have been crucial in hominid evolution, although aspects of culture can also be maladaptive.

There are different levels of cultural systems. Diffusion and migration carry the same cultural traits and patterns to different areas. These traits are shared across national boundaries. Nations include subcultural differences associated with ethnicity, region, and social class.

Anthropology finds no evidence that genetic differences explain cultural variation. Adopting a comparative perspective, anthropology examines biological, psychological, social, and cultural universals and generalities. It also considers unique and distinctive aspects of the human condition. In examining cultural elaborations on the fundamental biological plasticity of *Homo sapiens*, anthropology shows that American cultural traditions are no more natural than any others. Mechanisms of cultural change include diffusion, acculturation, independent invention, cultural convergence, and globalization.

CHAPTER THREE

Ethnicity and Ethnic Relations

ETHNIC GROUPS AND ETHNICITY
Status Shifting

ETHNIC GROUPS, NATIONS, AND NATIONALITIES
Nationalities and Imagined Communities

ETHNIC TOLERANCE AND ACCOMMODATION
Assimilation ~ The Plural Society ~ Multiculturalism and Ethnic Identity

ROOTS OF ETHNIC CONFLICT
Prejudice and Discrimination ~ Chips in the Mosaic ~ Aftermaths
of Oppression

W e know from the last chapter that culture is learned, symbolic, shared, patterned, all-encompassing, adaptive, and maladaptive. Now we consider the relation between culture and ethnicity. Ethnicity is based on cultural similarities and differences in a society or nation. The similarities are with members of the same ethnic group; the differences are between that group and others.

ETHNIC GROUPS AND ETHNICITY

As with any culture, members of an **ethnic group** *share* certain beliefs, values, habits, customs, and norms because of their common background. They define themselves as different and special because of cultural features. This distinction may arise from language, religion, historical experience, geographic isolation, kinship, or race (see the next chapter). Markers of an ethnic group may include a collective name, belief in common descent, a sense of solidarity, and an association with a specific territory, which the group may or may not hold (Ryan 1990, pp. xiii, xiv).

Ethnicity means identification with, and feeling part of, an ethnic group and exclusion from certain other groups because of this affiliation. Ethnic feelings and associated behavior vary in intensity within ethnic groups and countries and over time. A change in the degree of importance attached to an ethnic identity may re-

37

flect political changes (Soviet rule ends—ethnic feeling rises) or individual life-cycle changes (young people relinquish, or old people reclaim, an ethnic background).

We saw in the last chapter that people participate in various levels of culture. Subgroups within a culture (including ethnic groups in a nation) have different learning experiences as well as shared ones. Subcultures originate in ethnicity, class, region, and religion. Individuals often have more than one group identity. People may be loyal (depending on circumstances) to their neighborhood, school, town, state or province, region, nation, continent, religion, ethnic group, or interest group (Ryan 1990, p. xxii). In a complex society like the United States or Canada, people constantly negotiate their social identities. All of us "wear different hats," presenting ourselves sometimes as one thing, sometimes as another.

The term **status** can be used to refer to such "hats"—to any position that determines where someone fits in society (Light, Keller, and Calhoun 1994). Social statuses include parent, professor, student, factory worker, Democrat, shoe salesperson, labor leader, ethnic group member, and thousands of others. People always occupy multiple statuses (e.g., Hispanic, Catholic, infant, brother). Among the statuses we occupy, particular ones dominate in particular settings, such as son or daughter at home and student in the classroom.

Some statuses are **ascribed:** People have little or no choice about occupying them. Age is an ascribed status; people can't choose not to age. Race and ethnicity are usually ascribed; people are born members of a certain group and remain so all their lives. **Achieved** statuses, by contrast, aren't automatic but come through traits, talents, actions, efforts, activities, and accomplishments. (See Figure 3-1.)

In many societies an ascribed status is associated with a position in the social-political hierarchy. Certain groups, called **minority groups,** are subordinate. They have inferior power and less secure access to resources than do **majority groups** (which are superordinate, dominant, or controlling). Minorities need not have fewer members than the majority group does. Women in the United States and blacks in South Africa have been numerical majorities but minorities in terms of income, authority, and power. Often ethnic groups are minorities. When an ethnic group is assumed to have a biological basis, it is called a **race.** Discrimination against such a group is called **racism.** The next chapter considers race as a social and biological concept.

Status Shifting

Sometimes statuses, particularly ascribed ones, are mutually exclusive. It's hard to bridge the gap between black and white, or male and female (although some rock stars seem to be trying to do so). Sometimes, taking a status or joining a group requires a conversion experience, acquiring a new and overwhelming primary identity, such as becoming a "born again" Christian.

Some statuses aren't mutually exclusive, but contextual. People can be both black and Hispanic, or both a mother and a senator. One identity is used in certain

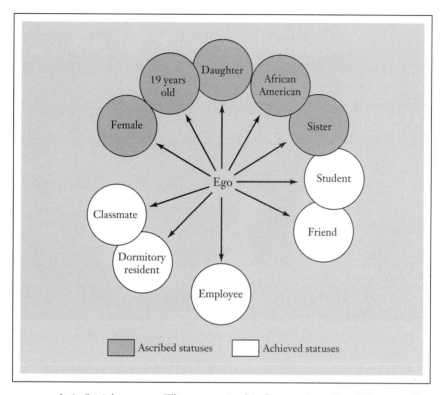

FIGURE 3-1 Social statuses. The person in this figure—"ego," or "I"—occupies many social statuses. The gray circles indicate ascribed statuses; the white circles represent achieved statuses.

settings, another in different ones. We call this the *situational negotiation of social identity.* When ethnic identity is flexible and situational (Moerman 1965), it can become an achieved status.

Hispanics, for example, may move through levels of culture (shifting ethnic affiliations) as they negotiate their identities. "Hispanic" is an ethnic category based mainly on language. It includes whites, blacks, and "racially" mixed Spanish speakers and their ethnically conscious descendants. (There are also "Native American," and even "Asian," Hispanics.) "Hispanic" lumps together millions of people of diverse geographic origin—Puerto Rico, Mexico, Cuba, El Salvador, Guatemala, the Dominican Republic, and other Spanish-speaking countries of Central and South America and the Caribbean. "Latino" is a broader category, which can also include Brazilians (who speak Portuguese).

Mexican Americans (Chicanos), Cuban Americans, and Puerto Ricans may mobilize to promote general Hispanic issues (e.g., opposition to "English-only" laws) but act as three separate interest groups in other contexts. Cuban Americans are richer on average than Chicanos and Puerto Ricans are, and their class interests and

The ethnic label "Hispanic" lumps together millions of people of diverse geographic origin—Puerto Rico, Mexico, Cuba, El Salvador, Guatemala, the Dominican Republic, and other Spanish-speaking countries of Central and South America and the Caribbean. Hispanics of diverse national backgrounds, like these Cuban Americans in Miami, may mobilize to promote general Hispanic issues (such as opposition to "English-only" laws) but act as separate interest groups in other contexts. Images of Cuba decorate this restaurant in Miami's "Little Havana."

voting patterns differ. Cubans often vote Republican, but Puerto Ricans and Chicanos generally favor Democrats. Some Mexican Americans whose families have lived in the United States for generations have little in common with new Hispanic immigrants, such as those from Central America. Many Americans (especially those fluent in English) claim Hispanic ethnicity in some contexts but shift to a general "American" identity in others.

ETHNIC GROUPS, NATIONS, AND NATIONALITIES

What is the relation between an ethnic group and a nation? The term **nation** was once synonymous with "tribe" or "ethnic group." All three of these terms referred to a single culture sharing a single language, religion, history, territory, ancestry, and kinship. Thus one could speak interchangeably of the Seneca (American Indian) nation, tribe, or ethnic group. Now *nation* has come to mean a **state**—an independent, centrally organized political unit, or a government. *Nation* and *state* have become synonymous. Combined in **nation-state** they refer to an autonomous political entity, a "country"—like the United States, "one nation, indivisible."

Because of migration, conquest, and colonialism (see below), most nation-states are not ethnically homogeneous. Of 132 nation-states existing in 1971, Connor (1972) found just 12 (9 percent) to be ethnically homogeneous. In another 25 (19 percent) a single ethnic group accounted for more than 90 percent of the population. Forty percent of the countries contained more than five significant ethnic groups. In a later study, Nielsson (1985) classified only 45 of 164 states as "single nation-group" (i.e., ethnic group) states (with one ethnic group accounting for more than 95 percent of the population).

Nationalities and Imagined Communities

Ethnic groups that once had, or wish to have or regain, autonomous political status (their own country) are called **nationalities.** In the words of Benedict Anderson (1991), they are "imagined communities." Even when they become nation-states, they remain imagined communities, because most of their members, though feeling deep comradeship, will never meet (Anderson 1991, pp. 6–10). They can only imagine that they all participate in the same unit.

Anderson traces Western European nationalism, which arose in imperial powers like England, France, and Spain, back to the eighteenth century. He stresses that language and print played a crucial role in the growth of European national consciousness. The novel and the newspaper were "two forms of imagining" communities (consisting of all the people who read the same sources and thus witnessed the same events) that flowered in the eighteenth century (Anderson 1991, pp. 24–25).

Making a similar point, Terry Eagleton (1983, p. 25) describes the vital role of the novel in fomenting English national consciousness and identity. The novel gave the English "a pride in their national language and literature; if scanty education and extensive hours of labor prevented them personally from producing a literary masterpiece, they could take pleasure in the thought that others of their kind—English people—had done so."

Over time, political upheavals and wars have divided many imagined national communities that arose in the eighteenth and nineteenth centuries. The German and Korean homelands were artificially divided after wars, and according to Communist and capitalist ideologies. World War I split the Kurds, who remain an imagined community, forming a majority in no state. Kurds are a minority group in Turkey, Iran, Iraq, and Syria. Similarly, Azerbaijanis, who are related to Turks, were a minority in the former Soviet Union, as they still are in Iran.

Migration is another reason certain ethnic groups live in different nation-states. Massive migration in the decades before and after 1900 brought Germans, Poles, and Italians to Brazil, Canada, and the United States. Through migration, Chinese, Senegalese, Lebanese, and Jews have spread all over the world. Some of these (e.g., descendants of Germans in Brazil and the United States) have assimilated to their host nations and no longer feel attached to the imagined community of their origin.

ETHNIC TOLERANCE AND ACCOMMODATION

Ethnic diversity may be associated with positive group interaction and coexistence or with conflict (discussed below). There are nation-states in which multiple cultural groups live together in reasonable harmony, including some less developed countries. In Indonesia, for example, a common language and school system have promoted ethnic harmony, national identity, and integration, as Anderson (1991, pp. 120–123, 132) describes. Indonesia, a large and populous nation, spans about 3,000 islands. Its national consciousness straddles religious, ethnic, and linguistic diversity. For example, Indonesia contains such religious groups as Muslims, Buddhists, Catholics, Protestants, Hindu-Balinese, and animists. Despite these contrasts, more than 100 distinct ethnolinguistic groups have come to view themselves as fellow Indonesians.

Under Dutch rule (which ended in 1949), the school system extended over the islands. Advanced study brought youths from different areas to Batavia, the colonial capital. The colonial educational system offered Indonesian youths uniform textbooks, standardized diplomas, and teaching certificates. It created a "self-contained, coherent universe of experience" (Anderson 1991, p. 121). Literacy acquired through the school system also paved the way for a single national print language. Indonesian developed as the national language out of an ancient lingua franca (common language) used in trade between the islands.

Most former colonies haven't been as lucky as Indonesia in terms of ethnic harmony and national integration. In creating multitribal and multiethnic states, colonialism often erected boundaries that corresponded poorly with preexisting cultural divisions. But colonial institutions also helped create new "imagined communities" beyond nations. A good example is the idea of **négritude** ("African identity") developed by African intellectuals in Francophone (French-speaking) West Africa. *Négritude* can be traced to the association and common experience of youths from Guinea, Mali, the Ivory Coast, and Senegal at the William Ponty school in Dakar, Senegal (Anderson 1991, pp. 123–124).

Assimilation

Assimilation describes the process of change that a minority ethnic group may experience when it moves to a country where another culture dominates. By assimilating, the minority adopts the patterns and norms of its host culture. It is incorporated into the dominant culture to the point that it no longer exists as a separate cultural unit. Some countries, like Brazil, are more assimilationist than others are. Germans,

Italians, Japanese, Mid-Easterners, and East Europeans started migrating to Brazil late in the nineteenth century. These immigrants have assimilated to a common Brazilian culture, which has Portuguese, African, and Native American roots. The descendants of these immigrants speak the national language (Portuguese) and participate in the national culture. (During World War II, Brazil, which was on the Allied side, forced assimilation by banning instruction in any language other than Portuguese—especially in German.)

Brazil has been more of a "melting pot" than have the United States and Canada, in which ethnic groups retain more distinctiveness and self-identity. I remember my first visit to the southern Brazilian city of Porto Alegre, the site of mass migration by Germans, Poles, and Italians. Transferring an expectation derived from my North American culture to Porto Alegre, I asked my tour guide to show me his city's ethnic neighborhoods. He couldn't understand what I was talking about. Except for a Japanese-Brazilian neighborhood in the city of São Paulo, the idea of an ethnic neighborhood is alien to Brazil.

The Plural Society

Assimilation isn't inevitable, and there can be ethnic harmony without it. Ethnic distinctions can persist despite generations of interethnic contact. Through a study of three ethnic groups in Swat, Pakistan, Fredrik Barth (1958/1968) challenged an old idea that interaction always leads to assimilation. He showed that ethnic groups can be in contact for generations without assimilating and can live in peaceful coexistence.

Barth (1958/1968, p. 324) defines **plural society** (an idea he extends from Pakistan to the entire Middle East) as a society combining ethnic contrasts, ecological specialization (i.e., use of different environmental resources by each ethnic group), and the economic interdependence of those groups. Consider his description of the Middle East (in the 1950s): "The 'environment' of any one ethnic group is not only defined by natural conditions, but also by the presence and activities of the other ethnic groups on which it depends. Each group exploits only part of the total environment, and leaves large parts of it open for other groups to exploit." The ecological interdependence (or, at least, the lack of competition) between ethnic groups may be based on different activities in the same region or on long-time occupation of different regions in the same nation-state.

In Barth's view, ethnic boundaries are most stable and enduring when the groups occupy different ecological niches. That is, they make their living in different ways and don't compete. Ideally, they should depend on each other's activities and exchange with one another. When different ethnic groups exploit the *same* ecological niche, the militarily more powerful group will normally replace the weaker one. If they exploit more or less the same niche, but the weaker group is better able to use marginal environments, they may also coexist (Barth 1958/1968, p. 331). Given niche specialization, ethnic boundaries, distinctions, and interdependence can be maintained, although the specific cultural features of each group may change. By shifting the analytic focus from individual cultures or ethnic groups to *relationships* between cultures or ethnic groups, Barth (1958/1968 and 1969) has made important contributions to ethnic studies.

Multiculturalism and Ethnic Identity

The view of cultural diversity in a country as something good and desirable is called **multiculturalism.** The multicultural model is the opposite of the assimilationist model, in which minorities are expected to abandon their cultural traditions and values, replacing them with those of the majority population. The multicultural view encourages the practice of cultural-ethnic traditions. A multicultural society socializes individuals not only into the dominant (national) culture but also into an ethnic culture. Thus in the United States millions of people speak both English and another language, eat both "American" (apple pie, steak, hamburgers) and "ethnic" foods, celebrate both national (July 4, Thanksgiving) and ethnic-religious holidays, and study both national and ethnic group histories. Multiculturalism succeeds best in a society whose political system promotes freedom of expression and in which there are many and diverse ethnic groups.

In the United States and Canada multiculturalism is of growing importance. This reflects an awareness that the number and size of ethnic groups have grown

In the United States and Canada, multiculturalism is of growing importance. Especially in large cities like Toronto (shown here), people of diverse backgrounds attend ethnic fairs and festivals, feast on ethnic foods, and pass one another in the streets each day.

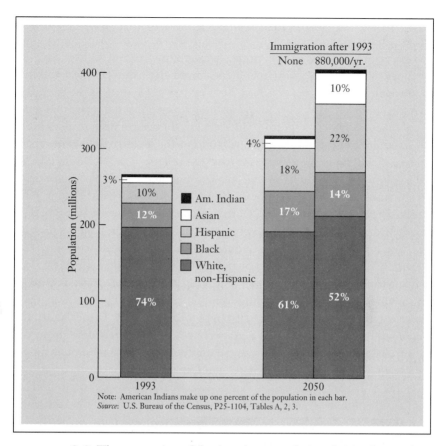

FIGURE 3-2 The proportion of the American population that is white and non-Hispanic is declining. Consider two projections of the ethnic composition of the United States in A.D. 2050. The first assumes an annual immigration rate of zero; the second assumes continuation of the current level—about 880,000 immigrants per year. With either projection, the non-Hispanic white proportion of the population declines dramatically. (Martin and Midgley 1994, p. 9)

dramatically in recent years. If this trend continues, the ethnic composition of the United States will change dramatically (see Figure 3-2).

Because of immigration and differential population growth, whites are now outnumbered by minorities in many urban areas. For example, of the 7,323,000 people living in New York City in 1990, 28.7 percent were black, 24.4 percent Hispanic, 7.0 percent Asian, 0.4 percent Native American, and 39.5 percent other—including non-Hispanic whites. The comparable figures for Los Angeles (3,485,000 people) were 14.0 percent black, 39.9 percent Hispanic, 9.8 percent Asian, 0.5 percent Native American, and 35.8 percent non-Hispanic whites (*Statistical Abstract* 1991, pp. 34–35).

One response to ethnic diversification and awareness has been for many whites to reclaim ethnic identities (Italian, Albanian, Serbian, Lithuanian, etc.) and to join ethnic associations (clubs, gangs). Some such groups are new. Others have existed for decades, although they lost members during the assimilationist years of the 1920s through the 1950s.

Multiculturalism seeks ways for people to understand and interact that don't depend on sameness but on respect for differences. Multiculturalism stresses the interaction of ethnic groups and their contribution to the country. It assumes that each group has something to offer and learn from the others.

We see evidence of multiculturalism all around us. Seated near you in the classroom are students whose parents were born in other countries. Islamic mosques have joined Jewish synagogues and Christian churches in American cities. To help in exam scheduling, colleges inform professors about the main holidays of many religions. You can attend ethnic fairs and festivals, watch ethnically costumed dancers on television, eat ethnic foods, even outside ethnic restaurants, and buy ethnic foods at your supermarket. Some such foods (e.g., bagels, pasta, tacos) have become so familiar that their ethnic origin is fading from our memories. There is even a popular shrine celebrating the union of diversity and globalization. At Disneyland and Walt Disney World we can see and hear a chorus of ethnically correct dolls drone on that "it's a small world after all." All these exemplify growing tolerance and support of ethnic communities in the United States and Canada.

Several forces have propelled North America away from the assimilationist model toward multiculturalism. First, multiculturalism reflects the fact of recent large-scale migration, particularly from the "less developed countries" to the "developed" nations of North America and Western Europe. The global scale of modern migration introduces unparalleled ethnic variety to host nations. Multiculturalism is related to globalization: People use modern means of transportation to migrate to nations whose lifestyles they learn about through the media and from tourists who increasingly visit their own countries.

Migration is also fueled by rapid population growth, coupled with insufficient jobs (both for educated and uneducated people), in the less developed countries. As traditional rural economies decline or mechanize, displaced farmers move to cities, where they and their children are often unable to find jobs. As people in the less developed countries get better educations, they seek more skilled employment. They hope to partake in an international culture of consumption that includes such modern amenities as refrigerators, televisions, and automobiles.

Contrary to popular belief, the typical migrant to the United States or Canada isn't poor and unskilled but middle-class and fairly well educated. Educated people migrate for several reasons. Often they can't find jobs to match their skills in their countries of origin (Grasmuck and Pessar 1991; Margolis 1994). Also, they are knowledgeable enough to manipulate international regulations. Many migrants have been raised to expect a lifestyle that their own nations can offer to just a few. On arrival in North America or Western Europe, immigrants find themselves in democracies where citizens are allowed (or even encouraged) to organize for economic gain and a "fair share" of resources, political influence, and cultural respect. Educated immigrants often become political organizers and particularly effective advocates of multiculturalism.

In a world with growing rural-urban and transnational migration, ethnic identities are used increasingly to form self-help organizations focused mainly on enhancing the group's economic competitiveness (Williams 1989). People claim and express ethnic identities for political and economic reasons. Michel Laguerre's (1984) study of Haitian immigrants in New York City shows that they make no conscious decision to form an ethnic group. Rather, they have to mobilize to deal with the discriminatory structure (racist in this case, since Haitians tend to be black) of American society. Ethnicity (their common Haitian creole language and cultural background) is an evident basis for their mobilization. Haitian ethnicity then helps distinguish them from Afro-Americans and other ethnic groups who may be competing for the same resources and recognition. In studying ethnic relations, it's not enough to look at the cultural content of the ethnic group. Equally important are the structural constraints and the political-economic context in which ethnic differentiation develops.

In the face of globalization, much of the world, including the entire "democratic West," is experiencing an "ethnic revival." The new assertiveness of long-resident ethnic groups extends to the Basques and Catalans in Spain, the Bretons and Corsicans in France, and the Welsh and Scots in the United Kingdom. The United States and Canada are becoming increasingly multicultural, focusing on their internal diversity. "Melting pots" no longer, they are better described as ethnic "salads" (each ingredient remains distinct, although in the same bowl, with the same dressing). In 1992, then New York mayor David Dinkins called his city a "gorgeous mosaic."

A document of the University of Michigan American Culture Program published in 1992 offers a good exposition of the multicultural model. It recognizes "the multiplicity of American cultures." It presents multiculturalism as a new approach to the central question in American studies: What does it mean to be an American? The document suggests a shift from the study of core myths and values, and people's relationships to them as generalized Americans, to "recognizing that 'America' includes people of differing community, ethnic, and cultural histories, different points of view and degrees of empowerment." Such a perspective spurs studies of specific ethnic groups rather than the country as a whole (Internal Review document of the Program in American Culture of the University of Michigan—3/12/92).

ROOTS OF ETHNIC CONFLICT

Ethnicity, based on perceived cultural similarities and differences in a society or nation, can be expressed in peaceful multiculturalism or in discrimination or violent interethnic confrontation. Culture is both adaptive and maladaptive. The perception of cultural differences can have disastrous effects on social interaction.

The roots of ethnic differentiation—and therefore, potentially, of ethnic conflict—can be political, economic, religious, linguistic, cultural, or "racial." We may hypothesize that the potentiality for ethnic conflict is proportional to the number and degree of contrasts—particularly in situations of competition for resources and power. Why do ethnic differences often lead to conflict and violence? The causes include a sense of injustice because of resource distribution, economic and/or political competition, and reaction to discrimination, prejudice, and other expressions of threatened or devalued identity (Ryan 1990, p. xxvii).

Prejudice and Discrimination

Ethnic conflict often arises in reaction to prejudice (attitudes and judgments) or discrimination (action). **Prejudice** means devaluing (looking down on) a group because of its assumed behavior, values, capabilities, or attributes. People are prejudiced when they hold stereotypes about groups and apply them to individuals. (**Stereotypes** are fixed ideas—often unfavorable—about what the members of a group are like.) Prejudiced people assume that members of the group will act as they are "supposed to act" (according to the stereotype) and interpret a wide range of individual behaviors as evidence of the stereotype. They use this behavior to confirm their stereotype (and low opinion) of the group.

Discrimination refers to policies and practices that harm a group and its members. Discrimination may be *de facto* (practiced, but not legally sanctioned) or *de jure* (part of the law). An example of *de facto* discrimination is the harsher treatment that American minorities (compared with other Americans) tend to get from the police and the judicial system. This unequal treatment isn't legal, but it happens anyway. Segregation in the southern United States and apartheid in South Africa provide two examples of *de jure* discrimination, which are no longer in existence. In the United States *de jure* segregation has been illegal since the 1950s, and the South African apartheid system was abandoned in 1991. In both systems, by law, blacks and whites had different rights and privileges. Their social interaction ("mixing") was legally curtailed. Slavery, of course, is the most extreme and coercive form of legalized inequality; people are treated as property.

We can also distinguish between attitudinal and institutional discrimination. With **attitudinal discrimination,** people discriminate against members of a group because they are prejudiced toward that group. For example, in the United States members of the Ku Klux Klan have expressed their prejudice against blacks, Jews, and Catholics through verbal, physical, and psychological harassment.

The most extreme form of anti-ethnic (attitudinal) discrimination is **genocide,** the deliberate elimination of a group through mass murder. The United Nations defines *genocide* as acts "committed with intent to destroy, in whole or in part, a national, ethnical, racial, or religious group, as such" (Ryan 1990, p. 11). Strongly prejudicial attitudes (hate) and resulting genocide have been directed against people viewed as "standing in the way of progress" (e.g., Native Americans) and people with jobs that the dominant group wants (e.g., Jews in Hitler's Germany, Chinese in Indonesia).

Institutional discrimination refers to programs, policies, and institutional arrangements that deny equal rights and opportunities to, or differentially harm, members of particular groups. This form of discrimination is usually less personal and intentional than attitudinal discrimination is, but it may be based on a long history of inequality that also includes attitudinal bias. One example of institutional discrimination is what Bunyan Bryant and Paul Mohai (1991, p. 4) call **environmental racism**— "the systematic use of institutionally based power by whites to formulate policy decisions that will lead to the disproportionate burden of environmental hazards in minority communities." Thus, toxic waste dumps tend to be located in areas with nonwhite populations.

Environmental racism is discriminatory but not always intentional. Sometimes toxic wastes *are* deliberately dumped in areas whose residents are considered unlikely to protest (because they are poor, powerless, "disorganized," or "uneducated"). In other cases property values fall after toxic waste sites are located in an area. The wealthier people move out, and poorer people, often minorities, move in, to suffer the consequences of living in a hazardous environment.

Chips in the Mosaic

Although the multicultural model is increasingly prominent in contemporary North America, ethnic competition and conflict are just as evident. We hear increasingly of conflict between new arrivals, like Central Americans and Koreans, and long-established ethnic groups, like African Americans. Ethnic antagonism flared in South-Central Los Angeles in spring 1992, in rioting that followed the acquittal of the four white police officers who were tried for the videotaped beating of Rodney King.

Angry blacks attacked whites, Koreans, and Hispanics. This violence expressed frustration by African Americans about their prospects in an increasingly multicultural society. A *New York Times*/CBS News Poll conducted May 8, 1992, just after the Los Angeles riots, found that blacks had a bleaker outlook than whites did about the effects of immigration on their lives. Only 23 percent of the blacks felt they had more opportunities than recent immigrants, compared with twice that many whites (Toner 1992).

South-Central Los Angeles, where most of the 1992 rioting took place, is an ethnically mixed area, which used to be mainly African-American. As blacks have moved out, there has been an influx of Latin Americans (Mexicans and Central Americans—mainly recent and illegal immigrants). The Hispanic population of South-Central Los Angeles increased by 119 percent in a decade, as the number of blacks declined by 17 percent. By 1992 the neighborhood had become 45 percent Hispanic and 48 percent black. Many store owners in South-Central Los Angeles are Korean immigrants.

Korean stores were hard hit during the 1992 riots, and more than a third of the businesses destroyed were Hispanic-owned. A third of those who died in the riots were Hispanics. These mainly recent migrants lacked deep roots to the neighborhood and, as Spanish speakers, faced language barriers (Newman 1992). Many Koreans also had trouble with English.

Koreans interviewed on ABC's *Nightline* on May 6, 1992, recognized that blacks resented them and considered them unfriendly. One man explained, "It's not part of our culture to smile." African Americans interviewed on the same program did complain about Korean unfriendliness. "They come into our neighborhoods and treat us like dirt." These comments suggest a shortcoming of the multicultural perspective: Ethnic groups (blacks here) expect other ethnic groups in the same nation-state to assimilate to some extent to a shared (national) culture. The African Americans' comments invoked a general American value system that includes friendliness, openness, mutual respect, community participation, and "fair play." Los Angeles blacks wanted their Korean neighbors to act more like generalized Americans—and good neighbors.

Whatever their ethnic background, people can't hope to live in social isolation from the communities from which they derive their livelihoods. They have to take steps to adapt. Some African Americans jointly interviewed with a few Koreans by ABC told the store owners they could improve relations in the neighborhood by hiring one or two local people. The Koreans said they couldn't afford to hire nonrelatives.

One way in which Koreans in cities like New York and Los Angeles have succeeded economically is through family enterprise. Family members work together in small grocery stores, like those in South-Central Los Angeles, pooling their labor and their wealth. Korean culture also stresses the value of education; children, supervised and encouraged by their parents, study hard to do well in school. In a society whose economy is shifting from manufacturing toward specialized services and information processing, good jobs demand education beyond high school. Asian family values and support systems encourage children to plan, study, and work hard, with such careers in mind.

These values also fit certain general American ideals. Work and achievement are American values that the Korean Americans being interviewed invoked to explain their behavior. (Family solidarity is also a general American value, but the specific meaning of "family" varies between groups.) The Koreans also felt that they couldn't succeed financially if they had to hire nonrelatives.

The key question is whether such groups can prosper in impoverished multiethnic areas like South-Central Los Angeles if they don't extend their social ties to their host communities. Providing an economic service is not enough. Without efforts designed to gain social acceptance, storekeepers (of whatever ethnic group) will continue to face looting, boycotts, and other **leveling mechanisms.** This term refers to customs or social actions that operate to reduce differences in wealth and bring standouts in line with community norms. Leveling mechanisms surface when there is an expectation of community solidarity and economic similarity—especially shared poverty—and some people are profiting more than, or at the expense of, others.

Leveling mechanisms tend to discourage people from surpassing their peers—punishing those who do, pushing them back to the common level. Such mechanisms, according to Max Weber (1904/1958), were common in European peasant communities before the rise of capitalism. Peasants, Weber believed, worked just hard enough to satisfy their immediate needs. Then they quit, mistrusting people who needlessly worked more than others. The individualism associated with capitalism had to surmount the collectivism of the peasant community, in which gossip and other social pressures brought overachievers back in line.

Anthropologist George Foster (1965) stresses the importance of leveling mechanisms in "classic" peasant societies throughout the world. According to Foster, peasants have an "image of limited good," according to which all valued things are finite. They regard the total amount of health, wealth, honor, or success available to community members as limited. Thus, one person can excel only at the expense of others. Unless good fortune clearly comes from outside (for example, external wage work or a lottery) and unless the fruits of success are shared with others, successful people face ostracism through leveling mechanisms including gossip, avoidance, insults, and physical attack.

Leveling mechanisms are found not only in peasant communities but also in many other societies anthropologists have studied. The 1992 Los Angeles riots show that leveling mechanisms continue to operate in urban, stratified, multiethnic America.

Aftermaths of Oppression

Also fueling ethnic conflict are such forms of discrimination as forced assimilation, ethnocide, and cultural colonialism. A dominant group may try to destroy the cultures of certain ethnic groups (**ethnocide**) or force them to adopt the dominant culture (**forced assimilation**). Many countries have penalized or banned the language and customs of an ethnic group (including its religious observances). One example of forced assimilation is the anti-Basque campaign that the dictator Francisco Franco (who ruled between 1939 and 1975) waged in Spain. Franco banned Basque books, journals, newspapers, signs, sermons, and tombstones and imposed fines for using the Basque language in schools. His policies led to the formation of a Basque terrorist group and spurred strong nationalist sentiment in the Basque region (Ryan 1990).

A policy of **ethnic expulsion** aims at removing groups who are culturally different from a country. There are many examples, including Bosnia-Herzegovina in the 1990s. Uganda expelled 74,000 Asians in 1972. The neofascist parties of contemporary Western Europe advocate repatriation (expulsion) of immigrant workers (West Indies in England, Algerians in France, and Turks in Germany) (Ryan 1990, p. 9).

A policy of expulsion may create **refugees**—people who have been forced (involuntary refugees) or who have chosen (voluntary refugees) to flee a country, to escape persecution or war. For example, Palestinian refugees moved to camps in Egypt, Jordan, and Lebanon after the Arab-Israeli wars of 1948 and 1967 (Ryan 1990).

Colonialism, another form of oppression, refers to the political, social, economic, and cultural domination of a territory and its people by a foreign power for an extended time (Bell 1981). The British and French colonial empires are familiar examples of colonialism, but we can extend the term to the former Soviet empire, formerly known as "the Second World."

Using the labels "First World," "Second World," and "Third World" is a common, although clearly ethnocentric, way of categorizing nations that may be defined here. The **First World** refers to the "democratic West"—traditionally conceived in opposition to a "Second World" ruled by "communism." The First World includes Canada, the United States, Western Europe, Japan, Australia, and New Zealand. The **Second World** refers to the Warsaw Pact nations, including the former Soviet Union, the Socialist and once-Socialist countries of Eastern Europe and Asia. Proceeding with this classification, the less developed countries (LDCs) make up the **Third World.** Some even assign the poorest nations to a **Fourth World.** This usage would, for example, distinguish Bangladesh (Fourth World) from India (Third World).

The frontiers imposed by colonialism weren't usually based on, and often didn't reflect, preexisting cultural units. In many countries, colonial nation-building left ethnic strife in its wake. Thus, over a million Hindus and Muslims were killed in the violence that accompanied the division of the Indian subcontinent into India and Pakistan. Problems between Arabs and Jews in Palestine began during the British mandate period. Ethnic conflicts in the less developed countries have proliferated since the early 1960s, when decolonization reached its height. There have been bitter ethnic conflicts in Zaire, Nigeria, Bangladesh, Sudan, India, Sri Lanka, Iraq, Ethiopia, Uganda, Rwanda, Burundi, Lebanon, and Cyprus. Few of these have been resolved.

Like other colonial powers, the Soviet Union politically suppressed ethnic expression, including potential and actual conflict, for decades. Multiculturalism may be growing in the United States and Canada, but the opposite is happening in the disintegrating Second World, where ethnic groups (nationalities) want their own nation-states. The flowering of ethnic feeling and conflict as the Soviet empire disintegrated illustrates that years of political repression and ideology provide insufficient common ground for lasting unity.

Cultural colonialism refers to internal domination—by one group and its culture/ideology over others. One example is the domination over the former Soviet empire by Russian people, language, and culture, and by Communist ideology. The dominant culture makes itself the official culture. This is reflected in schools, the media, and public interaction. Under Soviet rule ethnic minorities had very limited

For decades the Soviet Union suppressed ethnic expression. Cultural colonialism
refers to domination by one group and its culture-ideology over others. One example
is the privileged position of the Russian people, language, and culture in the former
Soviet Union. Ethnic Russian colonists were sent (as were tanks) to many areas,
such as Tajikistan (shown here), to diminish the cohesion and clout of the local
people—but there was resistance.

self-rule in republics and regions controlled by Moscow. All the republics and their
peoples were to be united by the oneness of "socialist internationalism."

One common technique in cultural colonialism is to flood ethnic areas with
members of the dominant ethnic group. Thus, in the former Soviet Union, ethnic
Russian colonists were sent to many areas, like Tajikistan (see Figure 3-3), to diminish the cohesion and clout of the local people. Tajikistan is a small, poor state (and
former Soviet republic) in Central Asia, near Afghanistan, with 5.1 million people.
In Tajikistan, as in Central Asia generally, most people are Muslims. Today Islam,
as an alternative way of ordering spiritual and social life, is replacing the ideology of
Soviet communism. This comes after more than seventy years of official atheism
and suppression of religion. The Soviet empire limited Islamic teaching and worship, converting and destroying mosques, discouraging religious practice by the
young, but allowing it for old people. Still, Islam was taught at home, around the
kitchen table, so it has been called "kitchen Islam."

Now, as the Russians leave Tajikistan, the force of Russian culture and language
is receding. Islamic influence is growing. Women have started covering their arms,

FIGURE 3-3 Former Soviet Socialist Republics of Central Asia, including Tajikistan.

legs, and hair. More and more people speak and pray in Tajik, a language related to Persian (which is spoken in Iran) (Erlanger 1992).

"The Commonwealth of Independent States" is all that remains of the Soviet Union. In this group of new nations, ethnic groups (nationalities) like the Tajiks are seeking to establish separate and viable nation-states based on cultural boundaries. This celebration of ethnic autonomy is an understandable reaction to the Soviet Union's years of suppressing diversity: historic, national, linguistic, ethnic, cultural, and religious. It is part of an ethnic florescence that—as surely as globalization and transnationalism—is a trend of the late twentieth century.

SUMMARY

Ethnicity is based on cultural similarities (among members of the same ethnic group) and differences (between that group and others). Ethnic distinctions can arise from language, religion, history, geography, kinship, or "race." A race is an ethnic group assumed to have a biological basis. Usually race and ethnicity are ascribed statuses; people are born members of a group and remain so all their lives.

The term *nation* was once synonymous with "ethnic group." Now *nation* has come to mean a state—a centrally organized political unit, a government. *Nation* and *state* have become synonymous. Combined in *nation-state*, they refer to such an autonomous political entity, a "country." Because of migration, conquest, and colonialism, most nation-states are not ethnically homogeneous. States sometimes encourage ethnic divisions for political and economic ends.

Ethnic groups that once had, or wish to have or regain, autonomous political status (their own country) are called *nationalities*. Language and print have played a crucial role in the growth of national consciousness. But over time, political upheavals, wars, and migrations have divided many imagined national communities.

Ethnic diversity may be associated with positive group interaction and coexistence (harmony) or with conflict. In creating multitribal and multiethnic states, colonial regimes often erected boundaries that corresponded poorly with preexisting cultural divisions. But certain colonial policies and institutions also helped create new "imagined communities."

Assimilation describes the process of change that an ethnic group may experience when it moves to a country where another culture dominates. By assimilating, the minority adopts the patterns and norms of its host culture. Assimilation isn't inevitable, and there can be ethnic harmony without it.

A plural society combines ethnic contrasts and economic interdependence. Such interdependence (or, at least, the lack of competition) between ethnic groups may be based on different activities in the same region or on long-time occupation of different regions in the same country.

The view of cultural diversity in a nation-state as good and desirable is multiculturalism. The multicultural model is the opposite of the assimilationist model, in which minorities are expected to abandon their cultural traditions and values, replacing them with those of the majority population. A multicultural society socializes individuals not only into the dominant (national) culture but also into an ethnic culture. Multiculturalism succeeds best in a society whose political system promotes freedom of expression and in which there are many and diverse ethnic groups.

Ethnicity can be expressed in peaceful multiculturalism or in discrimination or violent interethnic confrontation. Ethnic conflict often arises in reaction to prejudice (attitudes and judgments) or discrimination (action). *Prejudice* means devaluing (looking down on) a group because of its assumed behavior, values, capabilities, or attributes. *Discrimination* refers to policies and practices that harm a group and its members. Discrimination may be *de facto* (practiced, but not legally sanctioned) or *de jure* (part of the law). With *attitudinal discrimination*, people discriminate because they are prejudiced toward a group. The most extreme form of antiethnic discrimination is genocide, the deliberate elimination of a group through mass murder. *Institutional discrimination* refers to programs, policies, and arrangements that deny equal rights and opportunities to, or differentially harm, particular groups.

Although the multicultural model is increasingly prominent in North America, ethnic competition and conflict are also evident. One shortcoming of the multicultural perspective is that ethnic groups may expect other ethnic groups who live in the same country to assimilate to some extent to a more general, supposedly shared, national culture and value system.

A dominant group may try to destroy the cultures of certain ethnic groups (ethnocide) or force them to adopt the dominant culture (forced assimilation). A policy of ethnic expulsion may create refugees—people who have been forced (involuntary refugees) or who have chosen (voluntary refugees) to flee a country. *Colonialism* refers to the political, social, economic, and cultural domination of a territory and its people by a foreign power for an extended time. In many countries, colonial nation-building left ethnic strife in its wake. *Cultural colonialism* refers to internal domination—by one group and its culture and/or ideology over others. One example is the domination of the former Soviet empire by the Russian people, language, and culture. The flowering of ethnic feeling and conflict as the Soviet empire disintegrated illustrates that years of political repression provide insufficient common ground for lasting unity. Celebration of ethnic autonomy is an understandable reaction to years of suppressing diversity: historic, national, linguistic, ethnic, cultural, and religious. It is part of an ethnic florescence that is a trend of the late twentieth century.

CHAPTER FOUR

The Cultural Construction of Race

SOCIAL RACE
Hypodescent: Race in the United States   ~   Not Us: Race in Japan   ~
Phenotype and Fluidity: Race in Brazil

STRATIFICATION AND "INTELLIGENCE"
BOX: Culture, Biology, and Sports

embers of an ethnic group may define themselves—and/or be defined by others—as different and special because of their language, religion, geography, history, ancestry, or physical traits. When an ethnic group is assumed to have a biological basis (shared "blood" or genetic material), it is called a *race*. In this chapter, examples from different cultures will be used to show that race, like ethnicity in general, is a cultural category rather than a biological reality. That is, ethnic groups, including "races," derive from contrasts perceived and perpetuated in particular societies, rather than from scientific classifications based on common genes.

It is not possible at this time to define races biologically. Only cultural constructions of race are possible—even though the average person conceptualizes "race" in biological terms. The belief that races exist and are important is much more common among the public than it is among scientists. Most Americans, for example, believe that their population includes biologically based "races" to which various labels have been applied. These labels include "white," "black," "yellow," "red," "Caucasoid," "Negroid," "Mongoloid," "Amerindian," "Euro-American," "African American," "Asian American," and "Native American."

We hear the words *ethnicity* and *race* frequently, but American culture doesn't draw a very clear line between them. As illustration, consider two articles in the *New York Times* of May 29, 1992. One, discussing the changing ethnic composition of the United States, states (correctly) that Hispanics "can be of any race" (Barringer 1992, p. A12). In other words, "Hispanic" is an ethnic category that cross-cuts "racial" contrasts such as that between "black" and "white." The other article reports that during the Los Angeles riots of spring 1992, "hundreds of Hispanic residents were interrogated about their immigration status on the basis of their *race* alone [emphasis added]" (Mydans 1992a, p. A8). Use of "race" here seems inappropriate because "Hispanic" is usually perceived as referring to a linguistically based

57

TABLE 4-1   ETHNIC GROUPS IN THE UNITED STATES, 1990 CENSUS DATA

Claimed Identity	Millions of People
Whites, German ancestry	57.9
Whites, Irish ancestry	38.7
Whites, English ancestry	32.6
Blacks	30.0
Asians and Pacific Islanders	7.3
American Indians, Eskimos, and Aleuts	1.9
Hispanics (any "race")	22.3
Others	58.0
Total population	248.7

Source: Barringer 1992, p. A12

(Spanish-speaking) ethnic group, rather than a biologically based race. Since these Los Angeles residents were being interrogated because they were Hispanic, the article is actually reporting on ethnic, not racial, discrimination. However, given the lack of a precise distinction between race and ethnicity, it is probably better to use the term "ethnic group" instead of "race" to describe *any* such social group, for example, African Americans, Asian Americans, Irish Americans, Anglo-Americans, or Hispanics. (Table 4-1 lists the main ethnic groups in the United States.)

SOCIAL RACE

Races are ethnic groups assumed (by members of a particular culture) to have a biological basis, but actually race is socially constructed. The "races" we hear about every day are cultural, or social, rather than biological categories. In Charles Wagley's terms (Wagley 1959/1968), they are **social races** (groups assumed to have a biological basis but actually defined in a culturally arbitrary, rather than a scientific, manner). Many Americans mistakenly assume that "whites" and "blacks," for example, are biologically distinct and that these terms stand for discrete races. But these labels, like racial terms used in other societies, really designate culturally perceived rather than biologically based groups.

Hypodescent: Race in the United States

How is race culturally constructed in the United States? In American culture, one acquires his or her racial identity at birth, as an ascribed status, but race isn't based on biology or on simple ancestry. Take the case of the child of a "racially mixed"

culture, and common ancestry) to give the Engineer's part to an English actor than to a Filipino one. But Actors' Equity didn't see it that way. (The most "correct" choices for the part would have been a French man, a Vietnamese man, or a Eurasian of appropriate background.)

When Actors' Equity vetoed Pryce, Mackintosh canceled the New York production of *Miss Saigon*. Negotiations continued, and *Miss Saigon* eventually opened on Broadway, with a well-integrated cast, starring Pryce and Salonga (whose demanding part was shared, for two performances per week, with a Chinese-American actress). A year after the opening, Pryce and Salonga had left the production, and the three main "Asian" (Vietnamese) parts (including the Eurasian Engineer) were being played by Filipinos.

The culturally arbitrary hypodescent rule—not logic—is behind the notion that an Asian is more appropriate to play a Eurasian than a "Caucasian" is. Hypodescent governs ethnic ascription in the United States and channels discrimination against offspring of mixed unions, who are assigned minority status. But, as the case of *Miss Saigon* illustrates, what has been used against a group can also be used to promote the interests of that group. There has been a shortage of parts for Asian and Asian-American actors. In this case they used the hypodescent rule as a basis for political action—to stake their claim to "Eurasian" as well as "Asian" parts.

Not Us: Race in Japan

American culture ignores considerable diversity in biology, language, and geographic origin as it socially constructs race in the United States. North Americans also overlook diversity by seeing Japan as a nation that is homogeneous in race, ethnicity, language, and culture—an image the Japanese themselves cultivate. Thus in 1986 former Prime Minister Nakasone created an international furor by contrasting his country's supposed homogeneity (responsible, he suggested, for Japan's success in international business) with the ethnically mixed United States. To describe Japanese society, Nakasone used *tan'itsu minzoku*, an expression connoting a single ethnic-racial group (Robertson 1992).

Japan is hardly the uniform entity Nakasone described. Some dialects of Japanese are mutually unintelligible, and scholars estimate that 10 percent of the national population of 124 million are minorities of various sorts. These include aboriginal Ainu, annexed Okinawans, outcast *burakumin*, children of mixed marriages, and immigrant nationalities, especially Koreans, who number more than 700,000 (De Vos et al. 1983).

Americans tend to see Japanese and Koreans as alike, but the Japanese stress the difference between themselves and Koreans. To describe racial attitudes in Japan, Jennifer Robertson (1992) uses Kwame Anthony Appiah's (1990) term "intrinsic racism"—the belief that a (perceived) racial difference is a sufficient reason to value one person less than another.

In Japan the valued group is majority ("pure") Japanese, who are believed to share "the same blood." Thus, the caption to a printed photo of a Japanese-American model reads: "She was born in Japan but raised in Hawaii. Her nationality is American but no foreign blood flows in her veins" (Robertson 1992, p. 5). Something like hypodescent also operates in Japan, but less precisely than in the United States, where mixed offspring automatically become members of the minority group. The children of mixed marriages between majority Japanese and others (including Euro-Americans) may not get the same "racial" label as their minority parent, but they are still stigmatized for their non-Japanese ancestry (De Vos and Wagatsuma 1966).

How is race culturally constructed in Japan? The (majority) Japanese define themselves by opposition to others, whether minority groups in their own nation or outsiders—anyone who is "not us." Aspects of phenotype (detectable physical traits, such as perceived body odor) are considered part of being *racially different by opposition*. Other races don't smell as "we" do. The Japanese stigmatize Koreans by saying they smell different (as Europeans also do). The Japanese contend that Koreans have a pungent smell, which they mainly attribute to diet—Koreans eat garlicky foods and spicy kimchee. Japanese also stereotype their minorities with behavioral and psychological traits. Koreans are seen as underachievers, crime-prone, and working class, in opposition to dominant Japanese, who are positively stereotyped as harmonious, hardworking, and middle class (Robertson 1992).

The "not us" should stay that way; assimilation is generally discouraged. Cultural mechanisms, especially residential segregation and taboos on "interracial" marriage, work to keep minorities "in their place." (Still, many marriages between minorities and majority Japanese do occur.) However, perhaps to give the appearance of homogeneity, people (e.g., Koreans) who become naturalized Japanese citizens are expected to take Japanese-sounding names (Robertson 1992; De Vos et al. 1983).

In its construction of race, Japanese culture regards certain ethnic groups as having a biological basis, when there is no evidence that they do. The best example is the *burakumin*, a stigmatized group of at least 4 million outcasts, sometimes compared to India's untouchables. The *burakumin* are physically and genetically indistinguishable from other Japanese. Many of them "pass" as (and marry) majority Japanese, but a deceptive marriage can end in divorce if *burakumin* identity is discovered (Aoki and Dardess, eds. 1981).

Burakumin are perceived as standing apart from the majority Japanese lineage. Through ancestry, descent (and thus, it is assumed, "blood," or genetics) *burakumin* are "not us." Majority Japanese try to keep their lineage pure by discouraging mixing. The *burakumin* are residentially segregated in neighborhoods (rural or urban) called *buraku*, from which the racial label is derived. Compared with majority Japanese, the *burakumin* are less likely to attend high school and college. When *burakumin* attend the same schools as majority Japanese, they face discrimination. Majority children and teachers may refuse to eat with them because *burakumin* are considered unclean.

Japan's stigmatized *burakumin* are physically and genetically indistinguishable from other Japanese. In response to *burakumin* political mobilization, Japan has dismantled the legal structure of discrimination against *burakumin* and has worked to improve conditions in their neighborhoods, which are called *buraku*. This Sports Day for *burakumin* children is one kind of mobilization.

In applying for university admission or a job and in dealing with the government, Japanese must list their address, which becomes part of a household or family registry. This list makes residence in a *buraku*, and likely *burakumin* social status, evident. Schools and companies use this information to discriminate. (The best way to pass is to move so often that the *buraku* address eventually disappears from the registry.) Majority Japanese also limit "race" mixture by hiring marriage mediators to check out the family histories of prospective spouses. They are especially careful to check for *burakumin* ancestry (De Vos et al. 1983).

The origin of the *burakumin* lies in a historic tiered system of stratification (from the Tokugawa period—1603–1868). The top four ranked categories were warrior-administrators (*samurai*), farmers, artisans, and merchants. The ancestors of the *burakumin* were below this hierarchy, an outcast group who did unclean jobs, like animal slaughter and disposal of the dead. *Burakumin* still do similar jobs, including work with animal products, like leather. The *burakumin* are more likely than majority Japanese are to do manual labor (including farm work) and to belong to the national lower class. *Burakumin* and other Japanese minorities are also more likely to have careers in crime, prostitution, entertainment, and sports (De Vos et al. 1983).

Like blacks in the United States, the *burakumin* are class-stratified. Because certain jobs are reserved for the *burakumin*, people who are successful in those occupations (e.g., shoe factory owners) can be wealthy. *Burakumin* have also found jobs as government bureaucrats. Financially successful *burakumin* can temporarily escape their stigmatized status by travel, including foreign travel.

Today most discrimination against the *burakumin* is *de facto* rather than *de jure*. It is strikingly like the discrimination—attitudinal and institutional—that blacks have experienced in the United States. The *burakumin* often live in villages and neighborhoods with poor housing and sanitation. They have limited access to education, jobs, amenities, and health facilities. In response to *burakumin* political mobilization, Japan has dismantled the legal structure of discrimination against *burakumin* and has worked to improve conditions in the *buraku*. Still, Japan has yet to institute American-style affirmative action programs for education and jobs. Discrimination against nonmajority Japanese is still the rule in companies. Some employers say that hiring *burakumin* would give their company an unclean image and thus create a disadvantage in competing with other businesses (De Vos et al. 1983).

By contrast with the *burakumin*, who are citizens of Japan, most Japanese Koreans, who form one of the nation's largest minorities (about 750,000 people), are not. Koreans in Japan continue, as resident aliens, to face discrimination in education and jobs. They lack citizens' health care and social service benefits, and government and company jobs don't usually go to non-Japanese.

Koreans started arriving in Japan, mainly as manual laborers, after Japan conquered Korea in 1910 and ruled it through 1945. During World War II, there were more than 2 million Koreans in Japan. They were recruited to replace Japanese farm workers who left the fields for the imperial army. Some Koreans were women (numbering 70,000 to 200,000), forced to serve as prostitutes ("comfort women") for Japanese troops. By 1952 most Japanese Koreans had been repatriated to a divided Korea. Those who stayed in Japan were denied citizenship. They became "resident aliens," forced, like Japanese criminals, to carry an ID card, which resentful Koreans call a "dog tag." Unlike most nations, Japan doesn't grant automatic citizenship to people born in the country. One can become Japanese by having one parent born in Japan and living there three successive years (Robertson 1992).

Like the *burakumin*, many Koreans (who by now include third and fourth generations) fit physically and linguistically into the Japanese population. Most Koreans speak Japanese as their primary language, and many pass as majority Japanese. Still, they tend to be segregated residentially, often in the same neighborhoods as *burakumin*, with whom they sometimes intermarry. Koreans maintain strong kin ties and a sense of ethnic identity with other Koreans, especially in their neighborhoods. Most Japanese Koreans qualify for citizenship but choose not to take it because of Japan's policy of forced assimilation. Anyone who naturalizes is strongly encouraged to take a Japanese name. Many Koreans feel that to do so would cut them off from their kin and ethnic identity. Knowing they can never become majority Japanese, they choose not to become "not us" twice.

Phenotype and Fluidity: Race in Brazil

There are more flexible, less exclusionary ways of constructing social race than those used in the United States and Japan. Along with the rest of Latin America, Brazil has less exclusionary categories, which permit individuals to change their racial classification. Brazil shares a history of slavery with the United States, but it lacks the hypodescent rule. Nor does Brazil have racial aversion of the sort found in Japan. The history of Brazilian slavery dates back to the sixteenth century, when Africans were brought as slaves to work on sugar plantations in northeastern Brazil. Later, Brazilians used slave labor in mines and on coffee plantations. The contributions of Africans to Brazilian culture have been as great as they have been to American culture. Today, especially in areas of Brazil where slaves were most numerous, African ancestry is evident.

The system that Brazilians use to classify biological differences contrasts with those used in the United States and Japan. First, Brazilians use many more racial labels—over 500 have been reported (Harris 1970)—than Americans or Japanese do. In northeastern Brazil I found forty different racial terms in use in Arembepe, a village of only 750 people (Kottak 1992). Through their classification system Brazilians recognize and attempt to describe the physical variation that exists in their population. The system used in the United States, by recognizing only three or four races, blinds Americans to an equivalent range of evident physical contrasts. Japanese races, remember, don't even originate in physical contrasts. *Burakumin* are physically indistinguishable from other Japanese but are considered to be biologically different.

The system that Brazilians use to construct social race has other special features. In the United States one's race is an ascribed status; it is assigned automatically by hypodescent and doesn't usually change. In Japan race is also ascribed at birth, but it can change when, say, a *burakumin* or a naturalized Korean passes as a majority Japanese. In Brazil racial identity is more flexible, more of an achieved status. Brazilian racial classification pays attention to phenotype. **Phenotype** refers to an organism's evident traits, its "manifest biology"—anatomy and physiology. There are thousands of evident (detectable) physical traits, ranging from skin color, hair form, and eye color (which are visible), to blood type, colorblindness, and enzyme production (which become evident through testing). A Brazilian's phenotype, and racial label, may change due to environmental factors, such as the tanning rays of the sun.

For historical reasons, darker-skinned Brazilians tend to be poorer than lighter-skinned Brazilians are. When Brazil's Princess Isabel abolished slavery in 1889, the freed men and women received no land or other reparations. They took what jobs were available. For example, the freed slaves who founded the village of Arembepe, which I have been studying since 1962, turned to fishing. Many Brazilians (including slave descendants) are poor because they lack a family history of access to land or commercial wealth and because upward social mobility is difficult. Continuing today, especially in cities, it is poor, dark-skinned Brazilians, on average, who face the most intense discrimination.

Given the correlation between poverty and dark skin, the class structure affects Brazilian racial classification, so that someone who has light skin and is poor will be perceived and classified as darker than a comparably colored person who is rich. The racial term applied to a wealthy person who has dark skin will tend to "lighten" the skin color, which gives rise to the Brazilian expression "money whitens." In the United States, by contrast, race and class are correlated, but racial classification isn't changed by class. Because of hypodescent, racial identity in the United States is an ascribed status—fixed and lifelong—regardless of phenotype or economic status. One illustration of the absence of hypodescent in Brazil is the fact that (unlike the United States) full siblings there may belong to different races (if they are phenotypically different).

Arembepe has a mixed and physically diverse population, reflecting generations of immigration and intermarriage between its founders and outsiders. Some villagers have dark skin color; others, light. Facial features, eye and hair color, and hair type also vary. Although physically heterogeneous, Arembepe is economically homogeneous—local residents have not risen out of the national lower class. Given such economic uniformity, wealth contrasts don't affect racial classification, which Arembepeiros base on the physical differences they perceive between individuals. As physical characteristics change (sunlight alters skin color, humidity affects hair form), so do racial terms. Furthermore, racial differences are so insignificant in structuring community life that people often forget the terms they have applied to others. Sometimes they even forget the ones they've used for themselves. To reach this conclusion, I made it a habit to ask the same person on different days to tell me the races of others in the village (and my own). In the United States I am always "white" or "Euro-American," but in Arembepe I got lots of terms besides *branco* ("white"). I could be *claro* ("light"), *louro* ("blond"), *sarará* ("light-skinned redhead"), *mulato claro* ("light mulatto"), or *mulato* ("mulatto"). The racial term used to describe me or anyone else varied from person to person, week to week, even day to day. My best informant, a man with very dark skin color, changed the term he used for himself all the time—from *escuro* ("dark") to *preto* ("black") to *moreno escuro* ("dark brunet").

The American and Japanese racial systems are creations of particular cultures, rather than scientific—or even accurate—descriptions of human biological differences. Brazilian racial classification is also a cultural construction, but Brazilians have developed a way of describing human biological diversity that is more detailed, fluid, and flexible than the systems used in most cultures. Brazil lacks Japan's racial aversion, and it also lacks a rule of descent like that which ascribes racial status in the United States (Harris 1964; Degler 1970).

The operation of the hypodescent rule helps us understand why the populations labeled "black" and "Indian" (Native American) are growing in the United States but shrinking in Brazil. American culture places all "mixed" children in the minority category, which therefore gets all the resultant population increase. Brazil, by contrast, assigns the offspring of mixed marriages to intermediate categories, using a larger set of ethnic and racial labels. A Brazilian with a "white" (*branco*) parent and a "black" (*preto*) parent will almost never be called *branco* or *preto* but instead by some intermediate term (of which dozens are available). The United States lacks intermediate categories, but it is those categories that are swelling in Brazil. Brazil's assimilated Indians are called *cabôclos* (rather than *índios*, or a specific tribal name, like Kayapó or Yanomami). With hypodescent, by contrast, someone may have just one of four or eight Indian grandparents or great-grandparents and still "feel Indian," be so classified, and even have a tribal identity.

For centuries the United States and Brazil have had mixed populations, with ancestors from Native America, Europe, Africa, and Asia. Although "races" have mixed in both countries, Brazilian and American cultures have constructed the results differently. The historic reasons for this contrast lie mainly in the different characteristics of the settlers of the two countries. The mainly English early settlers of the United States came as women, men, and families, but Brazil's Portuguese colonizers were mainly men—merchants and adventurers. Many of these Portuguese men married Native American women and recognized their "racially mixed" children as their heirs. Like their North American counterparts, Brazilian plantation owners had sexual relations with their slaves. But the Brazilian landlords more often freed the children that resulted—for demographic and economic reasons. (Sometimes these were their only children.) Freed offspring of master and slave became plantation overseers and foremen and filled many intermediate positions in the emerging Brazilian economy. They were not classed with the slaves, but were allowed to join a new intermediate category. No hypodescent rule ever developed in Brazil to ensure that whites and blacks remained separate (see Harris 1964; Degler 1970).

STRATIFICATION AND "INTELLIGENCE"

Over the centuries groups with power have used racial ideology to justify, explain, and preserve their privileged social positions. Dominant groups have declared minorities to be *innately*, that is, biologically, inferior. Racial ideas are used to suggest that social inferiority and presumed shortcomings (in intelligence, ability, character, or attractiveness) are immutable and passed across the generations. This ideology defends stratification as inevitable, enduring, and "natural"—based in biology rather than society. Thus the Nazis argued for the superiority of the "Aryan race," and European colonialists asserted the "white man's burden." South Africa institutionalized apartheid. Again and again, to justify exploitation of minorities and native peoples, those in control have proclaimed the innate inferiority of the oppressed. In the United States the supposed superiority of whites was once standard segregationist doctrine. Belief in the biologically based inferiority of Native Americans has been an argument for their slaughter, confinement, and neglect.

However, anthropologists know that most of the behavioral variation among contemporary human groups rests on culture rather than biology. The cultural sim-

Culture, Biology, and Sports

Culture constantly molds human biology. Culture promotes certain activities, discourages others, and sets standards of physical well-being and attractiveness. Sports activity, which is influenced by culture, helps build phenotype. American girls are encouraged to pursue—and they therefore do well in—competitive track and field, swimming, and diving. Brazilian girls, in contrast, haven't fared nearly as well in international athletic competition. Why are girls encouraged to become athletes in some nations but discouraged from physical activities in others? Why don't Brazilian women, and Latin women generally, do better in athletics?

Cultural standards of attractiveness affect athletic activities. Americans run or swim not just to compete but to keep trim and fit. Brazil's beauty standards accept more fat, especially in female buttocks and hips. Brazilian men have had some international success in swimming and running, but Brazil rarely sends female swimmers or runners to the Olympics. One reason Brazilian women avoid competitive swimming in particular is that sport's effects on phenotype. Years of swimming sculpt a distinctive physique—an enlarged upper torso, a massive neck, and powerful shoulders and back. Successful female swimmers tend to be big, strong, and bulky. The countries that produce them include the United States, Canada, Germany, China, and the former Soviet Union, where this phenotype isn't as stigmatized as it is in Latin countries. Swimmers develop hard bodies, but Brazilian culture says that women should be soft, with big hips and buttocks, not big shoulders.

Cultural factors also help explain why blacks excel in certain sports and whites in others. In North American schools, parks, sandlots, and city playgrounds, African Americans have access to baseball diamonds, basketball courts, football fields, and tracks. However, because of restricted economic opportunities, many black families can't afford to buy hockey gear or ski equipment, take ski vacations, pay for tennis lessons, or belong to clubs with tennis courts and pools. In the United States mainly light-skinned boys (often in private schools) play soccer, the most popular sport in the world. In Brazil, however, soccer is the national pastime of all males—black and white, rich and poor. There is wide

Years of swimming sculpt a distinctive physique—an enlarged upper torso, a massive neck, and powerful shoulders and back. The countries that produce the most successful female swimmers are the United States, Canada, Germany, the former Soviet Union, and China, where this phenotype is not as stigmatized for women as it is in Latin countries.

public access. Brazilians play soccer on the beach and in streets, squares, parks, and playgrounds. Many of Brazil's best soccer players, including the world-famous Pelé, have dark skin. When blacks have opportunities to do well in soccer, tennis, or any other sport, they are physically capable of doing as well as whites.

Why does the United States have so many black football and basketball players and so few black swimmers and hockey players? The answer lies mainly in cultural factors, such as variable access and social stratification. Many Brazilians practice soccer, hoping to play for money for a professional club. Similarly, American blacks are aware that certain sports have provided career opportunities for African Americans. They start developing skills in those sports in childhood. The better they do, the more likely they are to persist, and the pattern continues. Countering a claim made by TV sports commentator Jimmy the Greek Snyder a few years ago, culture—specifically differential access to sports resources—has more to do with sports success than does "race."

ilarities revealed through thousands of ethnographic studies leave no doubt that capacities for cultural evolution are equal in all human populations. There is also excellent evidence that within any **stratified** (class-based) society, differences in performance between economic, social, and ethnic groups reflect different experiences and opportunities rather than genetic makeup. (Stratified societies are those with marked differences in wealth, prestige, and power between social classes.)

Stratification, political domination, prejudice, and ignorance continue to exist. They propagate the mistaken belief that misfortune and poverty result from lack of ability. Occasionally doctrines of innate superiority are even set forth by scientists, who, after all, tend to come from the favored stratum of society. Among recent examples, one of the best known is Jensenism, named for the educational psychologist Arthur Jensen (Jensen 1969; Herrnstein 1971), its leading proponent. Jensenism is a highly questionable interpretation of the observation that African Americans, on average, perform less well on intelligence tests than Euro-Americans do. Jensenism asserts that blacks are hereditarily incapable of performing as well as whites do. Richard Herrnstein, writing with Charles Murray, makes a similar argument in the 1994 book *The Bell Curve*, to which the following critique also applies.

Environmental explanations for test scores are much more convincing than are the genetic tenets of Jensen, Herrnstein, and Murray. An environmental explanation does not deny that some people may be smarter than others. In any society, for many reasons, genetic and environmental, the talents of individuals vary. An environmental explanation does deny, however, that these differences can be generalized to whole groups. Even when talking about individual intelligence, however, we have to decide which of several abilities is an accurate measure of intelligence.

Psychologists have devised several kinds of tests to measure intelligence, but there are problems with all of them. Early intelligence tests demanded skill in manipulating words. Such tests do not accurately measure learning ability for several reasons. For example, individuals who have learned two languages as children— bilinguals—don't do as well, on average, on verbal intelligence tests as do people who have learned a single language. It would be absurd to suppose that children who master two languages have inferior intelligence. One explanation seems to be that because bilinguals have vocabularies, concepts, and verbal skills in both languages, their ability to manipulate either one suffers a bit. Still, this is offset by the advantage of being fluent in two languages.

Most tests are written by educated people in Europe and North America. They reflect the experiences of the people who devise them. It is not surprising that middle- and upper-class children do better since they are more likely to share the test makers' educational background and standards. Numerous studies have shown that performance on Scholastic Achievement Tests (SATs) can be improved by coaching and preparation. Parents who can afford $500 for an SAT preparation course enhance their kids' chances of getting high scores. Standardized college entrance exams are similar to IQ tests in that they purportedly measure intellectual aptitude. They may do this, but they also measure type and quality of high school education, linguistic and cultural background, and parental wealth. No test is free of class, ethnic, and cultural biases.

Tests invariably measure particular learning histories, not the potential for learning. They use middle-class performance as a standard for determining what should be known at a given chronological age. Furthermore, tests are usually administered by middle-class white people who give instructions in a dialect or language that may not be totally familiar to the child being tested. Test performance improves when the subcultural, socioeconomic, and linguistic backgrounds of subjects and test personnel are similar (Watson 1972).

Recognizing the difficulties in devising a culture-free test, psychologists have developed several nonverbal tests, hoping to find an objective measure that is not bound to a single culture. In one such test, individuals score higher by adding body parts to a stick figure. In a maze test, subjects trace their way out of various mazes. The score increases with the speed of completion. Other tests also base scores on speed, for example, in fitting geometric objects into appropriately shaped holes. All these tests are culture-bound because American culture emphasizes speed and competition whereas most nonindustrial cultures do not.

Examples of cultural biases in intelligence testing abound. Biases affect performance by people in other cultures and by different groups within the same culture, such as Native Americans in the United States. Many Native Americans have grown up on reservations or under conditions of urban or rural poverty. They have suffered social, economic, political, and cultural discrimination. In one study, Native Americans had the lowest IQ test scores (a mean of 81, compared with a standard of 100) of any minority group in the United States (Klineberg 1951). But when the environment offers opportunities similar to those available to middle-class Americans, test performance tends to equalize. Consider the Osage Indians, on whose reservation oil was discovered. Profiting from oil sales, the Osage did not experience the stresses of poverty. They developed a good school system, and their average IQ was 104. Here the relationship between test performance and environment is particularly clear. The Osage did not settle on the reservation because they knew that oil was there. There is no reason to believe that these people were innately more intelligent than were Indians on different reservations. They were just luckier.

Similar relationships between social, economic, and educational environment and test performance show up in comparisons of American blacks and whites. At the beginning of World War I, intelligence tests were given to approximately 1 million American army recruits. Blacks from some northern states had higher average scores than did whites from some southern states. This was caused by the fact that early in this century northern blacks got a better public education than did many southern whites. Thus, their superior performance is not surprising. On the other hand, southern whites did better than southern blacks. This is also expectable, given the unequal school systems then open to whites and blacks in the South.

Some people tried to get around the environmental explanation for the superior performance of northern blacks over southern whites by suggesting selective migration—smarter blacks had moved north. However, it was possible to test this hypothesis, which turned out to be false. If smarter blacks had moved north, their superior intelligence should have been obvious in their school records while they were still living in the South. It was not. Furthermore, studies in New York, Washington, and Philadelphia showed that as length of residence increased, test scores also rose.

Studies of identical twins raised apart also illustrate the impact of environment on identical heredity. In a study of nineteen pairs of twins, IQ scores varied directly with years in school. The average difference in IQ was only 1.5 points for the eight twin pairs with the same amount of schooling. It was 10 points for the eleven pairs with an average of five years' difference. One subject, with fourteen years more education than his twin, scored 24 points higher (Bronfenbrenner 1975).

These and similar studies provide overwhelming evidence that test performance measures education and social, economic, and cultural background rather than genetically determined intelligence. During the past 500 years Europeans and their descendants extended their political and economic control over most of the world. They colonized and occupied environments that they reached in their ships and conquered with their weapons. Most people in the most powerful contemporary nations—located in North America, Europe, and Asia—have light skin color. Some people in these currently powerful countries may incorrectly assert and believe that their world position has resulted from innate biological superiority. However, all contemporary human populations seem to have comparable learning abilities.

We are living in and interpreting the world at a particular time. In the past there were far different associations between centers of power and human physical characteristics. When Europeans were barbarians, advanced civilizations thrived in the Middle East. When Europe was in the Dark Ages, there were civilizations in West Africa, on the East African coast, in Mexico, and in Asia. Before the Industrial Revolution, the ancestors of many white Europeans and Americans were living much more like precolonial Africans than like current members of the American middle class. Their average performance on twentieth-century IQ tests would have been abominable.

SUMMARY

An ethnic group assumed (by a particular culture) to have a biological basis is called a *race*. Race, like ethnicity in general, is a cultural category rather than a biological reality. That is, ethnic groups, including "races," derive from contrasts perceived and perpetuated in particular societies, rather than from scientific classifications based on common genes. In the United States "racial" labels like "white" and "black" designate social races—categories defined by American culture. Given the lack of a precise distinction between race and ethnicity, it is better to use "ethnic group" instead of "race" to describe any such social group.

In American culture, one acquires his or her racial identity at birth, as an ascribed status, but American racial classification, governed by the rule of hypodescent, is based neither on phenotype nor genetics. Children of mixed unions are automatically classified with the minority-group parent.

Japan is not the uniform society that many imagine. Ten percent of the Japanese population consists of minorities: Ainu, Okinawans, outcast *burakumin*, children of mixed marriages, and immigrant nationalities, especially Koreans. Racial attitudes in Japan illustrate "intrinsic racism"—the belief that a perceived racial difference is a sufficient reason to value one person less than another. The valued group is majority ("pure") Japanese, who are believed to share "the same blood." Majority Japanese define themselves by opposition to others, whether minority groups in their own nation or outsiders—anyone who is "not us." Assimilation is discouraged; residential segregation and taboos on "interracial" marriage work to keep minorities "in their place." Japanese culture regards certain ethnic groups as having a biological basis, when there is no evidence that they do. The *burakumin*, for example, are physically and genetically indistinguishable from other Japanese but still face discrimination as as social race.

Racial classification in Brazil shows that the exclusionary American and Japanese systems are not inevitable. Brazil shares a history of slavery with the United States, but it lacks the hypodescent rule. One illustration of the absence of hypodescent is the fact that (unlike the United States) full siblings may belong to different races if they are phenotypically different. Nor does Brazil have racial aversion of the sort found in Japan. Brazilians recognize more than 500 races. Brazilian racial identity is more of an achieved status; it can change during a person's lifetime, reflecting phenotypical changes. It also varies depending on who is doing the classifying. But given the correlation between poverty and dark skin, the class structure affects Brazilian racial classification, so that someone who has light skin and is poor will be perceived and classified as darker than a comparably colored person who is rich.

Some people assert that there are genetically determined differences in the learning abilities of "races," classes, and ethnic groups. However, environmental variables (particularly educational, economic, and social background) provide much better explanations for performance on intelligence tests by such groups. Intelligence tests reflect the cultural biases and life experiences of the people who develop and administer them. All tests are to some extent culture-bound. Equalized environmental opportunities show up in test scores.

CHAPTER FIVE

Language

THE STRUCTURE OF LANGUAGE
Phonemes and Phones

TRANSFORMATIONAL-GENERATIVE GRAMMAR

LANGUAGE, THOUGHT, AND CULTURE
The Sapir-Whorf Hypothesis ～ Focal Vocabulary ～ Meaning

SOCIOLINGUISTICS
Linguistic Diversity in Nation-States ～ Stratification and Symbolic
Domination ～ BOX: Jocks, Burnouts, and Runts

HISTORICAL LINGUISTICS

anguage, spoken (*speech*) and written (*writing*, which has existed for about 6,000 years), is humans' primary means of communication. Key features of language include cultural transmission, productivity, and displacement. Like culture in general, of which language is a part, language is transmitted through learning, as part of enculturation. Language is based on arbitrary, learned associations between words and the things they stand for. **Productivity** refers to our ability to produce expressions (words, phrases, sentences) that are comprehensible to other speakers of the same language. Linguistic **displacement** describes our ability to speak (or write) of things and events that are not present. Unlike monkeys and apes, our nearest relatives, which use *call systems* in the wild, we don't have to see the objects before we make the sounds (say the words) that stand for them. (**Call systems** are vocal systems of communication used by nonhuman primates; they consist of a limited number of sounds—*calls*—that are produced only when particular environmental stimuli are encountered.) Human conversations are not bounded by place or by personal experience. Language allows us to discuss the past and future, share our experiences with others, and benefit from theirs.

Like ethnicity, language may be associated with cultural similarities and differences in (or between) societies or nations. The similarities are with speakers of the same language or dialect; the differences are between that group and others.

Anthropologists study language in its social and cultural context. Linguistic anthropology illustrates anthropology's characteristic interest in comparison, variation, and change. Some linguistic anthropologists reconstruct ancient languages by comparing their contemporary descendants and in so doing make discoveries about history. Others make inferences about universal features of language, linking them to uniformities in the human brain. Still others study linguistic differences to discover varied worldviews and patterns of thought in a multitude of cultures. Sociolinguists examine dialects and styles in a single language to show how speech reflects social differences (Fasold 1990; Labov 1972*a, b*). Linguistic anthropologists also explore the role of language in colonization, capitalist expansion, state formation, class relations, and political and economic dependence (Geis 1987).

THE STRUCTURE OF LANGUAGE

Until the late 1950s, linguists thought that the study of a language should proceed through a sequence of stages of analysis. The first stage was **phonology,** the study of sounds used in speech. Phonological analysis would determine which speech sounds (**phones**) were present and significant in that language. Speech sounds can be recorded using the International Phonetic Alphabet, a series of symbols devised to describe dozens of sounds that occur in different languages. The next stage was **morphology,** the study of the forms in which sounds combine to form **morphemes**—words and their meaningful constituents. Thus, the word *cats* would be analyzed as containing two morphemes—*cat*, the name for a kind of animal, and *-s*, a morpheme indicating plurality. The language's **lexicon** was a dictionary containing all its morphemes and their meanings. The next step was to study **syntax,** the arrangement and order of words in phrases and sentences. This stage-by-stage analysis sometimes created the erroneous impression that phonology, morphology, lexicon, and syntax were unconnected. All this was revolutionized by an approach known as **transformational-generative grammar,** to which we shall return after a brief consideration of phonology.

Phonemes and Phones

No language includes all the sounds designated by the symbols in the International Phonetic Alphabet. Nor is the number of **phonemes**—significant sound contrasts in a given language—infinite. Phonemes lack meaning in themselves, but they are the smallest sound *contrasts* that distinguish meaning. We discover them by comparing **minimal pairs,** words that resemble each other in all but one sound. An example is the minimal pair *pit/bit*. These two words are distinguished by a single sound contrast between /p/ and /b/ (we enclose phonemes in slashes). Thus /p/ and /b/ are phonemes in English. Another example is the different vowel sound of *bit* and *beat* (Figure 5-1). This contrast serves to distinguish these two words and the two phonemes /I/ and /i/ in English.

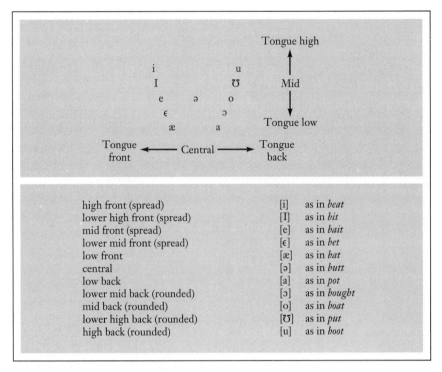

high front (spread)	[i]	as in *beat*
lower high front (spread)	[I]	as in *bit*
mid front (spread)	[e]	as in *bait*
lower mid front (spread)	[ɛ]	as in *bet*
low front	[æ]	as in *bat*
central	[ə]	as in *butt*
low back	[a]	as in *pot*
lower mid back (rounded)	[ɔ]	as in *bought*
mid back (rounded)	[o]	as in *boat*
lower high back (rounded)	[ʊ]	as in *put*
high back (rounded)	[u]	as in *boot*

FIGURE 5-1 Vowel phonemes in Standard American English shown according to height of tongue and tongue position at front, center, or back of mouth. Phonetic symbols are identified by English words that include them; note that most are minimal pairs. (Adaptation of excerpt and Figure 3-1 from *Aspects of Language*, 2nd ed., by Dwight Bolinger, copyright © 1975 by Harcourt Brace Jovanovich, Inc.; reprinted by permission of the publisher.)

Standard (American) English (SE), the "region-free" dialect of TV network newscasters, has about thirty-five phonemes—at least eleven vowels and twenty-four consonants. The number of phonemes varies from language to language—from fifteen to sixty, averaging between thirty and forty. The number of phonemes also varies between dialects of a given language. In American English, for example, vowel phonemes vary noticeably from dialect to dialect. Readers should pronounce the words in Figure 5-1, paying attention to (or asking someone else) whether they distinguish each of the vowel sounds. Most Americans don't pronounce them all.

Phonetics is the study of speech sounds in general, what people actually say in various languages. **Phonemics** studies the significant sound contrasts (phonemes) of a *particular* language. In English, /b/ and /v/ are phonemes, occurring in minimal pairs such as *bat* and *vat*. In Spanish, however, the contrast between [b] and [v] does not distinguish meaning, and they are therefore not phonemes (we enclose phones that are not phonemic in brackets). Spanish speakers normally use the [b] sound to pronounce words spelled with either *b* or *v*.

In any language a given phoneme extends over a phonetic range. In English the phoneme /p/ ignores the phonetic contrast between the [pʰ] in *pin* and the [p] in *spin*. Most English speakers don't even notice that there is a phonetic difference. [pʰ] is aspirated, so that a puff of air follows the [p]. The [p] in *spin* is not. (To see the difference, light a match, hold it in front of your mouth, and watch the flame as you pronounce the two words.) The contrast between [pʰ] and [p] is phonemic in some languages. That is, there are words whose meaning is distinguished only by the contrast between an aspirated and an unaspirated [p].

Native speakers vary in their pronunciation of certain phonemes. This variation is important in the evolution of language. With no shifts in pronunciation, there can be no linguistic change. The section on sociolinguistics below considers phonetic variation and its relationship to social divisions and the evolution of language.

TRANSFORMATIONAL-GENERATIVE GRAMMAR

Noam Chomsky's influential book *Syntactic Structures* (1957) advocated a new method of linguistic analysis—**transformational-generative grammar.** In Chomsky's view, a language is more than the surface phenomena just discussed (sounds, words, and word order). Beneath the surface features discovered through stage-by-stage analysis of particular languages, all languages share a limited set of organizing principles.

Chomsky views language as a uniquely human possession, qualitatively different from the communication systems of all other animals. Every normal child who grows up in a society develops language easily and automatically. Chomsky thinks that this occurs because the human brain contains a genetically transmitted blueprint, or basic linguistic plan, for building language. He calls this plan a **universal grammar.** When children learn a language, they don't start from scratch, because they already have the outline. As they learn their native language, children experiment with different parts of the blueprint. In so doing, they discover that their language uses some sections but not others. They gradually reject principles used in other languages and accept only the ones in their own.

The fact that children everywhere begin to speak at about the same age buttresses Chomsky's theory that humans are "wired" for language. Furthermore, people master features of language at similar rates. There are universals in language acquisition, such as improper generalizations (*foot, foots; hit, hitted*), which are eventually corrected. Children experiment with linguistic rules, accepting and refining some while rejecting others.

As we learn to speak, we master a specific **grammar,** a *particular* set of rules—the ones our language has taken from the universal set. These rules let us convert what we want to say into what we do say. People who hear us and speak our language understand our meaning. Our knowledge of the rules enables us to use lan-

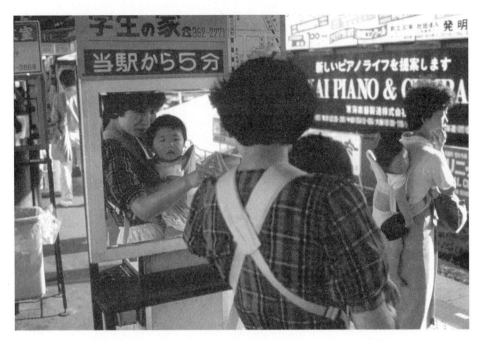

According to Noam Chomsky, the human brain contains a genetically transmitted blueprint, or basic linguistic plan, for building language. As they learn their native language, children experiment with different parts of that blueprint. They gradually reject principles used in other languages and accept only the ones in their own—Japanese in this case.

guage creatively, to *generate* an infinite number of sentences according to a finite number of rules. We can produce sentences that no one has ever uttered before, and we can understand other people's original statements.

Chomsky distinguishes between a native speaker's linguistic **competence** (what the speaker must—and does—know about his or her language in order to speak and understand) and **performance** (what the person actually says in social situations). Competence develops during childhood and becomes an unconscious structure. The linguist's job is to discover this structure by looking at deep structures, surface structures, and the transformational rules that link them.

When a speaker wishes to express a thought, a sentence is formed at what Chomsky calls the level of **deep structure** (the mental level) in the speaker's mind. That sentence rises to **surface structure** (actual speech)—expressed in sound—and passes from speaker to hearer. When a *sentence* (roughly defined as a complete thought) is spoken, the hearer figures out its meaning by translating it back into his or her own deep structure (Figure 5-2).

On the surface—the object of traditional linguistics—languages seem more different than they really are. Similarities are more evident at the level of deep structure. Chomsky proposed that by studying the deep structures of many languages,

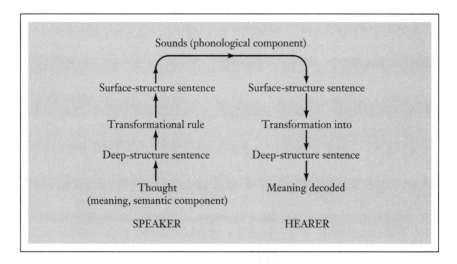

FIGURE 5-2 How a message passes from speaker to hearer, according to Chomsky's model. The speaker translates meaning (the semantic component) into sound (the phonological component) through grammar (deep structure, a transformation rule, and a surface-structure sentence). The hearer decodes in reverse order to find meaning.

linguists might eventually discover the grammatical building blocks on which all languages are based.

LANGUAGE, THOUGHT, AND CULTURE

According to Chomsky, the human brain contains a limited set of rules for organizing language. The fact that people can learn foreign languages and that words and ideas can be translated from one language into another tends to support Chomsky's position that all humans have similar linguistic abilities and thought processes.

The Sapir-Whorf Hypothesis

Other linguists and anthropologists take a different approach to the relationship between language and thought. Rather than seeking universal linguistic structures as clues to universal mental processes, they believe that different languages produce different ways of thinking. This position is sometimes known as the **Sapir-Whorf hypothesis** after Edward Sapir (1931) and Benjamin Lee Whorf (1956), its prominent early advocates. They argued that languages lead their speakers to think about things in particular ways. For example, the third-person singular pronouns of English (*he, she; him, her; his, hers*) distinguish gender, whereas those of the Palaung, a small tribe in Burma, do not (Burling 1970). Gender exists in English, although a fully developed noun-gender and adjective-agreement system, as in French and other Romance languages (*la belle fille, le beau fils*), does not. The Sapir-Whorf hypothesis therefore might suggest that English speakers can't help paying more attention to differences between males and females than do the Palaung and less than do French or Spanish speakers.

English divides time into past, present, and future. Hopi, a language of the Pueblo region of the Native American Southwest, does not. However, Hopi distinguishes between events that exist or have existed (what we use past and present to discuss) and those which don't or don't yet (our future events, along with imaginary and hypothetical events). Whorf argued that this difference gives English and Hopi speakers different perceptions of time and reality.

Focal Vocabulary

A lexicon (or vocabulary) is a language's dictionary, its set of names for things, events, and ideas. Lexicon influences perception. Thus, Eskimos have several distinct words for different types of snow that in English are all called *snow*. Most English speakers never notice the differences between these types of snow and might have trouble seeing them even if someone pointed them out. Eskimos recognize and think about differences in snow that English speakers don't see because our language provides us with just one word.

Similarly, the Nuer of Sudan have an elaborate vocabulary to describe cattle. Eskimos have several words for snow and the Nuer have dozens for cattle because of their particular histories, economies, and environments (Eastman 1975; Brown 1958). When the need arises, English speakers can also elaborate their snow and cattle vocabularies. For example, skiers name varieties of snow with words that are missing from the lexicons of Florida retirees. Similarly, the cattle vocabulary of Texas ranchers is much more extensive than that of a salesperson in a New York City department store. Such specialized sets of terms and distinctions that are particularly important to certain groups (those with particular *foci* of experience or activity) are known as **focal vocabulary.**

Vocabulary and lexical distinctions belong to the area of language that changes most readily. New words and distinctions, when needed, appear and spread. For example, who would have "faxed" anything a decade ago? Often-used words tend to be or become simple (*monolexemes*) rather than compound expressions (*rain* versus *tropical storm*) (Brown 1958). Names for items get simpler as they become common and important. A television has become a *TV*, an automobile a *car*, and a videocassette recorder a *VCR*.

Language, culture, and thought are interrelated. However, it would be more accurate to say that changes in culture produce changes in language and thought than the reverse. Consider differences between female and male Americans in regard to the color terms they use (Lakoff 1975). Distinctions implied by such terms as *salmon, rust, peach, beige, teal, mauve, cranberry,* and *dusky orange* aren't in the vocabularies of

A lexicon, or vocabulary, is a language's dictionary, its set of names for things, events, and ideas. Eskimos have several distinct words for different types of snow that in English are all called "snow." Eskimos recognize and think about differences in snow that English speakers don't see because our language provides us with just one word.

most American men. However, many of them weren't even in American women's lexicons fifty years ago. These changes reflect changes in American economy, society, and culture. Color terms and distinctions have increased with the growth of the fashion and cosmetic industries. A similar contrast in Americans' lexicons shows up in football, basketball, and hockey vocabularies. Sports fans, more often males than females, use more terms in reference to, and make more elaborate distinctions between, the games they watch. Thus cultural contrasts and changes affect lexical distinctions (for instance, *peach* versus *salmon*) within semantic domains (for instance, color terminology). **Semantics** refers to a language's meaning system.

Meaning

Speakers of particular languages use sets of terms to organize, or categorize, their experiences and perceptions. Linguistic terms and contrasts encode (embody) differences in meaning that people perceive. **Ethnoscience,** or **ethnosemantics,** studies such classification systems in various languages. Well-studied ethnosemantic *domains* (sets of related things, perceptions, or concepts named in a language) include kinship terminology and color terminology. When we study such domains, we are examining how those people perceive and distinguish between kin relationships or colors. Other ethnosemantic domains include ethnomedicine—the terminology for causes, symptoms, and cures of disease (Frake 1961); ethnobotany—native classification of plant life (Conklin 1954; Berlin, Breedlove, and Raven 1974); and ethnoastronomy (Goodenough 1953).

The ways in which people divide up the world—the contrasts they perceive as meaningful or significant—reflect their experiences. Anthropologists have discovered that certain lexical domains and vocabulary items evolve in a determined order. For example, after studying color terminology in more than 100 languages, Berlin and Kay (1969/1992) discovered ten basic color terms: *white, black, red, yellow, blue, green, brown, pink, orange,* and *purple* (they evolved in more or less that order). The number of terms varied with cultural complexity. Representing one extreme were Papua-New Guinea cultivators and Australian hunters and gatherers, who used only two basic terms, which translate as *black* and *white* or *dark* and *light*. At the other end of the continuum were European and Asian languages with all the color terms. Color terminology was most developed in areas with a history of using dyes and artificial coloring.

SOCIOLINGUISTICS

No language is a homogeneous system in which everyone speaks just like everyone else. Linguistic *performance* (what people actually say) is the concern of sociolinguists. The field of **sociolinguistics** investigates relationships between social and linguistic variation, or language in its social context. How do different speakers use a given language? How do linguistic features correlate with social stratification, including class, ethnic, and gender differences (Tannen 1986, 1990)? How is language used to express, reinforce, or resist power (Geis 1987)?

Sociolinguists don't deny that people who speak the same language share deep structures and rules, which permit mutually intelligible communication. However, sociolinguists focus on features that vary systematically with social position and situation. To study variation, sociolinguists must do fieldwork in order to define, observe, and measure variable aspects of language. Different aspects of variable speech must be quantified. To show that linguistic features correlate with social, economic, and political differences, the social attributes of speakers must also be measured and related to speech (Fasold 1990; Labov 1972*a*).

Variation within a language at a given time is historical change in progress. According to the principle of **linguistic uniformitarianism,** the same forces that have produced large-scale linguistic changes over the centuries, working gradually, are still at work and can be observed in linguistic events taking place today (Labov

1972*b*). Linguistic change doesn't occur in a vacuum but in society. Only when new ways of speaking are associated with social factors can they be imitated, spread, and play a role in linguistic change.

Linguistic Diversity in Nation-States

As an illustration of the linguistic variation encountered in all nation-states, consider the contemporary United States. Ethnic diversity is revealed by the fact that millions of Americans learn first languages other than English. Spanish is the most common. Most of these people eventually become bilinguals, adding English as a second language. In many multilingual (including colonized) nations, people use two languages on different occasions—one in the home, for example, and the other on the job or in public.

Whether bilingual or not, we all vary our speech in different contexts; we engage in **style shifts.** In certain parts of Europe, people regularly switch dialects. This phenomenon, known as **diglossia,** applies to "high" and "low" variants of the same language, for example, in German and Flemish (spoken in Belgium). People employ the "high" variant at universities and in writing, professions, and the mass media. They use the "low" variant for ordinary conversation with family members and friends.

Just as social situations influence our speech, so do geographic, cultural, and socioeconomic differences. Many dialects coexist in the United States with Standard (American) English (SE). SE itself is a dialect that differs, say, from "BBC English,"

Ethnic and linguistic diversity characterizes many nations,
especially in big cities, as is illustrated by this multilingual
advertising on New York City's Lower East Side.

In stratified societies, people constantly shift linguistic
styles. Linguistic performance varies in formal and informal
contexts. The Portuguese woman on the left uses an
animated, informal style with her neighbor in
Lisbon's Alfama neighborhood.

which is the preferred dialect in Great Britain. According to the principle of **linguistic relativity,** all dialects are equally effective as systems of communication,
which is language's main job. Our tendency to think of particular dialects as cruder
or more sophisticated than others is a social rather than a linguistic judgment. We
rank certain speech patterns because we recognize that they are used by groups that
we also rank. People who say *dese, dem,* and *dere* instead of *these, them,* and *there* communicate perfectly well with anyone who recognizes that the *d* sound systematically
replaces the *th* sound in their speech. However, this form of speech has become an
indicator of low social rank. We call it, like the use of *ain't,* "uneducated speech."
The use of *dem, dese,* and *dere* is one of many phonological differences that Americans recognize and look down on.

Stratification and Symbolic Domination

We use and evaluate speech—and language changes—in the context of *extralinguistic*
forces: social, political, and economic. Mainstream Americans evaluate the speech of
low-status groups negatively, calling it "uneducated." This is not because these ways
of speaking are bad in themselves but because they have come to symbolize low status. Consider variation in the pronunciation of *r.* In some parts of the United States
r is regularly pronounced, and in other (*r*less) areas it is not. Originally, American

*r*less speech was modeled on the fashionable speech of England. Because of its prestige, *r*lessness was adopted in many areas and continues as the norm around Boston and in the South.

New Yorkers sought prestige by dropping their *r*'s in the nineteenth century, after having pronounced them in the eighteenth. However, contemporary New Yorkers are going back to the eighteenth-century pattern of pronouncing *r*'s. What matters, and what governs linguistic change, is not the reverberation of a strong midwestern *r* but *social* evaluation, whether *r*'s happen to be "in" or "out."

Studies of *r* pronunciation in New York City have clarified the mechanisms of phonological change. William Labov (1972*b*) focused on whether *r* was pronounced after vowels in such words as *car*, *floor*, *card*, and *fourth*. To get data on how this linguistic variation correlated with social class, he used a series of rapid encounters with employees in three New York City department stores, each of whose prices and locations attracted a different socioeconomic group. Saks Fifth Avenue (68 encounters) catered to the upper middle class, Macy's (125) attracted middle-class shoppers, and S. Klein's (71) had predominantly lower-middle-class and working-class customers. The class origins of store personnel tended to reflect those of their clients.

Having already determined that a certain department was on the fourth floor, Labov approached ground-floor salespeople and asked where that department was. After the salesperson had answered, "Fourth floor," Labov repeated his "Where?" in order to get a second response. The second reply was more formal and emphatic, the salesperson presumably thinking that Labov hadn't heard or understood the first answer. For each salesperson, therefore, Labov had two samples of /r/ pronunciation in two words.

Labov calculated the percentages of workers who pronounced /r/ at least once during the interview. These were 62 percent at Saks, 51 percent at Macy's, but only 20 percent at S. Klein's. He also found that personnel on upper floors, where he asked "What floor is this?" (and where more expensive items were sold), pronounced *r* more often than ground-floor salespeople did.

In Labov's study, *r* pronunciation was clearly associated with prestige. Certainly the job interviewers who had hired the salespeople never counted *r*'s before offering employment. However, they did use speech evaluations to make judgments about how effective certain people would be in selling particular kinds of merchandise. In other words, they practiced sociolinguistic discrimination, using linguistic features in deciding who got certain jobs.

In stratified societies, our speech habits help determine our access to employment and other material resources. Because of this, "proper language" itself becomes a strategic resource—and a path to wealth, prestige, and power (Gal 1989). Illustrating this, many ethnographers have described the importance of verbal skill and oratory in politics (Beeman 1986; Bloch, ed. 1975; Brenneis 1988; Geis 1987). Remember, too, that a "great communicator," Ronald Reagan, dominated American society in the 1980s as a two-term president.

The French anthropologist Pierre Bourdieu views linguistic practices as *symbolic*

Jocks, Burnouts, and Runts

epending on where we live, Americans have certain stereotypes about how people in other regions talk. Some stereotypes, spread by the mass media, are more generalized than others. Most Americans think they can imitate a "southern accent." We also have nationwide stereotypes about speech in New York City (the pronunciation of *coffee*, for example) and Boston ("I pahked the kah in Hahvahd Yahd").

Many Americans also believe that midwesterners don't have accents. This belief stems from the fact that midwestern dialects don't have many stigmatized linguistic variants—speech patterns that people in other regions recognize and look down on, such as *r*lessness and *dem*, *dese*, and *dere* (instead of *them*, *these*, and *there*).

Actually, regional patterns influence the way all Americans speak. Midwesterners do have detectable accents. College students from out of state easily recognize that their in-state classmates speak differently. In-state students, however, have difficulty hearing their own speech peculiarities, because they are accustomed to them and view them as normal.

In Detroit-area high schools, sociolinguist Penelope Eckert, as described in her book *Jocks and Burnouts* (1990), studied variation in speech correlated with high school social categories. Eckert's study has revealed links between speech and social status—the high school manifestation of a larger and underlying American social class system. Social variation showed up most clearly in the division of the high school population into two main categories—"jocks" and "burnouts."

Along with teachers, administrators, and parents (particularly "jock parents"), jocks helped maintain the school's formal and traditional social structure. They participated more in athletics, student government, and organized school-based activities. In contrast, burnouts (a social label derived from their tendency to smoke cigarettes) had their main social networks in their neighborhoods. They took school social structure less seriously.

A comparable split exists in many public high schools, although the specific names of the two categories vary from place to place. Jocks have also been called "preppies" or "tweeds," and burnouts have been called "freaks," "greasers," "hoods," or "rednecks." This social division correlates with linguistic differences. Many adult speech habits are set when people are teens, as adolescents copy the speech of people they like and admire. Because jocks and burnouts move in different social systems, they come to talk differently. Eckert is still analyzing the specific differences.

The first step in a sociolinguistic study is to find out which speech forms vary. In New York City, the pronunciation of *r* varies systematically with social class and thus can be used in studies of sociolinguistic variation. However, this feature doesn't vary much among midwesterners, most of whom are adamant *r* pronouncers. However, vowel pronunciation does vary considerably among midwesterners and can be used in a sociolinguistic study.

Far from having no accents, midwesterners, even in the same high school, exhibit sociolinguistic variation. Furthermore, dialect differences in Michigan are immediately obvious to people, like myself, who come from other parts of the country. One of the best examples of variable vowel pronunciation is the /e/ phoneme, which occurs in words like *ten, rent, French, section, lecture, effect, best,* and *test.* In southeastern Michigan there are four different ways of pronouncing this phoneme. Speakers of Black English and immigrants from Appalachia often pronounce *ten* as *tin,* just as southerners habitually do. Some Michiganians say *ten,* the correct pronunciation in Standard English. However, two other pronunciations are more common. Instead of *ten,* many Michiganians say *tan,* or *tun* (as though they were using the word *ton,* a unit of weight).

My students often astound me with their pronunciation. One day I met one of my Michigan-raised teaching assistants in the hall. She was deliriously happy. When I asked why, she replied, "I've just had the best suction."

"What?" I said.

"I've just had a wonderful suction," she repeated.

"What?" I still wasn't understanding.

She finally spoke more precisely. "I've just had the best saction." She considered this a clearer pronunciation of the word *section.*

Another TA complimented me, "You luctured to great effuct today." After an exam a student lamented that she hadn't been able to do her "bust on the tust." Once I lectured about uniformity in fast-food restaurant chains. One of my students had just vacationed in Hawaii, where, she told me, hamburger prices were higher than they were on the mainland. It was, she said, because of the runt. Who, I wondered, was this runt? The very puny owner of Honolulu's McDonald's franchise? Perhaps he advertised on television "Come have a hamburger with the runt." Eventually I figured out that she was talking about the high cost of *rent* on those densely packed islands.

capital which properly trained people may convert into economic and social capital. The value of a dialect—its standing in a "linguistic market"—depends on the extent to which it provides access to desired positions in the labor market. In turn, this reflects its legitimation by formal institutions—the educational establishment, state, church, and prestige media. In stratified societies, even people who don't use the prestige dialect accept its authority and correctness, its "symbolic domination" (Bourdieu 1982, 1984). Thus, linguistic forms, which lack power in themselves, take on the power of the groups and relationships they symbolize. The education system, however (defending its own worth), denies this, misrepresenting prestige speech as being inherently better. The linguistic insecurity of lower-class and minority speakers is a result of this symbolic domination.

HISTORICAL LINGUISTICS

Sociolinguists study contemporary variation in speech—language change in progress. **Historical linguistics** deals with longer-term change. Historical linguists can reconstruct many features of past languages by studying contemporary **daughter languages.** These are languages that descend from the same parent language and that have been changing separately for hundreds or even thousands of years. We call the original language from which they diverge the **protolanguage.** French and Spanish, for example, are daughter languages of Latin, their common protolanguage. Historical linguists also classify languages according to their degree of relationship.

Language changes over time. It evolves—varies, spreads, divides into **subgroups** (languages within a taxonomy of related languages that are most closely related). Dialects of a single parent language become distinct daughter languages, especially if they are isolated from one another. Some of them split, and new, "granddaughter" languages develop. If people remain in the ancestral homeland, their speech patterns also change. The evolving speech in the ancestral homeland should be considered a daughter language like the others.

A close relationship between languages doesn't necessarily mean that their speakers are closely related biologically or culturally, because people can adopt new languages. In the equatorial forests of Africa, Pygmy hunters have discarded their ancestral languages and now speak those of the cultivators who have migrated to the area. Immigrants to the United States spoke many different languages on arrival, but their descendants now speak fluent English.

Knowledge of linguistic relationships is often valuable to anthropologists interested in history, particularly events during the past 5,000 years. Cultural features may (or may not) correlate with the distribution of language families. Groups that speak related languages may (or may not) be more culturally similar to each other than they are to groups whose speech derives from different linguistic ancestors. Of course, cultural similarities aren't limited to speakers of related languages. Even groups whose members speak unrelated languages have contact through trade, intermarriage, and warfare. Ideas and inventions diffuse widely among human groups. Many items of vocabulary in contemporary English come from French. Even without written documentation of France's influence after the Norman Conquest of England in 1066, linguistic evidence in contemporary English would reveal a long period of important firsthand contact with France. Similarly, linguistic evidence may confirm cultural contact and borrowing when written history is lacking. By considering which words have been borrowed, we can also make inferences about the nature of the contact.

SUMMARY

Language, the main system that humans use to communicate, features productivity and displacement and is culturally transmitted. Linguistic anthropologists share anthropology's general interest in uniformity and diversity in time and space. Linguistic anthropology examines meaning systems, relationships between language and culture, linguistic universals, sociolinguistics, and linguistic change.

No language includes all the sound (phones) that the human vocal apparatus can make. Phonology—the study of speech sounds—focuses on sound contrasts (phonemes) that distinguish meaning in a given language. In sociolinguistics, variation among speakers of the same language correlates with social contrasts and exemplifies linguistic change in progress.

In his transformational-generative approach, Chomsky argues for an innate blueprint for building language in the human brain. All people share this genetically determined capacity for language, though not for any particular language. Each language's grammar is a particular set of rules taken from the universal set. Once we master our language's rules, we can generate an infinite number of statements. Surface structures, the object of traditional linguistic study, make languages seem more different than they are. The similarities lie deeper, at the level of deep structure.

There are culturally distinctive as well as universal relationships between language and mental processes. The lexicons and grammars of particular languages can lead speakers to perceive and think in particular ways. Studies of domains such as kinship, color terminologies, and pronouns show that speakers of different languages categorize their experiences differently. However, language does not tightly restrict thought, because cultural changes can produce changes in thought and in language, particularly in surface structure.

Sociolinguistics investigates relationships between social and linguistic variation. It focuses on performance (the actual use of language) rather than competence (rules shared by all speakers of a given language). Sociolinguists do fieldwork with several informants and quantify their observations. Only when features of speech acquire social meaning are they imitated. If they are valued, they spread.

People vary their speech on different occasions, shifting styles, dialects, and languages, particularly in the modern world system. As linguistic systems, all languages and dialects are equally complex, rule-governed, and effective for communication. However, speech is used, is evaluated, and changes in the context of political, economic, and social forces. The linguistic traits of a low-status group are negatively evaluated (often even by members of that group) not because of their *linguistic* features but because they are associated with and symbolize low *social* status. One dialect, supported by the dominant institutions of the state, exercises symbolic domination over the others.

Historical linguistics is useful for anthropologists interested in historical relationships between populations. Cultural similarities and differences often correlate with linguistic ones. Linguistic clues can suggest past contacts between cultures. Related languages—members of the same language family—descend from an original protolanguage. Relationships between languages don't necessarily mean that there are biological ties between their speakers, because people can learn new languages.

Linguistic relativity views each language as a communication system that is as adequate as any other for the exchange of information.

CHAPTER SIX

Religion

ORIGINS, FUNCTIONS, AND EXPRESSIONS OF RELIGION
Animism ~ Mana and Taboo ~ Magic and Religion ~ Anxiety, Control, Solace ~ The Social Functions of Ritual Acts ~ Rites of Passage ~ Totems: Symbols of Society ~ The Nature of Ritual

ANALYSIS OF MYTH
Structural Analysis ~ Fairy Tales ~ Secular Rituals

RELIGION AND CULTURE

RELIGION AND CHANGE
Revitalization Movements ~ BOX: Halloween: An American Ritual of Rebellion

he anthropologist Anthony F. C. Wallace has defined **religion** as "belief and ritual concerned with supernatural beings, powers, and forces" (1966, p. 5). Like ethnicity and language, religion may be associated with social divisions within and between societies and nations. Religious behavior and beliefs both unite and divide. Participation in common rites may affirm, and thus maintain, the social solidarity of a religion's adherents. On the other hand, religious differences may be associated with bitter enmity.

In studying religion cross-culturally, anthropologists pay attention not only to the social roles of religion but also to the nature and content of religious acts, actions, events, processes, settings, practitioners, specialists, and organizations. We also consider such verbal manifestations of religious beliefs as prayers, chants, invocations, myths, fables, tales, texts, and statements about ethics, standards, and morality.

The supernatural is the extraordinary realm outside (but believed to touch on) the observable world. It is nonempirical, unverifiable, mysterious, and inexplicable in ordinary terms. Supernatural beings—gods and goddesses, ghosts, and souls—are not of the material world. Nor are supernatural forces, some of which are wielded by beings. Other sacred forces are impersonal—they simply exist. In many societies, however, people believe that they can benefit from, become imbued with, or manipulate supernatural forces.

Religion, as defined here, exists in all human societies. It is a cultural universal. However, we shall see that it isn't always easy to distinguish the supernatural from the natural and that different cultures conceptualize supernatural entities very differently.

ORIGINS, FUNCTIONS, AND EXPRESSIONS OF RELIGION

Any statement about when, where, why, and how religion arose or any description of its original nature is pure speculation. Nevertheless, although such speculations are inconclusive, many of them have revealed important functions and effects of religious behavior. We will examine several theories now.

Animism

The Englishman Sir Edward Burnett Tylor (1871/1958) was a founder of the anthropology of religion. Religion was born, Tylor thought, as people tried to understand conditions and events they could not explain by reference to daily experience. Tylor believed that our ancestors—and contemporary nonindustrial peoples—were particularly intrigued with death, dreaming, and trance. In dreams and trances people experience a form of suspended animation. On waking, they recall images from the dream world.

Tylor concluded that attempts to explain dreams and trances led early humans to believe that two entities inhabit the body, one active during the day and the other—a double or soul—active during sleep and trance states. Although they never meet, the two entities are vital to each other. When the double permanently leaves the body, the person dies. Death is departure of the soul. From the Latin for soul, *anima*, Tylor named this belief animism.

Tylor proposed that religion had evolved through stages, beginning with animism. **Polytheism** (the belief in multiple gods) and then monotheism (the belief in a single, all-powerful deity) developed later. Because religion originated to explain things people didn't understand, Tylor thought it would decline as science offered better explanations. To an extent, he was right. We now have scientific explanations for many things that religion once elucidated. Nevertheless, because religion persists, it must do something more than explain the mysterious. It must, and does, have other functions.

Mana and Taboo

There was a competing view to Tylor's theory of **animism** (the belief in souls and other spiritual *beings*) as the first religion. The alternative was that early humans saw the supernatural as a domain of impersonal power, or *force*, which people could control under certain conditions. Such a conception of the supernatural was particularly

Beliefs in mana—a supernatural force or power, which
people may manipulate for their own ends—are
widespread. Mana can reside in people, animals, plants, and
objects, such as the skull held here by a member of the
headhunting Iban tribe of Malaysia.

prominent in Melanesia, the area of the South Pacific that includes Papua-New
Guinea and adjacent islands. Melanesians believed in **mana,** a sacred impersonal
force existing in the universe. Mana can reside in people, animals, plants, and objects.

Melanesian mana was similar to our notion of luck. Melanesians attributed success to mana, which people could acquire or manipulate in different ways, such as
through magic. Objects with mana could change someone's luck. For example, a
charm belonging to a successful hunter might transmit the hunter's mana to the next
person who held it. A woman might put a rock in her garden, see her yields improve
dramatically, and attribute the change to the force contained in the rock.

Beliefs in manalike forces are widespread, although the specifics of the religious
doctrines vary. Consider the contrast between mana in Melanesia and Polynesia (the
islands included in a triangular area marked by Hawaii to the north, Easter Island to
the east, and New Zealand to the southwest). In Melanesia, one could acquire mana
by chance, or by working hard to get it. In Polynesia, however, mana was not potentially available to everyone but was attached to political offices. Chiefs and nobles
had more mana than ordinary people did.

So charged with mana were the highest chiefs that contact with them was dangerous to commoners. The mana of chiefs flowed out of their bodies wherever they went. It could infect the ground, making it dangerous for others to walk in the chief's footsteps. It could permeate the containers and utensils chiefs used in eating. Contact between chief and commoners was dangerous because mana could have an effect like an electric shock. Because high chiefs had so much mana, their bodies and possessions were **taboo** (set apart as sacred and off-limits to ordinary people). Contact between a high chief and commoners was forbidden. Because ordinary people couldn't bear as much sacred current as royalty could, when commoners were accidentally exposed, purification rites were necessary.

We see that one function of religion is to explain. The belief in souls explains what happens in sleep, trance, and death. Melanesian mana explains success that people can't understand in ordinary, natural terms. People fail at hunting, warfare, or gardening not because they are lazy, stupid, or inept but because success comes— or doesn't come—from the supernatural world.

The beliefs in spiritual beings (e.g., animism) and supernatural forces (e.g., mana) fit within the definition of religion given at the beginning of this chapter. Most religions include both spirits and impersonal forces. Likewise, the supernatural beliefs of contemporary North American people include beings (gods, saints, souls, demons) and forces (charms, talismans, and sacred objects).

Magic and Religion

Magic refers to supernatural techniques intended to accomplish specific aims. These techniques include spells, formulas, and incantations used with deities or with impersonal forces. Magicians use *imitative magic* to produce a desired effect by imitating it. If magicians wish to injure or kill someone, they may imitate that effect on an image of the victim. Sticking pins in "voodoo dolls" is an example. With *contagious magic*, whatever is done to an object is believed to affect a person who once had contact with it. Sometimes practitioners of contagious magic use body products from prospective victims—their nails or hair, for example. The spell performed on the body product is believed to reach the person eventually and work the desired result.

We find magic in cultures with diverse religious beliefs. It can be associated with animism, mana, polytheism, and even monotheism. Magic is neither simpler nor more primitive than animism or the belief in mana.

Anxiety, Control, Solace

Religion and magic don't just explain things and help people accomplish goals. They also enter the domain of feelings. In other words, they do not have just explanatory (cognitive) functions but emotional ones as well. For example, supernatural beliefs and practices can help reduce anxiety. Magical techniques can dispel doubts that arise when outcomes are beyond human control. Similarly, religion helps people face death and endure life crises.

Although all societies have techniques to deal with everyday matters, there are certain aspects of people's lives over which they lack control. When people face uncertainty and danger, according to Malinowski, they turn to magic.

> [H]owever much knowledge and science help man in allowing him to obtain what he wants, they are unable completely to control chance, to eliminate accidents, to foresee the unexpected turn of natural events, or to make human handiwork reliable and adequate to all practical requirements. (1931/1978, p. 39)

Malinowksi found that the Trobriand Islanders used magic when sailing, a hazardous activity. He proposed that because people can't control matters such as wind, weather, and the fish supply, they turn to magic. People may call on magic when they come to a gap in their knowledge or powers of practical control yet have to continue in a pursuit (Malinowski 1931/1978).

According to Malinowski, magic is used to establish control, but religion "is born out of . . . the real tragedies of human life" (Malinowski 1931/1978, p. 45). Religion offers emotional comfort, particularly when people face a crisis. Malinowski saw tribal religions as concerned mainly with such crises of life as birth, puberty, marriage, and death.

The Social Functions of Ritual Acts

Magic and religion can reduce anxiety and allay fears. Ironically, rituals and beliefs can also *create* anxiety and a sense of insecurity and danger (Radcliffe-Brown 1962/1965). Anxiety may arise *because* a rite exists. Indeed, participation in a rite may build up a common stress whose reduction, through completion of the rite, enhances the solidarity of participants.

Rites of Passage

The traditional vision quests of Native Americans, particularly the Plains Indians, illustrate **rites of passage** (customs associated with the transition from one place or stage of life to another), which are found throughout the world. Among the Plains Indians, to move from boyhood to manhood, a youth temporarily separated from his community. After a period of isolation in the wilderness, often featuring fasting and drug consumption, the young man would see a vision, which would become his guardian spirit. He would then return to his community as an adult.

The rites of passage of contemporary cultures include confirmations, baptisms, bar and bat mitzvahs, and fraternity hazing. Passage rites involve changes in social status, such as from boyhood to manhood and from nonmember to sorority sister. More generally, a rite of passage may mark any change in place, condition, social position, or age.

Liminal people, like these members of the N'Jembe women's group in Omboue, Gabon, West Africa, are temporarily set apart from ordinary distinctions and expectations. Their liminal status may be marked by a variety of contrasts with ordinary life, such as the painted faces and headdresses shown here.

All rites of passage have three phases: separation, margin, and aggregation. In the first phase, people withdraw from the group and begin moving from one place or status to another. In the third phase, they reenter society, having completed the rite. The *margin* phase is the most interesting. It is the period between states, the limbo during which people have left one place or state but haven't yet entered or joined the next. We call this the liminal phase of the passage rite (Turner 1974).

Liminality always has certain characteristics. Liminal people occupy ambiguous social positions. They exist apart from ordinary distinctions and expectations, living in a time out of time. They are cut off from normal social contacts. A variety of contrasts may demarcate liminality from regular social life. For example, among the Ndembu of Zambia, a chief had to undergo a passage rite before taking office. During the liminal period, his past and future positions in society were ignored, even reversed. He was subjected to a variety of insults, orders, and humiliations.

Unlike the vision quest and the Ndembu initiation, which are individual experiences, passage rites are often collective. A group—boys being circumcised, fraternity or sorority initiates, men at military boot camps, football players in summer training camps, women becoming nuns—pass through the rites together. Table 6-1 summarizes the contrasts or oppositions between liminality and normal social life.

Most notable is a social aspect of *collective liminality* called **communitas** (Turner 1974), an intense community spirit, a feeling of great social solidarity, equality, and togetherness. People experiencing liminality together form a community of equals. The social distinctions that have existed before or will exist afterward are temporarily forgotten. Liminal people experience the same treatment and conditions and must act alike. Liminality may be marked ritually and symbolically by *reversals* of ordinary behavior. For example, sexual taboos may be intensified or, conversely, sexual excess may be encouraged.

Liminality is part of every passage rite. Furthermore, in certain societies, it can become a permanent feature of particular groups. This happens most notably in complex societies, nation-states. Religious groups often use liminal characteristics to set themselves off from others. Humility, poverty, equality, obedience, sexual abstinence, and silence may be conditions of membership in a sect. Liminal features may also signal the sacredness of persons, settings, and events by setting them off as extraordinary—outside normal social space and regular time.

TABLE 6-1   OPPOSITIONS BETWEEN LIMINALITY AND NORMAL SOCIAL LIFE

Liminality	*Normal Social Structure*
transition	state
homogeneity	heterogeneity
communitas	structure
equality	inequality
anonymity	names
absence of property	property
absence of status	status
nakedness or uniform dress	dress distinctions
sexual continence or excess	sexuality
minimization of sex distinctions	maximization of sex distinctions
absence of rank	rank
humility	pride
disregard of personal appearance	care for personal appearance
unselfishness	selfishness
total obedience	obedience only to superior rank
sacredness	secularity
sacred instruction	technical knowledge
silence	speech
simplicity	complexity
acceptance of pain and suffering	avoidance of pain and suffering

Source: Adapted from Victor W. Turner, *The Ritual Process.* Copyright © 1969 by Victor W. Turner. By permission of Aldine de Gruyter. New York.

Totems: Symbols of Society

Thus rituals may serve the social function of creating temporary or permanent solidarity between people—forming a social community. We see this also in religious practices known as totemism. Totemism was important in the religions of the Native Australians. *Totems* could be animals, plants, or geographic features. In each tribe, groups of people had particular totems. Members of each totemic group believed themselves to be descendants of their totem. They customarily neither killed nor ate it, but this taboo was lifted once a year, when people assembled for ceremonies dedicated to the totem. These annual rites were believed to be necessary for the totem's survival and reproduction.

Totemism is a religion that uses nature as a model for society. The totems are usually animals and plants, which are part of nature. People relate to nature through their totemic association with natural species. Because each group has a different totem, social differences mirror natural contrasts. Diversity in the natural order becomes a model for separation in the social order. However, although totemic plants and animals occupy different niches in nature, on another level they are united because they all are part of nature. The unity of the human social order is enhanced by symbolic association with and imitation of the natural order (Durkheim 1912/1961; Radcliffe-Brown 1962/1975; Lévi-Strauss 1963).

One role of religious rites and beliefs is to affirm, and thus maintain, the solidarity of a religion's adherents. ("A family that prays together stays together.") Totems are sacred emblems symbolizing common identity. In totemic rites, people gather together to honor their totem. In so doing, they use ritual to maintain the social oneness that the totem symbolizes.

The Nature of Ritual

Several features distinguish **rituals** from other kinds of behavior (Rappaport 1974). Rituals are formal—stylized, repetitive, and stereotyped. People perform them in special (sacred) places and at set times. Rituals include **liturgical orders**—sequences of words and actions invented prior to the current performance of the ritual in which they occur.

These features link rituals to plays, but there are important differences. Plays have audiences rather than participants. Actors merely *portray* something, but ritual performers—who make up congregations—are *in earnest*. Rituals convey information about the participants and their traditions. Repeated year after year, generation after generation, rituals translate enduring messages, values, and sentiments into action.

Rituals are *social* acts. Inevitably, some participants are more committed than others are to the beliefs that lie behind the rites. However, just by taking part in a joint public act, the performers signal that they accept a common social and moral order, one that transcends their status as individuals.

Passage rites are often collective. Members of a group—
such as these initiates in Togo and Marine recruits in South
Carolina—pass through the rites together. Such liminal
people experience the same treatment and conditions and
must act alike. They share communitas, an intense
community spirit, a feeling of great social
solidarity or togetherness.

ANALYSIS OF MYTH

Cross-cultural research has documented a rich variety of ideas about the supernatural, including animism, mana, taboo, and totemism. We have seen that participation in a ritual creates solidarity. Regardless of their particular thoughts and varied degrees of commitment, the participants temporarily submerge their individuality in a community. Like ethnicity, religion can be a powerful molder of social solidarity.

Nevertheless, the anthropological study of religion is not limited to religion's social effects or its expression in rites and ceremonies. Anthropology also studies religious and quasi-religious stories about supernatural entities—the myths and tales of long ago or far away that are retold across the generations in every society.

Myths often include people's own account of their creation, of the beginning of their world and the extraordinary events that affected their ancestors. They may also tell of the continuing exploits and activities of deities or spirits either in an alternative world or as they come into occasional contact with mortals. Myths, legends, and folktales express cultural beliefs and values. They offer hope, excitement, and escape. They also teach lessons that society wants taught.

Structural Analysis

One way of studying myth is structural analysis, or **structuralism,** developed by Claude Lévi-Strauss, a prolific French anthropologist. Lévi-Straussian structuralism (1967) aims not at *explaining* relations, themes, and connections among aspects of culture but at *discovering* them. It differs in its goals and results from the methods of gathering and interpreting data usually used in the sciences. Because structuralism is as close to the humanities as it is to science, structuralist methods have been used in analyzing literature and art as well as in anthropology.

Myths and folktales are the (oral) literature of nonliterate societies. Lévi-Strauss used structuralism to analyze the cultural creations of such societies, including their myths. Structuralism rests on Lévi-Strauss's belief that human minds have certain characteristics which originate in features of the *Homo sapiens* brain. These common mental structures lead people everywhere to think similarly regardless of their society or cultural background. Among these universal mental characteristics are the need to classify: to impose order on aspects of nature, on people's relation to nature, and on relations between people.

According to Lévi-Strauss, a universal aspect of classification is opposition, or contrast. Although many phenomena are continuous rather than discrete, the mind, because of its need to impose order, treats them as being more different than they are. Things that are quantitatively rather than qualitatively different are made to seem absolutely dissimilar. Scientific classification is the Western academic outgrowth of the universal need to impose order. One of the most common means of classifying is by using **binary opposition.** Good and evil, white and black, old and young, high and low are oppositions that, according to Lévi-Strauss, reflect the human need to convert differences of degree into differences of kind.

Lévi-Strauss has applied his assumptions about classification and binary opposition to myths and folktales. He has shown that these narratives have simple building blocks—elementary structures or "mythemes." Examining the myths of different cultures, Lévi-Strauss shows that one tale can be converted into another through a series of simple operations, for example, by doing the following:

1. Converting the positive element of a myth into its negative
2. Reversing the order of the elements
3. Replacing a male hero with a female hero
4. Preserving or repeating certain key elements

Through such operations, two apparently dissimilar myths can be shown to be variations on a common structure, that is, to be transformations of each other. One example is Lévi-Strauss's analysis of "Cinderella" (1967), a well-known tale whose elements vary between neighboring cultures. Through reversals, oppositions, and negations, as the tale is told, retold, diffused, and incorporated within the traditions of successive societies, "Cinderella" becomes "Ash Boy," after a series of contrasts related to the change in hero's gender.

Fairy Tales

In his book *The Uses of Enchantment: The Meaning and Importance of Fairy Tales* (1975), the psychologist Bruno Bettelheim drew a useful distinction between two kinds of tale: the tragic myth and the hopeful folktale. Tragic myths include many biblical accounts (that of Job, for example) and Greco-Roman myths that confront humans with powerful, capricious, and awesome supernatural entities. Such tales focus on the huge gap between mortals and the supernatural. In contrast, the folk- or fairy tales found in many cultures use fantasy to offer hope and to suggest the possibility of growth and self-realization. Bettelheim argues that this message is particularly important for children. The characters in the myths and tales of many cultures are not powerful beings but plants, animals, humans, and nature spirits who use intelligence, physical prowess, or cunning to accomplish their ends.

Bettelheim urges parents to read or tell folk- or fairy tales to their children. He chides American parents and librarians for pushing children to read "realistic" and "prosocial" stories, which often are dull, complex, and psychologically empty. Folk- or fairy tales, in contrast, allow children to identify with heroes who win out in the end. These stories offer confidence that no matter how bad things seem now, they will improve. They give reassurance that although small and insignificant now, the child will eventually grow up and achieve independence from parents and siblings.

Similar to the way Lévi-Strauss focuses on binary oppositions, Bettelheim analyzes how fairy tales permit children to deal with their ambivalent feelings (love and hate) about their parents and siblings. Fairy tales often split the good and bad aspects of the parent into separate figures of good and evil. Thus, in "Cinderella," the mother is split in two, an evil stepmother and a fairy go(o)dmother. Cinderella's two evil stepsisters disguise hostile and rivalrous feelings toward real siblings. A tale such as "Cinderella" permits the child to deal with hostile feelings toward parents and siblings, since positive feelings are preserved in the idealized good figure.

Secular Rituals

We must recognize certain problems in the cross-cultural study of religion and in the definition of religion given earlier. The first problem: If we define religion with reference to supernatural beings, powers, and forces, how do we classify rituallike behavior that occurs in secular contexts? Some anthropologists believe that there are both sacred and secular rituals. Secular rituals include formal, invariant, stereotyped, earnest, repetitive behavior that takes place in nonreligious settings.

A second problem: If the distinction between the ordinary and the supernatural is not consistently made in certain societies, how can we tell what is religion and what is not? The Betsileo of Madagascar, for example, view witches and dead ancestors as real people who play roles in ordinary life. Nevertheless, their powers are not empirically demonstrable.

A third problem: The kind of behavior considered appropriate for religious occasions varies tremendously from culture to culture. One society may consider drunken frenzy the surest sign of faith, whereas another may inculcate quiet reverence. Who is to say which is "more religious"?

RELIGION AND CULTURE

Religion is a cultural universal because it has so many causes, effects, and meanings for the people who take part in it. But religions are parts of particular cultures, and cultural differences show up systematically in religious beliefs, practices, and institutions. Religious forms do not vary randomly from society to society. The religions associated with nation-states and stratified societies differ from those of cultures in which social contrasts and power differentials are less marked.

Considering several cultures, Wallace (1966) identified four types of religion: shamanic, communal, Olympian, and monotheistic. The simplest type is shamanic religion. Unlike priests, **shamans** aren't full-time religious officials but part-time religious figures who mediate between people and supernatural beings and forces. All cultures have medico-magico-religious specialists. *Shaman* is the general term encompassing curers ("witch doctors"), mediums, spiritualists, astrologers, palm readers, and other diviners. Wallace found shamanic religions to be most characteristic of hunting and gathering societies, particularly those found in the northern latitudes, such as the Eskimos and the native peoples of Siberia.

Although they are only part-time specialists, shamans often set themselves off symbolically from ordinary people by assuming a different or ambiguous sex or gender role. (In nation-states, priests, nuns, and vestal virgins do something similar by taking vows of celibacy and chastity.) Transvestism is one way of being sexually ambiguous. Among the Chukchee of Siberia (Bogoras 1904), where coastal populations fished and interior groups hunted, male shamans copied the dress, speech, hair arrangements, and lifestyles of women. These shamans took other men as husbands and sex partners and received respect for their supernatural and curative expertise. Female shamans could join a fourth gender, copying men and taking wives.

Among the Crow of the North American Plains, certain ritual duties were reserved for **berdaches,** men who rejected the male role of bison hunter, raider, and warrior and joined a third gender (Lowie 1935). *Berdaches* dressed, spoke, and styled their hair like women and pursued such traditionally female activities as cooking and sewing. The fact that certain key rituals could be done only by *berdaches* indicates their regular and normal place in Crow social life.

Communal religions have, in addition to shamans, community rituals such as harvest ceremonies and rites of passage. Although communal religions lack *full-time* religious specialists, they believe in several deities (**polytheism**) who control aspects of nature. Although some hunter-gatherers, including Australian totemites, have communal religions, these religions are more typical of farming societies.

Olympian religions, which arose with nation-state organization and marked social stratification, add full-time religious specialists—professional priesthoods. Like the nation-state itself, the priesthood is hierarchically and bureaucratically organized. The term *Olympian* comes from Mount Olympus, home of the classical Greek gods. Olympian religions are polytheistic. They include powerful anthropomorphic gods with specialized functions, for example, gods of love, war, the sea, and death. Olympian **pantheons** (collections of supernatural beings) were prominent in the religions of many nonindustrial nation-states, including the Aztecs of Mexico, several African and Asian kingdoms, and classical Greece and Rome. Wallace's fourth type—**monotheism**—also has priesthoods and notions of divine power, but it views the supernatural differently. In monotheism, all supernatural phenomena are manifestations of, or are under the control of, a single eternal, omniscient, omnipotent, and omnipresent supreme being.

RELIGION AND CHANGE

Revitalization Movements

Religion helps maintain social order, but it can also be an instrument of change, sometimes even of revolution. As a response to conquest or foreign domination, religious leaders often undertake to alter or revitalize a society. We call such movements *nativistic movements* (Linton 1943) or **revitalization movements** (Wallace 1956).

Christianity originated as a revitalization movement. Jesus was one of several prophets who preached new religious doctrines while the Middle East was under Roman rule. It was a time of social unrest, when a foreign power ruled the land.

Halloween: An American Ritual of Rebellion

B razil is famous for *Carnaval,* a pre-Lenten festival celebrated the four days before Ash Wednesday. Carnival occurs, but has a limited distribution, in the United States. Here we know it as the Mardi Gras for which New Orleans is famous. Mardi Gras (Fat Tuesday) is part of a Latin tradition that New Orleans, because of its French background, shares with Brazil. France and Italy also have carnival. Nowhere, however, do people invest as much in carnival—in money, costumes, time, and labor—as they do in Rio de Janeiro. There, on the Saturday and Sunday before Mardi Gras, a dozen samba schools, each with thousands of members, take to the streets to compete in costumes, rhythmic dancing, chanting, singing, and overall presentation.

The United States lacks any national celebration that is exactly equivalent to carnival, but we do have Halloween, which is similar in some respects. Even if Americans don't dance in the street on Halloween, children do go out ringing bells and demanding "trick or treat." As they do things they don't do on ordinary nights, they also disguise themselves in costumes, as Brazilians do at carnival.

The common thread in the two events is that they are times of culturally permitted *inversion*—carnival much more strongly and obviously than Halloween (see the box in the chapter "Gender"). In the United States Halloween is the only nationally celebrated occasion that dramatically inverts the normal relationship between children and adults. Halloween is a night of disguises and reversals. Normally, children are at home or in school, taking part in supervised activities. Kids are domesticated and diurnal—active during the day. Halloween permits them to become—once a year—nocturnal invaders of public space. Furthermore, *they can be bad.* Halloween's symbolism is potent. Children love to cloak themselves in evil as they enjoy special privileges of naughtiness. Darth

Vader and Freddy Krueger are much more popular Halloween figures than are Luke Skywalker and the Smurfs.

Properly enculturated American kids aren't normally let loose on the streets at night. They aren't usually permitted to ask their neighbors for doles. They don't generally walk around the neighborhood dressed as witches, goblins, or vampires. Traditionally, the expectation that children be good little boys and girls has been overlooked on Halloween. "Trick or treat" recalls the days when children who didn't get treats would pull tricks such as soaping windows, turning over flower boxes, and setting off firecrackers on a grouch's porch.

Halloween is like the "rituals of rebellion" that anthropologists have described in African societies, times when normal power relations are inverted, when the powerless turn on the powerful, expressing resentments they suppress during the rest of the year. Halloween lets kids meddle with the dark side of the force. Children can command adults to do their bidding and punish the adults if they don't. Halloween behavior inverts the scoldings and spankings that adults inflict on kids. For adults, Halloween is a minor occasion, not even a holiday. For children, however, it's a favorite time, a special night. Kids know what rituals of rebellion are all about.

Halloween is therefore a festival that inverts two oppositions important in American life: the adult-child power balance and expectations about good and evil. Halloween's origin can be traced back 2,000 years to Samhain, the Day of the Dead, the most significant holiday in the Celtic religion (Santino 1983). Given its historical development through pagan rites, church suppression, and beliefs about witches and demons, Halloween continues to turn the distinction between good and bad on its head. Innocent children dress as witches and demons and act out their fantasies of rebellion and destruction. Once during the year, real adult witches are interviewed on talk shows, where they have a chance to describe their beliefs as solemnly as orthodox religious figures do. Puritan morality and the need for proper public behavior are important themes in American society. The rules are in abeyance on Halloween, and normal things are inverted. This is why Halloween, like *Carnaval* in Brazil, persists as a ritual of reversal and rebellion, particularly as an escape valve for the frustrations and resentments that build during enculturation.

Jesus inspired a new, enduring, and major religion. His contemporaries were not so successful.

The Handsome Lake religion arose around 1800 among the Iroquois of New York State (Wallace 1970). Handsome Lake, the founder of this revitalization movement, was a chief of one of the Iroquois tribes. The Iroquois had suffered because of their support of the British against the American colonials. After the colonial victory and a wave of immigration to their homeland, the Iroquois were dispersed on small reservations. Unable to pursue traditional horticulture and hunting in their homeland, the Iroquois became heavy drinkers and quarreled among themselves.

Handsome Lake was a heavy drinker who started having visions from heavenly messengers. The spirits warned him that unless the Iroquois changed their ways, they would be destroyed. His visions offered a plan for coping with the new order. Witchcraft, quarreling, and drinking would end. The Iroquois would copy European farming techniques, which, unlike traditional Iroquois horticulture, stressed male rather than female labor. Handsome Lake preached that the Iroquois should also abandon their communal longhouses and matrilineal descent groups (large kinship groups based exclusively on genealogical links through females) for more permanent marriages and individual family households. The teachings of Handsome Lake produced a new church and religion, one that still has members in New York and Ontario. This revitalization movement helped the Iroquois adapt to and survive in a modified environment. They eventually gained a reputation among their non-Indian neighbors as sober family farmers.

SUMMARY

Religion, a cultural universal capable of uniting or dividing social groups, consists of belief and behavior concerned with supernatural beings, powers, and forces. Cross-cultural studies have revealed many functions of religion. Tylor focused on religion's explanatory role, suggesting that animism—the belief in souls—is religion's most primitive form. He argued that religion evolved from animism through polytheism to monotheism. As science provided better explanations, Tylor thought that religion would eventually disappear. However, a different view of the supernatural also occurs in nonindustrial societies. This sees the supernatural as a domain of raw, impersonal power or force (called *mana* in Polynesia and Melanesia). People can manipulate and control mana under certain conditions.

When ordinary technical and rational means of doing things fail, people may turn to magic, using it when they lack control over outcomes. Religion offers comfort and psychological security at times of crisis. However, rites can also create anxiety. Rituals are formal, invariant, stylized, earnest acts that require people to subordinate their particular beliefs to a social collectivity. Rites of passage have three stages: separation, liminality or margin, and aggregation. Passage rites can mark any change in social status, age, place, or social condition. Collective rites are often cemented by communitas, a feeling of intense solidarity.

The study of religion also leads anthropologists to the cross-cultural analysis of myths and folktales. These forms of creative expression reveal native theories about the creation of the world and supernatural entities. Myths express cultural values, offer hope, and teach enculturative lessons. The myths typically found in nation-states include cautionary tragedies as well as hopeful tales. Lévi-Strauss, the inventor of the structural analysis of myth, has argued that people universally classify aspects of nature and culture by means of binary opposition. Such opposition makes phenomena that are continuous seem more distinct. Structural analysis aims not to explain but to discover otherwise hidden connections among aspects of culture. This approach links anthropology to the humanities.

Wallace defines four types of religion: shamanic, communal, Olympian, and monotheistic. Each has characteristic ceremonies and practitioners. Religion helps maintain social order, but it can also promote change. Revitalization movements incorporate old and new beliefs and have helped people adapt to changing environments.

CHAPTER SEVEN

Adaptive Strategies and Economic Systems

ultural diversity survives, even thrives, in an increasingly interconnected world. Cultures and communities are being incorporated, at an accelerating rate, into larger systems. An important impetus to the formation of regional social systems, and eventually of nation-states, was the origin of **food production**—plant cultivation and animal domestication. By 10,000 years ago, people in the Middle East were intervening in the reproduction of plants and animals. Those ancient Middle Easterners, pioneers in food production, added new, domesticated foods (wheat and barley, sheep and goats) to their diet. For hundreds of thousands of years before then, people had relied on wild foods, nature's bounty. Humans had always supported themselves by **foraging**—hunting and gathering. Food production led to major changes in human life, as the pace of cultural transformation increased enormously. This chapter provides a framework for understanding human adaptive strategies and economic systems.

ADAPTIVE STRATEGIES

The anthropologist Yehudi Cohen (1974) used the term *adaptive strategy* to describe a group's system of economic production. He argued that the most important reason for similarities between two (or more) unrelated cultures is their possession of a similar adaptive strategy. Similar economic causes, in other words, produce similar cultural effects. For example, there are striking similarities among most cultures that have a foraging strategy. Cohen developed a typology of cultures based on correlations between economies and social features. His typology includes six adaptive strategies: foraging, horticulture, agriculture, pastoralism, mercantilism (trade), and industrialism. I examine the last two strategies in the chapter "The World System, Industrialism, and Stratification." I focus on the first four here.

FORAGING

Until 10,000 years ago all humans were foragers. However, environmental specifics created contrasts between foraging populations. Some were big-game hunters; others hunted and collected a wider range of animals and plants. Nevertheless, ancient foraging economies shared one essential feature: People relied on nature for food and other necessities.

Domestication (initially of sheep and goats) and cultivation (of wheat and barley) began 10,000 to 12,000 years ago in the Middle East. Cultivation (of different crops, such as maize, manioc, and potatoes) arose independently 3,000 to 4,000 years later in the Western Hemisphere. In both hemispheres the new economy spread rapidly. Most foragers eventually turned to food production. Today almost all foragers have at least some dependence on food production or food producers (Kent 1992).

The foraging way of life held on (and sometimes *re*emerged) in a few areas. In most of those places, foraging should be described as "recent" rather than "contemporary." All modern foragers live in nation-states, depend to some extent on government assistance, and have contacts with food-producing neighbors, missionaries, and other outsiders. We should not view contemporary foragers as isolated or pristine survivors of the Stone Age. Modern foragers are late-twentieth-century people who are influenced by regional forces (e.g., trade and war), national and international policies, and political and economic events in the world system (see the box in Chapter 8).

Although foraging is on the wane, the outlines of Africa's two broad belts of recent foraging remain evident. One is the Kalahari Desert of southern Africa. This is

All modern foragers live in nation-states, depend to some
extent on government assistance, and have contact with
outsiders. Contemporary hunter-gatherers are not isolated
or pristine survivors of the Stone Age. Modern foragers—
such as this rifle-wielding Australian hunter—are influenced
by regional forces, national and international policies, and
political and economic events in the world system.

the home of the **San** (Bushmen), who include the **!Kung.** (The exclamation point
stands for a distinctive sound made in their language, a click.) (Lee 1984; Lee and
DeVore 1977.) The other main African foraging area is the equatorial forest of central and eastern Africa, home of the Mbuti and other Pygmies (Turnbull 1965; Bailey et al. 1989).

People still do subsistence foraging in certain remote forests in Madagascar,
Southeast Asia, Malaysia, the Philippines, and on certain islands off the Indian coast.
Some of the best-known recent foragers are the aborigines of Australia. Those Native Australians lived on their island continent for more than 40,000 years without
developing food production.

The Western Hemisphere also had recent foragers. The Eskimos, or Inuit, of
Alaska and Canada are well-known hunters. These (and other) northern foragers
now use modern technology, including rifles and snowmobiles, in their subsistence
activities (Pelto 1973). The native populations of California, Oregon, Washington,

and British Columbia were all foragers, as were those of inland subarctic Canada and the Great Lakes. For many Native Americans fishing, hunting, and gathering remain important subsistence (and sometimes commercial) activities.

Coastal foragers also lived near the southern tip of South America, in Patagonia. On the grassy plains of Argentina, southern Brazil, Uruguay, and Paraguay, there were other hunter-gatherers. The contemporary Aché of Paraguay are usually called "hunter-gatherers" even though they get just a third of their livelihood from foraging. The Aché also grow crops, have domesticated animals, and live in or near mission posts, where they receive food from missionaries (Hawkes et al. 1982; Hill et al. 1987).

Throughout the world, foraging survived mainly in environments that posed major obstacles to food production. (Some foragers took refuge in such areas after the rise of food production, the state, colonialism, or the modern world system.) The difficulties of cultivating at the North Pole are obvious. In southern Africa the Dobe !Kung San area studied by Richard Lee is surrounded by a waterless belt 70 to 200 kilometers in depth. The Dobe area is hard to reach even today, and there is no archeological evidence of occupation of this area by food producers before the twentieth century (Solway and Lee 1990, p. 115). However, environmental limits to other adaptive strategies aren't the only reason foragers survived. Their niches have one thing in common—their marginality. Their environments haven't been of immediate interest to groups with other adaptive strategies.

I should note, too, that foraging held on in a few areas that could be cultivated, even after contact with cultivators. Those tenacious foragers did not become food producers because they were supporting themselves adequately by hunting and gathering. As the modern world system spreads, the number of foragers continues to decline. (I consider issues of the cultural survival of foragers and other groups in later chapters, especially the chapter "Cultural Exchange and Survival.")

Correlates of Foraging

Typologies, such as Cohen's adaptive strategies, are useful because they suggest **correlations**—that is, associations or covariation between two or more variables. (Correlated variables are factors that are linked and interrelated, such as food intake and body weight, such that when one increases or decreases, the other tends to change, too.) Ethnographic studies in hundreds of cultures have revealed many correlations between the economy and social life. Associated (correlated) with each adaptive strategy is a bundle of particular cultural features. Correlations, however, are rarely perfect. Some foragers lack cultural features usually associated with foraging, and some of those features are found in groups with other adaptive strategies.

What, then, are the usual correlates of foraging? People who subsist by hunting, gathering, and fishing often live in band-organized societies. Their basic social unit, the **band,** is a small group of fewer than a hundred people, all related by kinship or marriage. Band size varies between cultures and often from one season to the next in a given culture. In some foraging societies, band size stays about the same year-round. In others, the band splits up for part of the year. Families leave to gather resources that are better exploited by just a few people. Later, they regroup for cooperative work and ceremonies. Several examples of seasonal splits and recongregation are known from archeology and ethnography. In southern Africa, some San aggregate around water holes in the dry season and split up in the wet season, whereas other bands disperse in the dry season (Barnard 1979; Kent 1992). This reflects environmental variation. San who lack permanent water must disperse and forage widely for moisture-filled plants.

One typical characteristic of the foraging life is mobility. In many San groups, as among the Mbuti of Zaire, people shift band membership several times in a lifetime. One may be born, for example, in a band where one's mother has kin. Later, one's family may move to a band where the father has relatives. Because bands are exogamous (i.e., people marry outside their own band), one's parents come from two different bands, and one's grandparents may come from four. People may affiliate with any band to which they have kinship or marriage links. A couple may live in, or shift between, the husband's and the wife's band.

One may also affiliate with a band through **fictive kinship**—personal relationships modeled on kinship, such as that between godparents and godchildren. San, for example, have a limited number of personal names. People with the same name have a special relationship; they treat each other like siblings. San expect the same hospitality in bands where they have **namesakes** as they do in a band in which a real sibling lives. Namesakes share a strong identity. They call everyone in a namesake's band by the kin terms the namesake uses. Those people reply as if they were addressing a real relative. Kinship, marriage, and fictive kinship permit San to join several bands, and nomadic (regularly on the move) foragers do change bands often. Band membership can therefore change tremendously from year to year.

All human societies have some kind of division of labor based on gender. Among foragers, men typically hunt and fish while women gather and collect, but the specific nature of the work varies among cultures. Sometimes women's work contributes most to the diet. Sometimes male hunting and fishing predominate. Among foragers in tropical and semitropical areas, gathering tends to contribute more to the diet than hunting and fishing do—even though the labor costs of gathering tend to be much higher than those of hunting and fishing.

All foragers make social distinctions based on age. Often old people receive great respect as guardians of myths, legends, stories, and traditions. Younger people value the elders' special knowledge of ritual and practical matters. Most foraging societies are *egalitarian*. This means that contrasts in prestige are minor and are based on age and gender.

When considering issues of "human nature," we should remember that the egalitarian band was a basic form of human social life for most of our history. Food production has existed less than 1 percent of the time *Homo* has spent on earth. However, it has produced huge social differences. We now consider the main economic features of food-producing strategies.

CULTIVATION

The three adaptive strategies based on food production in nonindustrial societies are horticulture, agriculture, and pastoralism. In non-Western cultures, just as in the United States and Canada, people carry out a variety of economic activities. Each adaptive strategy refers to the main economic activity. Pastoralists (herders), for example, consume milk, butter, blood, and meat from their animals as mainstays of their diet. However, they also add grain to their diet by doing some cultivating or by trading with neighbors. Food producers may also hunt or gather to supplement a diet based on domesticated species.

Horticulture

Horticulture and agriculture are two types of cultivation found in nonindustrial societies. Both differ from the farming systems of industrial nations like the United States and Canada, which use large land areas, machinery, and petrochemicals. **Horticulture** makes intensive use of *none* of the factors of production: land, labor, capital, and machinery. Horticulturalists use simple tools such as hoes and digging sticks to grow their crops. Their fields are not permanent property and lie fallow for varying lengths of time.

Horticulture is also known as **slash-and-burn** cultivation. Each year horticulturalists clear land by cutting down (slashing) and burning forest or bush or by setting fire to the grass covering the plot. The vegetation is broken down, pests are killed, and the ashes remain to fertilize the soil. Crops are then sown, tended, and harvested. Use of the plot is not continuous. Often it is cultivated for only a year. This depends, however, on soil fertility and weeds, which compete with cultivated plants for nutrients.

When horticulturalists abandon a plot because of soil exhaustion or a thick weed cover, they clear another piece of land, and the original plot reverts to forest. After several years of fallowing (the duration varies in different societies), the cultivator returns to farm the original plot again. Because the relationship between people and land is not permanent, horticulture is also called *shifting cultivation*. Shifting cultivation does not mean that whole villages must move when plots are abandoned. Horticulture can support large permanent villages. Among the Kuikuru of the South American tropical forest, for example, one village of 150 people remained in the same place for ninety years (Carneiro 1956). Kuikuru houses are large and well made. Because the work involved in building them is great, the Kuikuru would rather walk farther to their fields than construct a new village. They shift their plots rather than their settlements. On the other hand, horticulturalists in the montaña (Andean foothills) of Peru live in small villages of about thirty people (Carneiro 1961/1968). Their houses are small and simple. After a few years in one place, these people build new villages near virgin land. Because their houses are so simple, they prefer rebuilding to walking even a half mile to their fields.

Agriculture

Agriculture is cultivation that requires more labor than horticulture does, because it uses land intensively and continuously. The greater labor demands associated with agriculture reflect its common use of domesticated animals, irrigation, or terracing.

DOMESTICATED ANIMALS Many agriculturalists use animals as means of production—for transport, as cultivating machines, and for their manure. For example, the Betsileo of central Madagascar incorporate cattle into their agricultural economy based on rice production (Kottak 1980). First the Betsileo sow rice in nursery beds. Then, once the seedlings are big enough, women transplant them into flooded rice fields. Before transplanting, the men till and flood the fields. They bring cattle to trample the prepared fields just before transplanting. Young men yell at and beat the cattle, striving to drive them into a frenzy so that they will trample the fields properly. Trampling breaks up clumps of earth and mixes irrigation water with soil to form a smooth mud into which women transplant seedlings. Like many other agriculturalists, the Betsileo collect manure from their animals, using it to fertilize their plots and thus increasing the yield.

IRRIGATION While horticulturalists must await the rainy season, agriculturalists can schedule their planting in advance, because they control water. The Betsileo irrigate their fields with canals from rivers, streams, springs, and ponds.

In some areas of Irian Jaya, Indonesia (which is on the island of New Guinea), labor-intensive cultivation in valleys involves the construction of long drainage ditches. Here, members of the Dani tribe use their bare hands and feet to maintain such a canal.

Irrigation makes it possible to cultivate a plot year after year. Irrigation enriches the soil because the irrigated field is a unique ecosystem with several species of plants and animals, many of them minute organisms, whose wastes fertilize the land.

An irrigated field is a capital investment that usually increases in value. It takes time for a field to start yielding; it reaches full productivity only after several years of cultivation. The Betsileo, like other irrigators, have farmed the same fields for generations. In some agricultural areas, including the Middle East, however, salts carried in the irrigation water can make fields unusable after fifty or sixty years.

TERRACING   Terracing is another agricultural technique the Betsileo have mastered. Central Madagascar has small valleys separated by steep hillsides. Because the population is dense, people need to farm the hills. However, if they simply planted on the steep hillsides, fertile soil and crops would be washed away during the rainy season. To prevent this, the Betsileo, like the rice-farming Ifugao of the

Agriculture requires more labor than horticulture does and uses land intensively and continuously. Labor demands associated with agriculture reflect its use of domesticated animals, irrigation, and terracing. The Ifugao of the Philippines are famous for their terraced rice fields.

Philippines, cut into the hillside and build stage after stage of terraced fields rising above the valley floor. Springs located above the terraces supply their irrigation water. The labor necessary to build and maintain a system of terraces is great. Terrace walls crumble each year and must be partially rebuilt. The canals that bring water down through the terraces also demand attention.

COSTS AND BENEFITS OF AGRICULTURE   Agriculture requires human labor to build and maintain irrigation systems, terraces, and other works. People must feed, water, and care for their animals. Given sufficient labor input and management, agricultural land can yield one or two crops annually for years or even generations. An agricultural field does not necessarily produce a higher single-year yield than does a horticultural plot. The first crop grown by horticulturalists on long-idle land may be larger than that from an agricultural plot of the same size. Furthermore, because agriculturalists work harder than horticulturalists do, agriculture's yield relative to labor is also lower. Agriculture's main advantage is that the long-term yield per area is far greater and more dependable. Because a single field sustains its owners year after year, there is no need to maintain a reserve of uncultivated land as horticulturalists do. This is why agricultural societies are more densely populated than are horticultural ones.

The Cultivation Continuum

Because nonindustrial economies can have features of both horticulture and agriculture, it is useful to discuss cultivators as being arranged along a **cultivation continuum.** Horticultural systems stand at one end—the "low-labor, shifting-plot" end. Agriculturalists are at the other—the "labor-intensive, permanent-plot"—end.

We speak of a continuum because there are today intermediate economies, combining horticultural and agricultural features—more intensive than annually shifting horticulture but less intensive than agriculture. These recall the intermediate economies revealed by archeological sequences leading from horticulture to agriculture in the Middle East, Mexico, and other areas of early food production. Unlike nonintensive horticulturalists, who farm a plot just once before fallowing it, the South American Kuikuru grow two or three cops of **manioc,** or cassava—an edible tuber—before abandoning their plots. Cultivation is even more intense in certain densely populated areas of Papua-New Guinea, where plots are planted for two or three years, allowed to rest for three to five, and then recultivated. After several of these cycles the plots are abandoned for a longer fallow period. Such a pattern is called **sectorial fallowing** (Wolf 1966). Besides Papua-New Guinea, such systems occur in places as distant as West Africa and highland Mexico. Sectorial fallowing is associated with denser populations than is simple horticulture. The simpler system is the norm in tropical forests, where weed invasion and delicate soils prevent more intensive cultivation.

The key difference between horticulture and agriculture is that horticulture always uses a fallow period whereas agriculture does not. The earliest cultivators in the Middle East and Mexico were rainfall-dependent horticulturalists. Until recently, horticulture was the main form of cultivation in several areas, including parts of Africa, Southeast Asia, Indonesia, the Philippines, the Pacific islands, Mexico, Central America, and the South American tropical forest.

Implications of Intensification

The range of environments open to human use widens as people increase their control over nature. Agricultural populations exist in many areas that are too arid for nonirrigators or too hilly for nonterracers. Many ancient civilizations in arid lands arose on an agricultural base. Increasing labor intensity and permanent land use have major demographic, social, and political consequences.

Thus, because of their permanent fields, intensive cultivators are sedentary. People live in larger and more permanent communities located closer to other settlements. Growth in population size and density increases contact between individuals and groups. There is more need to regulate interpersonal relations, including conflicts of interest. Economies that support more people usually require more coordination in the use of land, labor, and other resources.

Agriculture poses many regulatory problems—which central governments have often arisen to solve. Most agriculturalists live in **states** (nation-states)—complex sociopolitical systems that administer a territory and populace with substantial contrasts in occupation, wealth, prestige, and power. In such societies, cultivators play their role as one part of a differentiated, functionally specialized, and tightly integrated sociopolitical system. The social and political implications of food production and intensification are examined more fully in the next chapter.

PASTORALISM

Pastoralists live in North Africa, the Middle East, Europe, Asia, and sub-Saharan Africa. These herders are people whose activities focus on such domesticated animals as cattle, sheep, goats, camels, and yak. East African pastoralists, like many others, live in symbiosis with their herds. (**Symbiosis** is an obligatory interaction between groups—here, humans and animals—that is beneficial to each.) Herders attempt to protect their animals and ensure their reproduction in return for food and other products, like leather. Herds provide dairy products and meat. East Africans also consume cooked cattle blood. Animals are killed at ceremonies, which occur throughout the year, and so beef is available regularly.

People use livestock in a variety of ways. Natives of North America's Great Plains, for example, didn't eat, but only rode, their horses. (Europeans reintroduced horses to the Western Hemisphere; the native American horse had become extinct thousands of years earlier.) For Plains Indians horses served as "tools of the trade," means of production used to hunt buffalo, a main target of their economies. So the Plains Indians were not true pastoralists but *hunters* who used horses—as many agriculturalists use animals—as means of production.

Unlike the use of animals merely as productive machines, pastoralists typically make direct use of their herds for food. They consume their meat, blood, and milk, from which they make yogurt, butter, and cheese. Although some pastoralists rely on their herds more completely than others do, it is impossible to base subsistence solely on animals. Most pastoralists therefore supplement their diet by hunting, gathering, fishing, cultivating, or trading. To get crops, pastoralists either trade with cultivators or do some cultivating or gathering themselves.

Unlike foraging and cultivation, which existed throughout the world before the Industrial Revolution, pastoralism was almost totally confined to the Old World. Before European conquest, the only pastoralists in the Americas lived in the Andean region of South America. They used their llamas and alpacas for food and wool and in agriculture and transport. Much more recently, the Navajo of the southwestern United States developed a pastoral economy based on sheep, which were brought to North America by Europeans. The populous Navajo are now the major pastoral population in the Western Hemisphere.

Two patterns of movement occur with pastoralism: nomadism and transhumance. Both are based on the fact that herds must move to use pasture available in particular places in different seasons. In **pastoral nomadism,** the entire group—women, men, and children—moves with the animals throughout the year. With **transhumance,** only part of the group follows the herds while the rest remain in home villages. During their annual trek, nomads trade for crops and other products with more sedentary people. Transhumants don't have to trade for crops. Because only part of the population accompanies the herds, transhumants can maintain year-round villages and grow their own crops.

MODES OF PRODUCTION

An **economy** is a system of production, distribution, and consumption of resources; *economics* is the study of such systems. Economists tend to focus on modern nations and capitalist systems, whereas anthropologists have broadened the understanding of economic principles by gathering data on nonindustrial economies. Economic anthropology studies economies in a comparative perspective.

A **mode of production** is a way of organizing production—that is, "a set of social relations through which labor is deployed to wrest energy from nature by means of tools, skills, organization, and knowledge" (Wolf 1982, p. 75). In the capitalist mode of production, money buys labor power, and there is a social gap between the people (bosses and workers) involved in the production process. By contrast, in non-

The cultivation of rice, one of the world's most important food
crops, often features a division of task by age and
gender. Women often transplant; men often thresh. These young
women are transplanting rice seedlings in Sulawesi, Indonesia,
and these men are threshing rice, to separate
the grains from the stem, in Bangladesh.

industrial societies, labor is not usually bought but is given as a social obligation. In
such a *kin-based* mode of production, mutual aid in production is one among many
expressions of a larger web of social relations.

Societies representing each of the adaptive strategies just discussed (e.g., foraging societies) tend to have similar modes of production. Differences in the mode of

production within a given strategy may reflect differences in environments, target resources, or cultural traditions. Thus a foraging mode of production may be based on individual hunters or teams, depending on whether the game is a solitary or a herd animal. Gathering is usually more individual than hunting. People may fish alone or in crews.

Organization of Production in Nonindustrial Populations

Although some kind of division of economic labor related to age and gender is a cultural universal, the specific tasks assigned to each sex and to people of different ages vary. Some horticulturalists assign a major productive role to women; others make men's work primary. Similarly, among pastoralists men generally tend large animals, but in some cultures women do the milking. Jobs accomplished through teamwork in some cultivating societies are done by smaller groups or individuals working over a longer period of time in others.

Among the Betsileo of Madagascar there are two stages of teamwork in rice cultivation: transplanting and harvesting. Team size varies with the size of the field. Both transplanting and harvesting feature a traditional division of labor by age and gender which is well known to all Betsileo and is repeated across the generations. The first job in transplanting is the trampling of a flooded field by young men driving cattle in order to mix earth and water. Once the tramplers leave the field, older men arrive. With their spades they break up the clumps that the cattle missed. Meanwhile, the owner and other adults uproot rice seedlings and bring them to the field. Women plant the seedlings.

At harvest time, four or five months later, young men cut the rice off the stalks. Young women carry it to a clearing above the field. Older women arrange and stack it. The oldest men and women then stand on the stack, stomping and compacting it. Three days later, young men thresh the rice, beating the stalks against a rock to remove the grain. Older men then attack the stalks with sticks to make sure all the grains have fallen off.

Most of the other tasks in Betsileo rice cultivation are done by individual owners and their immediate families. Men maintain and repair the irrigation and drainage systems and the earth walls that separate one plot from the next. Men also till with spade or plow. All members of the household help weed the rice field.

Means of Production

In nonindustrial societies there is a more intimate relationship between the worker and the means of production than there is in industrial nations. **Means, or factors, of production** include land, labor, and technology.

TERRITORY   Among foragers, ties between people and land are less permanent than they are among food producers. Although many bands have territories, the boundaries are not usually marked, and there is no way they can be enforced. The hunter's stake in an animal that is being stalked or has been hit with a poisoned arrow is more important than where the animal finally dies. A person acquires the right to use a band's territory by being born in the band or by joining it through a tie of kinship, marriage, or fictive kinship. In Botswana in southern Africa, !Kung San women, whose work provides over half the food, habitually use specific tracts of berry-bearing trees. However, when a woman changes bands, she immediately acquires a new gathering area.

Among food producers, rights to the means of production also come through kinship and marriage. Descent groups (groups whose members claim common ancestry) are common among nonindustrial food producers, and those who descend from the founder share the group's territory and resources. If the adaptive strategy is horticulture, the estate includes garden and fallow land for shifting cultivation. As members of a descent group, pastoralists have access to animals to start their own herds, to grazing land, to garden land, and to other means of production.

LABOR, TECHNOLOGY, TECHNICAL KNOWLEDGE, AND SPECIALIZATION   Like land, labor is a means of production. In nonindustrial societies, access to both land and labor comes through social links such as kinship, marriage, and descent. Mutual aid in production is merely one aspect of ongoing social relationships that are expressed on many other occasions.

Nonindustrial societies contrast with industrial nations in regard to another means of production—technology. In bands and tribes manufacturing is often linked to age and gender. Women may weave and men may make pottery or vice versa. Most people of a particular age and gender share the technical knowledge associated with that age and gender. If married women customarily make baskets, most married women know how to make baskets. Neither technology nor technical knowledge is as specialized as it is in states.

However, some tribal societies do promote specialization. Among the Yanomami of Venezuela and Brazil, for instance, certain villages manufacture clay pots and others make hammocks. They don't specialize, as one might suppose, because certain raw materials happen to be available near particular villages. Clay suitable for pots is widely available. Everyone knows how to make pots, but not everybody does so. Craft specialization reflects the social and political environment rather than the natural environment. Such specialization promotes trade, which is the first step in creating an alliance with enemy villages (Chagnon 1983/1992). Specialization contributes to keeping the peace, although it has not prevented intervillage warfare.

Alienation and Impersonality in Industrial Economies

What are the most significant contrasts between industrial and nonindustrial economies? When factory workers produce for sale and for the employer's profit rather than for their own use, they may be alienated from the items they make. Such alienation means they do not feel strong pride in or personal identification with their products. In nonindustrial societies people usually see their work through from start to finish and have a sense of accomplishment in the product.

In nonindustrial societies the economic relationship between coworkers is just one aspect of a more general social relationship. They aren't just coworkers but kin, in-laws, or celebrants in the same ritual. In industrial nations, people don't usually work with relatives and neighbors. If coworkers are friends, the personal relationship usually develops during their common employment rather than being based on a previous association.

Thus, industrial workers have impersonal relationships with their products, coworkers, and employers. People sell their labor for cash, and the economic domain stands apart from ordinary social life. In nonindustrial societies, however, the relations of production, distribution, and consumption are *social relations with economic aspects*. The economy is not a separate entity but is *embedded* in the society.

ECONOMIZING AND MAXIMIZATION

Economic anthropologists have been concerned with two main questions:

1. How are production, distribution, and consumption organized in different societies? This question focuses on *systems* of human behavior and their organization.
2. What motivates people in different cultures to produce, distribute or exchange, and consume? Here the focus is not on systems of behavior but on the *individuals* who participate in those systems.

Anthropologists view both economic systems and motivations in a cross-cultural perspective. Motivation is a concern of psychologists, but it has also been, implicitly or explicitly, a concern of economists and anthropologists. American economists assume that producers and distributors make decisions rationally using the *profit motive*, as do consumers when they shop around for the best value.

Although anthropologists know that the profit motive is not universal, the assumption that individuals try to maximize profits is basic to the capitalist world economy and to Western economic theory. In fact, the subject matter of economics is often defined as **economizing,** or the rational allocation of scarce means (or resources) to alternative ends (or uses). What does that mean? Classical economic theory assumes that our wants are infinite and that our resources are limited. Since means are always scarce, people have to make choices. They must decide how they will use their scarce resources—their time, labor, money, and capital. Western economists assume that when confronted with alternatives, people tend to choose the one that maximizes profit. This is assumed to be the most rational (reasonable) choice.

The idea that individuals maximize profits was a basic assumption of the classical economists of the nineteenth century and one that is held by many contemporary economists. However, certain economists now recognize that individuals in Western cultures, as in others, may be motivated by many other goals. Depending on the society and the situation, people may try to maximize profit, wealth, prestige, pleasure, comfort, or social harmony. Individuals may want to realize their personal or family ambitions or those of another group to which they belong.

Alternative Ends

To what uses do people in various societies put their scarce resources? Throughout the world, people devote some of their time and energy to building up a **subsistence fund** (Wolf 1966). In other words, they have to work to eat, to replace the calories they use in their daily activity. People must also invest in a **replacement fund.** They must maintain their technology and other items essential to production. If a hoe or plow breaks, they must repair or replace it. They must also obtain and replace items that are essential not to production but to everyday life, such as clothing and shelter.

People everywhere also have to invest in a **social fund.** They have to help their friends, relatives, in-laws, and especially in nonindustrial states, unrelated neighbors. It is useful to distinguish between a social fund and a **ceremonial fund.** The latter term refers to expenditures on ceremonies or rituals. To prepare a festival honoring one's ancestors, for example, requires time and the outlay of wealth.

Citizens of nonindustrial states must also allocate scarce resources to a **rent fund.** We think of rent as payment for the use of property. However, *rent fund* has a wider meaning. It refers to resources that people must render to an individual or agency that is superior politically or economically. Tenant farmers and sharecroppers, for example, either pay rent or give some of their produce to their landlords, as peasants did under feudalism.

Peasants are small-scale agriculturalists who live in nonindustrial states and have rent fund obligations. They produce to feed themselves, to sell, and to pay rent. All peasants have two things in common:

1. They live in state-organized societies.
2. They produce food without the elaborate technology—chemical fertilizers, tractors, airplanes to spray crops, and so on—of modern farming or agribusiness.

In addition to paying rent to landlords, peasants must satisfy government obligations, paying taxes in the form of money, produce, or labor. The rent fund is not simply an *additional* obligation for peasants. Often it becomes their foremost and unavoidable duty. Sometimes, to meet the obligation to pay rent, their own diets suffer. The demands of social superiors may divert resources from subsistence, replacement, social, and ceremonial funds.

Motivations vary from society to society, and people often lack freedom of choice in allocating their resources. Because of obligations to pay rent, peasants may

Scarcity and the Betsileo

From October 1966 through December 1967, my wife and I lived among the Betsileo people of Madagascar, studying their economy and social life (Kottak 1980). Soon after our arrival we met two well-educated schoolteachers who were interested in our research. The woman's father was a congressman who became a cabinet minister during our stay. Our schoolteacher friends told us that their family came from a historically important and typical Betsileo village called Ivato, which they invited us to visit with them.

We had traveled to many other villages, where we were often displeased with our reception. As we drove up, children would run away screaming. Women would hurry inside. Men would retreat to doorways, where they lurked bashfully. Eventually someone would summon the courage to ask what we wanted. This behavior expressed the Betsileos' great fear of the *mpakafo*. Believed to cut out and devour his victim's heart and liver, the *mpakafo* is the Malgasy vampire. These cannibals are said to have fair skin and to be very tall. Because I have light skin and stand six feet four inches tall, I was a natural suspect. The fact that such creatures were not known to travel with their wives helped convince the Betsileo that I wasn't really a *mpakafo*.

When we visited Ivato, we found that its people were different. They were friendly and hospitable. Our very first day there we did a brief census and found out who lived in which households. We learned people's names and relationships to our schoolteacher friends and to each other. We met an excellent informant who knew all about the local history. In a few afternoons I learned much more than I had in the other villages in several sessions.

Ivatans were willing to talk because I had powerful sponsors, village natives who had made it in the outside world, people the Ivatans knew would protect them. The schoolteachers vouched for us, but even more significant was the cabinet minister, who was like a grandfather and benefactor to everyone in town. The Ivatans had no reason to fear me because their most influential native son had asked them to answer my questions.

allocate their scarce means toward ends that are not their own but those of government officials. Thus, even in societies where there is a profit motive, people are often prevented from rationally maximizing self-interest by factors beyond their control.

Once we moved to Ivato, the elders established a pattern of visiting us every evening. They came to talk, attracted by the inquisitive foreigners but also by the wine, cigarettes, and food we offered. I asked questions about their customs and beliefs. I eventually developed interview schedules about various subjects, including rice production. I mimeographed these forms to use in Ivato and in two other villages I was studying less intensively. Never have I interviewed as easily as I did in Ivato. So enthusiastic were the Ivatans about my questions that even people from neighboring villages came to join the study. Since these people know nothing about social scientists' techniques, I couldn't discourage them by saying that they weren't in my sample. Instead, I agreed to visit each village, where I filled out the interview schedule in just one house. Then I told the other villagers that the household head had done such a good job of teaching me about their village I wouldn't need to ask questions in the other households.

As our stay drew to an end, the elders of Ivato began to lament, saying, "We'll miss you. When you leave, there won't be any more cigarettes, any more wine, or any more questions." They wondered what it would be like for us back in the United States. Ivatans had heard of American plans to send a man to the moon. Did I think it would succeed? They knew that I had an automobile and that I regularly purchased things, including the wine, cigarettes, and food I shared with them. I could afford to buy products they would never have. They commented, "When you go back to your country, you'll need a lot of money for things like cars, clothes, and food. We don't need to buy those things. We make almost everything we use. We don't need as much money as you, because we produce for ourselves."

The Betsileo are not unusual among people whom anthropologists have studied. Strange as it may seem to an American consumer, who may believe that he or she can never have enough money, some rice farmers actually believe that *they have all they need.* The lesson from the Betsileo is that scarcity, which economists view as universal, is variable. Although shortages do arise in nonindustrial societies, the concept of scarcity (insufficient means) is much less developed in stable subsistence-oriented societies than in societies characterized by industrialism, particularly as consumerism increases.

DISTRIBUTION, EXCHANGE

The economist Karl Polanyi (1957) stimulated the comparative study of exchange, and several anthropologists followed his lead. To study exchange cross-culturally,

Polanyi defined three principles orienting exchanges: the **market principle, redistribution,** and **reciprocity.** These principles can all be present in the same society, but in that case they govern different kinds of transactions. In any society, one of them usually dominates. The principle of exchange that dominates in a given society is the one that allocates the means of production.

The Market Principle

In today's world capitalist economy, the market principle dominates. It governs the distribution of the means of production—land, labor, natural resources, technology, and capital. "Market exchange refers to the organizational process of purchase and sale at money price" (Dalton 1967). With market exchange, items are bought and sold with an eye toward maximizing profit, and value is determined by the **law of supply and demand** (things cost more the scarcer they are and the more people want them).

Bargaining is characteristic of market-principle exchanges. The buyer and seller strive to maximize—to get their "money's worth." Bargaining doesn't require that the buyer and seller meet. Consumers bargain whenever they shop around or use advertisements in their decision making.

Redistribution

Redistribution operates when goods, services, or their equivalent move from the local level to a center. The center may be a capital, a regional collection point, or a storehouse near a chief's residence. Products move through a hierarchy of officials for storage at the center. Along the way officials and their dependents consume some of them, but the exchange principle here is *re*distribution. The flow of goods eventually reverses direction—out from the center, down through the hierarchy, and back to the common people.

Reciprocity

Reciprocity is exchange between social equals, who are normally related by kinship, marriage, or another close personal tie. Because it occurs between social equals, it is dominant in the more egalitarian societies—among foragers, cultivators, and pastoralists. There are three degrees of reciprocity: generalized, balanced, and negative (Sahlins 1968, 1972; Service 1966). These may be imagined as areas on a continuum defined by these questions:

1. How closely related are the parties to the exchange?
2. How quickly are gifts reciprocated?

Generalized reciprocity, the purest form of reciprocity, is characteristic of exchanges between closely related people. In **balanced reciprocity,** social distance increases, as does the need to reciprocate. In **negative reciprocity,** social distance is greatest and reciprocation is most urgent.

With generalized reciprocity, someone gives to another person and expects nothing concrete or immediate in return. Such exchanges (including parental gift giving in contemporary North America) are not primarily economic transactions but expressions of personal relationships. Most parents don't keep accounts of every penny they spend on their children. They merely hope that the children will respect their culture's customs involving love, honor, loyalty, and other obligations to parents.

Among foragers, generalized reciprocity tends to govern exchanges. People routinely share with other band members (Bird-David 1992; Kent 1992). A study of the !Kung San found that 40 percent of the population contributed little to the food supply (Lee 1974). Children, teenagers, and people over sixty depended on other people for their food. Despite the high proportion of dependents, the average worker hunted or gathered less than half as much (twelve to nineteen hours a week) as the average American works. Nonetheless, there was always food because different people worked on different days.

So strong is the ethic of reciprocal sharing that most foragers lack an expression for "thank you." To offer thanks would be impolite because it would imply that a particular act of sharing, which is the keystone of egalitarian society, was unusual. Among the Semai, foragers of central Malaysia (Dentan 1979), to express gratitude would suggest surprise at the hunter's generosity or success (Harris 1974).

Balanced reciprocity applies to exchanges between people who are more distantly related than are members of the same band or household. In a horticultural society, for example, a man presents a gift to someone in another village. The recipient may be a cousin, a trading partner, or a brother's fictive kinsman. The giver expects something in return. This may not come immediately, but the social relationship will be strained if there is no reciprocation.

Many nonindustrial societies also feature negative reciprocity, which applies to people on the fringes of their social systems. To people who live in a world of close personal relations, exchanges with outsiders are full of ambiguity and distrust. Exchange is one way of establishing friendly relations with outsiders, but when trade begins, the relationship is still tentative. The initial exchange is close to being purely economic; people want something back immediately. Just as in market economies, they try to get the best possible immediate return for their investment.

One example of negative reciprocity is silent trade or barter between the Mbuti Pygmy foragers of the African equatorial forest and neighboring horticultural villagers. There is no personal contact during the exchange. A Mbuti hunter leaves game, honey, or another forest product at a customary site. Villagers collect it and leave crops in exchange. The parties can bargain silently. If one feels that the return is insufficient, he or she simply leaves it at the trading site. If the other party wants to continue trade, it will be increased.

Coexistence of Exchange Principles

In contemporary North America, the market principle governs the means of production and most exchanges, for example, those involving consumer goods. We also have redistribution, but it is not highly developed. Much of our tax money goes to support the government, but some of it comes back as social services, education, Medicare, and road building. We also have reciprocal exchanges. Generalized reciprocity characterizes the relationship between parents and children. However, even here the dominant market mentality surfaces in comments about the high cost of raising children and in the stereotypical statement of the disappointed parent: "We gave you everything money could buy."

Exchanges of gifts, cards, and invitations exemplify reciprocity, usually balanced. Everyone has heard remarks like "They invited us to their daughter's wedding, so when ours gets married, we'll have to invite them" and "They've been here for dinner three times and haven't invited us yet. I don't think we should ask them back until they do." Such precise balancing of reciprocity would be out of place in a foraging band, where resources are communal (common to all) and daily sharing based on generalized reciprocity is an essential ingredient of social life and survival.

POTLATCHING

One of the most famous cultural practices studied by ethnographers is the **potlatch,** which was widely practiced by tribes of the North Pacific Coast of North America, including the Salish and **Kwakiutl** of Washington and British Columbia. The potlatch, which some tribes still practice (sometimes as a memorial to the dead) (Kan 1986, 1989), was a festive event. Assisted by members of their communities, potlatch sponsors gave away food, blankets, pieces of copper, and other items. In return, they got prestige. To give a potlatch enhanced one's reputation. Prestige increased with the lavishness of the potlatch, the value of the goods given away.

The potlatching tribes were hunters and gatherers, but compared with other foragers, they were more like food producers. They lived in sedentary tribes and had chiefs. Unlike those of most recent foragers, their environments were not marginal. They had access to a wide variety of land and sea resources. Their most important foods were salmon, herring, candlefish, berries, mountain goats, seals, and porpoises (Piddocke 1969).

Within the spreading world capitalist economy of the nineteenth century, the potlatching tribes, particularly the Kwakiutl, began to trade with Europeans (fur for blankets, for example), and their wealth increased as a result. Simultaneously, a huge proportion of the population died from previously unknown diseases brought by the Europeans. The increased wealth from trade flowed into a drastically reduced population. With many of the traditional sponsors dead, the Kwakiutl extended the right to give a potlatch to the entire population, and this stimulated intense competition for prestige. Given trade, increased wealth, and a decreased population, the Kwakiutl also started converting wealth into prestige by destroying wealth items such as blankets and pieces of copper (Vayda 1961/1968).

Scholars once regarded Kwakiutl potlatching as economically wasteful behavior, the result of an irrational drive for social status and prestige. They stressed the destructiveness of the Kwakiutl to support their contention that in some societies people strive irrationally to maximize prestige—even by destroying valuable resources.

However, a more recent interpretation views potlatching not as wasteful but as a useful cultural adaptive mechanism. This view not only helps us understand potlatching, it also has comparative value because it helps us understand similar patterns of feasting throughout the world. This is the new interpretation: *Customs such as the potlatch are adaptations to alternating periods of local abundance and shortage.*

How did this work? The overall natural environment of the North Pacific Coast is favorable, but resources fluctuate from year to year and place to place. Salmon and herring aren't equally abundant every year in a given locality. One village can have a good year while another is experiencing a bad one. Later their fortunes reverse. In this context, the potlatch cycle of the Kwakiutl and Salish had adaptive value, and the potlatch was not an irrational competitive display.

A village enjoying an especially good year had a surplus of subsistence items, which it could exchange for wealth, and wealth could be converted into prestige. Potlatches distributed food and wealth to other communities that needed it. In return, the sponsors and their villages got prestige. The decision to potlatch was determined by the health of the local economy. If there had been a subsistence surplus, and thus a buildup of wealth over several good years, the village could afford a potlatch to convert food and wealth into prestige.

The adaptive value of intercommunity feasting becomes clear when we consider what happened when a formerly prosperous village had a bad year. Its people started accepting invitations to potlatches in villages that were doing better. The tables were turned as the temporarily rich became temporarily poor, and vice versa. The newly needy accepted food and wealth items. They were willing to receive rather than bestow gifts and thus to relinquish some of their stored-up prestige. Later, if the village's fortunes continued to decline, its people could exchange wealth items for food, for example, slaves for herring or canoes for cherries (Vayda 1961/1968). They hoped that their luck would eventually improve so that resources could be recouped and prestige regained.

Note that potlatching also impeded the development of socioeconomic stratification. Wealth relinquished or destroyed was converted into a nonmaterial item—prestige. Under capitalism we reinvest our profits (rather than burning our cash) with the hope of making an additional profit. However, the potlatching tribes were content to destroy their surpluses rather than use them to widen the social distance between themselves and fellow tribe members.

The potlatch linked local groups along the North Pacific Coast into a regional alliance and exchange network. Potlatching and intervillage exchange had adaptive functions, regardless of the motivations of the individual participants. The anthropologists who stressed rivalry for prestige were not wrong. They were merely emphasizing motivations at the expense of an analysis of economic and ecological systems.

The use of feasts to enhance individual and community reputations and to redistribute wealth is not peculiar to the Kwakiutl and the Salish. Competitive but adaptive feasting is widely characteristic of nonindustrial food producers. But among foragers in marginal areas, unlike the Northwest Coast, resources are too meager to support feasting on such a level, and sharing rather than competition prevails.

SUMMARY

Yehudi Cohen's six adaptive strategies are foraging (hunting and gathering), horticulture, agriculture, pastoralism, mercantilism (trade), and indusrialism. Foraging was the only human strategy until food production (cultivation and animal domestication) appeared around 10,000 years ago. Food production eventually replaced foraging in most areas. Almost all modern foragers have at least some dependence on food production or food producers.

Among most foragers, the band is a basic social unit. Often band members split up seasonally into microbands or families. Kinship, marriage, and other arrangements link band members. Foragers assign tasks by gender and age. Men usually hunt and fish, and women gather. Old people guard traditions.

Cultivation is often combined with other adaptive strategies, such as pastoralism or foraging. Horticulture and agriculture stand at different ends of a continuum based on labor intensity and continuity of land use. Horticulture does not use land or labor intensively. Horticulturalists cultivate a plot for one or two years and then abandon it. Further along the continuum, horticulture becomes more intensive, but there is always a fallow period. Horticulturalists can shift plots while living in permanent villages. The first cultivating economies were horticultural. Horticulture still occurs in many areas of both hemispheres.

Agriculturalists farm the same plot of land continuously and use labor intensively. They use one or more of the following practices: irrigation, terracing, domesticated animals as means of production, and manuring. Because of permanent land use, agricultural populations are denser than are those associated with other adaptive strategies. Agriculturalists often have complex regulatory systems, including state organization.

The mixed nature of the pastoral strategy is evident. Nomadic pastoralists trade with cultivators. Transhumants grow their own crops. Part of the transhumant population cultivates while another part takes the herds to pasture. Except for some Peruvians and the Navajo, who are recent herders, the New World lacks native pastoralists.

Economic anthropologists study systems of production, distribution, and consumption cross-culturally. In nonindustrial societies, a kin-based mode of production prevails, and production is personal. The relations of production are aspects of continuous social relationships. One acquires rights to resources through membership in bands, descent groups, villages, and other social units, not impersonally through purchase and sale. Labor is also recruited through personal ties. Work is merely one aspect of social relationships that are expressed in a variety of social and ceremonial contexts.

Manufacturing specialization can exist in nonindustrial societies, promoting trade and alliance between groups. In nonindustrial societies there is usually a personal relationship between producer and commodity, in contrast to the alienation of labor, product, and management in industrial economies.

Economics has been defined as the science of allocating scarce means to alternative ends. Western economists assume that the notion of scarcity is universal—which it isn't—and that in making choices, people strive to maximize personal profit. However, in nonindustrial societies, as in our own, people maximize values other than individual profit. Furthermore, people often lack free choice in allocating their resources. In nonindustrial societies, people invest in subsistence, replacement, social, and ceremonial funds. States add a rent fund: People must share their output with government officials and other social superiors. In states, the obligation to pay rent often becomes primary, and family subsistence may suffer.

Besides production, economic anthropologists study and compare exchange systems. The three principles of exchange are the market principle, redistribution, and reciprocity. The market principle, based on supply and demand and the profit motive, is dominant in states. Its characteristics are impersonal purchase and sale and bargaining. With redistribution, goods are collected at a central place, and some of them are eventually given back, or redistributed, to the people. Reciprocity governs exchanges between social equals. It is the characteristic mode of exchange among foragers and nonintensive cultivators. There are different degrees of reciprocity. With generalized reciprocity, there is no immediate expectation of return. With balanced reciprocity, which is characteristic of exchanges between more distantly related people, donors expect their gifts to be returned, although not immediately. Exchanges on the fringes of the social system are governed by negative reciprocity. As with the market principle, there is concern about immediate return, as well as bargaining. Reciprocity, redistribution, and the market principle may coexist in a society, but the primary exchange mode is the one that allocates the means of production.

Patterns of feasting and exchanges of wealth between villages in a region are common among nonindustrial food producers, as among the potlatching cultures of North America's Northwest Coast. Such systems have adaptive value because they help even out the availability of resources over time. The destruction of wealth, characteristic of some such systems, also impedes the emergence of socioeconomic stratification.

CHAPTER EIGHT

The Political Systems of Nonindustrial Societies

TYPES AND TRENDS

FORAGING BANDS
BOX: The Great Forager Debate

TRIBAL CULTIVATORS
Descent-Group Organization ~ The Village Head ~ Village Raiding ~
The "Big Man" ~ Segmentary Lineage Organization ~ Pantribal Sodalities,
Associations, and Age Grades

CHIEFDOMS
Political and Economic Systems in Chiefdoms ~ Social Status
in Chiefdoms ~ Status Systems in Chiefdoms and States

STATES
Population Control ~ Judiciary ~ Enforcement ~ Fiscal Systems

nthropologists and political scientists share an interest in political organi-zation, but the anthropological approach is global and comparative. An-thropological data reveal substantial variations in power, authority, and legal sys-tems in different cultures. (*Power* is the ability to exercise one's will over others; *authority* is the socially approved use of power.)

Several years ago anthropologist Elman Service (1962) listed four types, or lev-els, of political organization: band, tribe, chiefdom, and state. *Bands,* as we have seen, are small kin-based groups (all members of the group are related to each other by kinship or marriage ties) found among foragers. **Tribes,** which are associated with nonintensive food production (horticulture and pastoralism), have villages and/or descent groups but lack a formal government and social classes (socioeco-nomic stratification). In a tribe, there is no reliable means of enforcing political deci-sions. The **chiefdom,** a form of sociopolitical organization that is intermediate be-tween the tribe and the state, is kin-based, but it has differential access to resources (some people have more wealth, prestige, and power than others do) and a permanent political structure. The **state** is a form of sociopolitical organization based on a formal government structure and socioeconomic stratification.

Many anthropologists have criticized Service's typology as being too simple. However, it does offer a handy set of labels for highlighting cross-cultural similarities and differences in social and political organization. For example, in bands and tribes, the political order, or **polity,** is not a separate entity but is submerged in the total social order. It is difficult to characterize an act or event as political rather than merely social.

Recognizing that political organization is sometimes just an aspect of social organization, Morton Fried offered this definition:

> Political organization comprises those portions of social organization that specifically relate to the individuals or groups that manage the affairs of *public policy* or seek to control the appointment or activities of those individuals or groups. (Fried 1967, pp. 20–21, emphasis added)

This definition certainly fits contemporary North America. Under "individuals or groups that manage the affairs of public policy" come federal, state (provincial), and local (municipal) governments. Those who "seek to control . . . appointment or activities" include such interest groups as political parties, unions, corporations, consumers, activists, action committees, and religious groups.

Fried's definition is much less applicable to bands and tribes, where it is often difficult to detect any "public policy." For this reason, I prefer to speak of *socio*political organization in discussing cross-cultural similarities and differences in the **regulation** or management of interrelationships among groups and their representatives. In a general sense regulation is the process that ensures that variables stay within their normal ranges, corrects deviations from the norm, and thus maintains a system's integrity. In the case of political regulation this includes such things as the settling of conflicts between individuals and groups and methods of decision making within the group. The study of political regulation draws our attention to questions about who performs these tasks (Are there formal leaders?) and how they are managed.

TYPES AND TRENDS

Ethnographic and archeological studies in hundreds of places have revealed many correlations between economy and social and political organization. Band, tribe, chiefdom, and state are categories or types in a system of **sociopolitical typology.** These types are correlated with the adaptive strategies (**economic typology**) discussed in the last chapter. Thus, foragers (an economic type) tend to have band organization (a sociopolitical type). Similarly, many horticulturalists and pastoralists live in tribal societies (or, more simply, tribes). The economies of chiefdoms tend to be based on intensive horticulture or agriculture, but some pastoralists also participate in chiefdoms. Nonindustrial states usually have an agricultural base.

Food producers tend to have larger, denser populations and more complex economies than do foragers. These features create new regulatory problems, which give rise to more complex relationships and linkages. Many sociopolitical trends reflect the increased regulatory demands associated with food production. Archeologists have studied these trends through time, and cultural anthropologists have observed them among contemporary groups.

This chapter examines societies that differ in their economic and political systems. A common set of questions will be considered for different types of societies: What kinds of social groups do they have? How do people affiliate with those groups? How do the groups link up with larger ones? How do the groups represent themselves to each other? How are their internal and external relations regulated?

FORAGING BANDS

In most foraging societies only two kinds of groups are significant: the nuclear family and the band. Unlike sedentary villages (which appear in tribal societies), bands are impermanent. They form seasonally as component nuclear families assemble. The particular combination of families in a band may vary from year to year. In such settings the main social building blocks (linking principles) are the personal relationships of individuals. For example, marriage and kinship create ties between members of different bands. Because one's parents and grandparents come from different bands, a person has relatives in several of these groups. Trade and visiting also link local groups, as does fictive kinship, such as the San namesake system described in the last chapter. Similarly, Eskimo men traditionally had trade partners, whom they treated almost like brothers, in different bands.

In a foraging band, there is very little differential authority and no differential power, although particular talents lead to special respect. For example, someone can sing or dance well, is an especially good storyteller, or can go into a trance and communicate with spirits. Band leaders are leaders in name only. They are first among equals. Sometimes they give advice or make decisions, but they have no means of enforcing their decisions.

Although foragers lack formal **law** in the sense of a legal code that includes trial and enforcement, they do have methods of social control and dispute settlement. The absence of law does not mean total anarchy. The aboriginal Eskimos (Hoebel 1954, 1968), or Inuit, as they are called in Canada, provide a good example of methods of settling disputes in stateless societies. As described by E. A. Hoebel (1954) in a study of Eskimo conflict resolution, a sparse population of some 20,000 Eskimos spanned 9,500 kilometers (6,000 miles) of the Arctic region. The most significant Eskimo social groups were the nuclear family and the band. Personal relationships linked the families and bands. Some bands had headmen. There were also shamans (part-time religious specialists). However, these positions conferred little power on those who occupied them.

Unlike tropical foraging societies, in which gathering—usually a female task—is more important, hunting and fishing by men were the primary Eskimo subsistence activities. The diverse and abundant plant foods available in warmer areas were absent in the Arctic. Traveling on land and sea in a bitter environment, Eskimo men faced more dangers than women did. The traditional male role took its toll in lives. Adult women would have outnumbered men substantially without occasional female **infanticide** (killing of a baby), which Eskimo culture permitted.

Despite this crude (and to us unthinkable) means of population regulation, there were still more adult women than men. This permitted some men to have two or three wives. The ability to support more than one wife conferred a certain amount of prestige, but it also encouraged envy. (**Prestige** is esteem, respect, or approval for culturally valued acts or qualities.) If a man seemed to be taking additional wives just to enhance his reputation, a rival was likely to steal one of them. Most disputes were between men and originated over women, caused by wife stealing or adultery. If a man discovered that his wife had been having sexual relations without his permission, he considered himself wronged.

Although public opinion would not let the husband ignore the matter, he had several options. He could try to kill the wife stealer. However, if he succeeded, one of his rival's kinsmen would surely try to kill him in retaliation. One dispute could escalate into several deaths as relatives avenged a succession of murders. No government existed to intervene and stop such a **blood feud** (a feud between families). However, one could also challenge a rival to a song battle. In a public setting, contestants made up insulting songs about each other. At the end of the match, the audience judged one of them the winner. However, if a man whose wife had been stolen won, there was no guarantee she would return. Often she would decide to stay with her abductor.

Several acts of killing that are crimes in contemporary North America were not considered criminal by the Eskimos. Infanticide has already been mentioned. Furthermore, people who felt that because of age or infirmity they were no longer useful might kill themselves or ask others to kill them. Old people or invalids who wished to die would ask a close relative, such as a son, to end their lives. It was necessary to ask a close relative in order to ensure that the kin of the deceased did not take revenge on the killer.

Thefts are common in state-organized societies, which have marked property differentials. However, thefts were not a problem for the Eskimos—or for most foragers. Each Eskimo had access to the resources needed to sustain life. Every man could hunt, fish, and make the tools necessary for subsistence. Every woman could obtain the implements and materials needed to make clothing, prepare food, and do domestic work. Eskimos could even hunt and fish in territories of other local groups. There was no notion of private ownership of territory or animals.

The Great Forager Debate

ow representative are modern hunter-gatherers of Paleolithic (Stone Age) peoples, all of whom were foragers? G. P. Murdock (1934) described living hunter-gatherers as "our primitive contemporaries." This label gave an image of foragers as living fossils—frozen, primitive, unchanging social forms that had managed to hang on in remote areas (like the Hollywood natives on King Kong's island).

Later, many anthropologists followed the prolific ethnographer Richard Lee (1984) in using the San (Bushmen) of the Kalahari Desert of southern Africa to represent the hunting-gathering way of life. But critics increasingly wonder about how much modern foragers can tell us about the economic and social relations that characterized humanity before food production. Modern foragers, after all, live in nation-states and an increasingly interlinked world. For generations, the Pygmies of Zaire have traded with their neighbors who are cultivators. They exchange forest products (e.g., honey and meat) for crops (e.g., bananas and manioc). The San have been influenced by Bantu speakers for 2,000 years and by Europeans for centuries. All foragers now trade with food producers, and most rely on governments and missionaries for at least part of what they consume. The Aché of Paraguay get food from missionaries, grow crops, and have domesticated animals (Hawkes et al. 1982; Hill et al. 1987). They spend only a third of their subsistence time foraging.

A debate is now raging in hunter-gatherer studies between "traditionalists" (e.g., Richard Lee) and "revisionists" (e.g., Edwin Wilmsen). Reconsideration of the status of contemporary foragers is related to the reaction against the ethnographic present discussed in the box in Chapter 1. Anthropologists have rejected the old tendency to depict societies as uniform and frozen in time and space. Attempts to capture the ethnographic present often ignored internal variation, change, and the influence of the world system.

The debate over foragers has focused on the San, whom the traditionalists view as autonomous foragers with a cultural identity different from that of their neighbors who are herders and cultivators (Lee 1979; Silberbauer 1981; Tanaka 1980). These scholars depict most San as egalitarian, band-organized people who until recently were nomadic or seminomadic. Traditionalists recognize contact between the San and food producers, but they don't think this contact has destroyed San culture.

The revisionists claim the San tell us little about the ancient world in which all humans were foragers. They argue that the San have been linked to food producers for generations, and that this contact has changed the basis of their culture. For Edwin Wilmsen (1989), the San are far from being isolated survivors of a pristine era. They are a rural underclass in a larger political and economic system dominated by Europeans and Bantu food producers. Many San now tend cattle for wealthier Bantu, rather than foraging independently. Wilmsen also argues that many San descend from herders who were pushed into the desert by poverty or oppression.

The isolation and autonomy of foragers have also been questioned for African Pygmies (Bailey et al. 1989) and for foragers in the Philippines (Headland and Reid 1989). The Mikea of southwest Madagascar may have moved into their remote forest habitat to escape the nearby Sakalava state. Eventually the Mikea became an economically specialized group of hunter-gatherers on the fringes of that state. The Tasaday of the Philippines maintain ties with food producers and probably descend from cultivating ancestors. This is true despite the initial "Lost Tribe" media accounts. The reports that followed the "discovery" of the Tasaday portrayed them as survivors of the Stone Age, hermetically sealed in a pristine world all their own. Many scholars now question the authenticity of the Tasaday as a separate cultural group (Headland, ed. 1992).

The debate about foragers raises a larger question: Why do ethnographic accounts and interpretations vary? The reasons include variation in space and time in the society, and different assumptions by ethnographers. Susan Kent (1992) notes a tendency to stereotype foragers, to treat them as all alike. Foragers used to be stereotyped as isolated, primitive survivors of the Stone Age. A new stereotype sees them as culturally deprived people forced by states, colonialism, or world events into marginal environments. This view is probably more accurate, although often exaggerated. All modern foragers have links with external systems, including food producers and nation-states. Because of this they differ substantially from Paleolithic hunter-gatherers.

Challenging both stereotypes, Kent (1992) stresses variation among foragers. She focuses on diversity in time and space among the San. The traditionalist-revisionist debate, suggests Kent, is largely based on failure to recognize the extent of diversity among the San. Researchers on both sides may be correct, depending on the group of San being described and the time period of the research.

San economic adaptations range from hunting and gathering to fishing, farming, herding, and wage work. Solway and Lee (1990) describe environmental degradation caused by herding and population increase. These factors are depleting game and forcing more and more San to give up foraging. Even traditionalists recognize that all San are being drawn inexorably into the modern world system. (Many of us remember the Coke bottle that fell from the sky into a San band in the movie *The Gods Must Be Crazy*—a film filled with many stereotypes.)

The nature of San life has changed appreciably since the 1950s and 1960s, when a series of anthropologists from Harvard University, including Richard Lee, embarked on a systematic study of life in the Kalahari. Lee and others have documented many of the changes in various publications. Such longitudinal research monitors variation in time, while fieldwork in many San areas has revealed variation in space. One of the most important contrasts is between settled (sedentary) and nomadic groups (Kent and Vierich 1989). Sedentism is increasing, but some San groups (along rivers) have been sedentary, or have traded with outsiders, for generations. Others, including Lee's Dobe !Kung San and Kent's Kutse San, have been more cut off and have retained more of the hunter-gatherer lifestyle.

Modern foragers are not Stone Age relics, living fossils, lost tribes, or noble savages. Still, to the extent that foraging is the basis of subsistence, modern hunter-gatherers can illustrate links between a foraging economy and other aspects of culture. For example, San groups that are still mobile, or that were so until recently, emphasize social, political, and gender equality. Social relations that stress kinship, sharing, and reciprocity work well in an economy with limited resources and few people. The nomadic pursuit of wild plants and animals tends to discourage permanent settlements, accumulation of wealth, and status distinctions. People have to share meat when they get it; otherwise it rots. Kent (1992) suggests that by studying diversity among the San, we can better understand foraging and how it is influenced by sedentism and other factors. Such study will enhance our knowledge of past, present, and future small-scale societies.

To describe certain property notions of people who live in societies without state organization, Elman Service (1966) coined the term **personalty** (note the spelling). Personalty refers to items other than strategic resources that are indelibly associated with a specific person. These items include such things as arrows, a tobacco pouch, clothing, and personal ornaments. The term points to the personal relationship between such items and their owner. Personalty is so tied to specific people that theft is inconceivable (think of your toothbrush). The "grave goods" that are often found in archeological sites dating to the period before food production probably represent personalty. These items were not passed on to heirs. Their association with the deceased was too definite.

One of the most basic Eskimo beliefs was that "all natural resources are free or common goods" (Hoebel 1968). Band-organized societies usually lack differential access to strategic resources. The only private property is personalty. If people want something from someone else, they ask for it, and it is usually given.

TRIBAL CULTIVATORS

Tribes usually have a horticultural or pastoral economy and are organized by village life and/or descent-group membership. Socioeconomic stratification (i.e., a class structure) and a formal government are absent. Many tribes have small-scale warfare, often in the form of intervillage raiding. Tribes have more effective regulatory mechanisms than do foragers, but tribalists have no sure means of enforcing political decisions. The main regulatory officials are village heads, "big men," descent-group leaders, village councils, and leaders of pantribal associations. All these figures and groups have limited authority.

Like foragers, horticulturalists tend to be egalitarian, although some have marked gender stratification—an unequal distribution of resources, power, prestige, and personal freedom between men and women. Horticultural villages are usually small, with low population density and open access to strategic resources. Age, gender, and personal traits determine how much respect people receive and how much support they get from others. Egalitarianism diminishes, however, as village size and population density increase. Horticultural villages usually have headmen—rarely, if ever, headwomen.

Descent-Group Organization

Kin-based bands are basic social units among foragers. An analogous group among food producers is the **descent group.** A descent group is a permanent social unit whose members claim common ancestry. The group endures even though its membership changes as members are born and die, move in and move out. Often, descent-group membership is determined at birth and is lifelong.

Descent groups frequently are exogamous (members must seek their mates from other descent groups). Two common rules serve to admit certain people as descent-group members while excluding others. With a rule of **matrilineal descent,** people join the mother's group automatically at birth and stay members throughout life. Matrilineal descent groups therefore include only the children of the group's women. With **patrilineal descent,** people automatically have lifetime membership in the father's group. The children of all the men join the group, but the children of the women are excluded. Matrilineal and patrilineal descent are types of **unilineal**

descent. This means that the descent rule uses *one line* only, either the male or the female (Figures 8-1 and 8-2). Patrilineal descent is much more common than is matrilineal descent. In a sample of 564 societies (Murdock 1957), about three times as many were found to be patrilineal (247 to 84).

Descent groups may be **lineages** or **clans.** Common to both is the belief that members descend from the same **apical ancestor.** This person stands at the apex, or top, of the common genealogy. How do lineages and clans differ? A lineage uses **demonstrated descent.** Members can recite the names of their forebears in each generation from the apical ancestor through the present. (This doesn't mean that their recitations are accurate, only that lineage members think they are.) Clans use **stipulated descent.** Clan members merely say they descend from the apical ancestor. They don't try to trace the actual genealogical links between themselves and that ancestor.

Some societies have both lineages and clans. In this case, clans have more members and cover a larger geographic area than lineages do. Sometimes a clan's apical ancestor is not a human at all but an animal or a plant (called a **totem**). Whether human or not, the ancestor symbolizes the social unity and identity of the members, distinguishing them from other groups.

A tribal society normally contains several descent groups. Any one of them may be confined to a single village, but they usually span more than one village. Any branch of a descent group that lives in one place is a **local descent group.** Two or

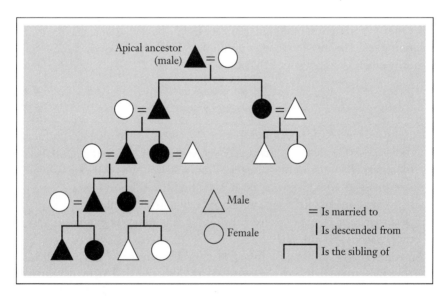

FIGURE 8-1 A patrilineage five generations deep. Lineages are based on demonstrated descent from an apical ancestor. With patrilineal descent, children of men (black) are included as descent-group members. Children of women are excluded; they belong to *their* father's patrilineage. Also, notice lineage exogamy.

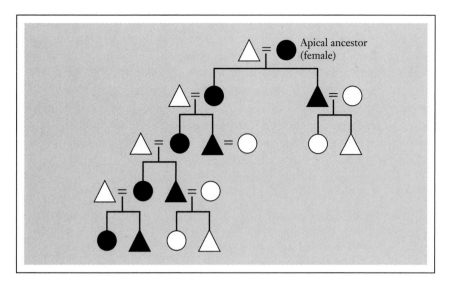

FIGURE 8-2 A matrilineage five generations deep. Matrilineages are based on demonstrated descent from a female ancestor. Only the children of women (black) belong to the matrilineage. The children of men are excluded; they belong to *their* mother's matrilineage.

more local branches of different descent groups may live in the same village. Descent groups in the same village or different villages may establish alliances through frequent intermarriage.

The Village Head

The Yanomami (Chagnon 1992) are Native Americans who live in southern Venezuela and adjacent Brazil. Their tribal society has about 20,000 people living in 200 to 250 widely scattered villages, each with a population between 40 and 250. The Yanomami are horticulturalists who also hunt and gather. Their staple crops are bananas and plantains (a bananalike crop). There are more significant social groups among the Yanomami than exist in a foraging society. The Yanomami have nuclear families, villages, and descent groups. Their descent groups are patrilineal and exogamous. They span more than one village. However, local branches of two different descent groups may live in the same village and intermarry.

As in many village-based tribal societies, the only leadership position among the Yanomami is that of **village head** (always a man). His authority, like that of the foraging band leader, is severely limited. If a headman wants something done, he must lead by example and persuasion. The headman lacks the right to issue orders. He can only persuade, harangue, and try to influence public opinion. For example, if he wants people to clean up the central plaza in preparation for a feast, he must start sweeping it himself, hoping that his covillagers will take the hint and relieve him.

When conflict erupts, the headman may be called on as a mediator who listens to both sides. He will give an opinion and advice. If a disputant is unsatisfied, the headman can do nothing. He has no power to back his decisions and no way to impose punishments. Like the band leader, he is first among equals.

A Yanomami village headman must also lead in generosity. Because he must be more generous than any other villager, he cultivates more land. His garden provides much of the food consumed when his village holds a feast for another village. The headman represents the village in its dealings with outsiders. Sometimes he visits other villages to invite people to a feast.

The way a person acts as headman depends on his personal traits and the number of supporters he can muster. One village headman, Kaobawa, intervened in a dispute between a husband and wife and kept him from killing her (Chagnon 1992). He also guaranteed safety to a delegation from a village with which a covillager of his wanted to start a war. Kaobawa was a particularly effective headman. He had demonstrated his fierceness in battle, but he also knew how to use diplomacy to avoid offending other villagers. No one in the village had a better personality for the headmanship. Nor (because Kaobawa had many brothers) did anyone have more supporters. Among the Yanomami, when a group is dissatisfied with a village headman, its members can leave and found a new village; this is done from time to time.

Village Raiding

Yanomami society, with its many villages and descent groups, is more complex than a band-organized society. The Yanomami also face more regulatory problems. A headman can sometimes prevent a specific violent act, but there is no government to maintain order. In fact, intervillage raiding in which men are killed and women are captured has been a feature of some areas of Yanomami territory, particularly those studied by Chagnon (1992).

We must also stress that the Yanomami are not isolated from outside events (although there are still uncontacted villages). The Yanomami live in two nation-states, Venezuela and Brazil, and external warfare waged by Brazilian ranchers and miners has increasingly threatened them (*Cultural Survival Quarterly* 1989; Chagnon 1992). During the recent Brazilian gold rush (1987–1991), one Yanomami died each day, on average, from external attacks (including biological warfare—introduced diseases to which the Indians lack resistance). By 1991, there were some 40,000 Brazilian miners in the Yanomami homeland. Some Indians were killed outright. The miners introduced new diseases, and the swollen population ensured that old diseases became epidemic. In 1991 a commission of the American Anthropological Association reported on the plight of the Yanomami (*Anthropology Newsletter*, September 1991). Brazilian Yanomami were dying at a rate of 10 percent annually, and their fertility rate had dropped to zero. Since then, both the Brazilian and the Venezuelan governments have intervened to protect the Yanomami. Former Brazilian president Fernando Collor declared a huge Yanomami territory off-limits to outsiders. Unfortunately, by mid-1992, local politicians, miners, and ranchers were increasingly evading the ban. These external attacks pose a much more serious threat to Yanomami survival than does traditional intervillage raiding.

The "Big Man"

In many areas of the South Pacific, particularly the Melanesian Islands and Papua-New Guinea, native cultures have a kind of political leader that we call the **big man.** The big man (almost always a male) is an elaborate version of the village head, but there is one very significant difference. The village head's leadership is within one village; the big man has supporters in several villages. He is therefore a more effective (but still limited) regulator of *regional* political organization. Here we see a trend toward expansion in the scale of sociopolitical regulation—from village to region.

The Kapauku Papuans live in Irian Jaya, Indonesia (which is on the island of New Guinea). Anthropologist Leopold Pospisil (1963) studied the Kapauku (45,000

The "big man" is an important regulator of regional events.
He persuades people to organize feasts, which distribute
pork and wealth. Shown here is such a regional event,
drawing on several villages, in Papua-New Guinea. Big
men owe their status to their individual personalities rather
than to inherited wealth or position.

people), who grow crops (with the sweet potato as their staple) and raise pigs. Their economy is too complex to be described as simple horticulture. Beyond the household, the only political figure among the Kapauku is the big man, known as a *tonowi*. A *tonowi* achieves his status through hard work, amassing wealth in the form of pigs and other native riches. Characteristics that can distinguish a big man from his fellows include wealth, generosity, eloquence, physical fitness, bravery, and supernatural powers. Notice that big men are what they are because they have certain personalities and have amassed their resources during their lifetimes, not because they have inherited their wealth or position.

Any man who is determined enough can become a big man, because people create their own wealth through hard work and good judgment. Wealth depends on successful pig breeding and trading. As a man's pig herd and prestige grow, he attracts supporters. He sponsors ceremonial pig feasts in which pigs are slaughtered and their meat is distributed to guests.

The big man has some advantages that the Yanomami village headman lacks. His wealth exceeds that of his fellows. His primary supporters, in recognition of past favors and anticipation of future rewards, recognize him as a leader and accept his decisions as binding. He is an important regulator of regional events in Kapauku life. He helps determine the dates for feasts and markets. He persuades people to sponsor feasts, which distribute pork and wealth. He regulates intervillage contacts by sponsoring dance expeditions. He initiates economic projects that require the cooperation of a regional community.

The Kapauku big man again exemplifies a generalization about leadership in tribal societies: If people achieve wealth and widespread respect and support, they must be generous. The big man works hard not to hoard wealth but to be able to *give away* the fruits of his labor, to convert wealth into prestige and gratitude. If a big man is stingy, he loses his supporters, and his reputation plummets. The Kapauku take even more extreme measures against big men who hoard. Selfish and greedy rich men may be murdered by their fellows.

Political figures such as the big man emerge as regulators of both demographic growth and economic complexity. Kapauku cultivation uses varied techniques for specific kinds of land. Labor-intensive cultivation in valleys involves mutual aid in turning the soil before planting. The digging of long drainage ditches is even more complex. Kapauku plant cultivation supports a larger and denser population than does the simpler horticulture of the Yanomami. Kapauku society could not survive in its present form without collective cultivation and political regulation of the more complex economic tasks.

Segmentary Lineage Organization

The big man is a *temporary* regional regulator. Big men can mobilize supporters in several villages to pool produce and labor on specific occasions. Another temporary form of regional political organization in tribal society is **segmentary lineage orga-**

nization (SLO). This means that the descent-group structure (usually patrilineal) has several levels—nested segments—that are like dolls nesting inside other dolls or boxes placed within boxes (Figure 8-3). The largest segments are maximal lineages, segments of which are known as major lineages. Major lineages are divided up into minor lineages. Minor lineages in turn are segmented into minimal lineages, whose common ancestor lived fairly recently—no more than four generations ago. The larger segments have spread throughout a region, but members of the minimal lineage occupy the same village. New minimal lineages develop when people move away and establish new settlements. Over time, minimal lineages grow into minor ones, minor into major ones, and major into maximal ones.

Segmentary lineage organization exists in broad outline in many cultures, such as the traditional societies of North Africa and the Middle East, including prestate Arabs and biblical Jews. However, the classic examples of SLO are two African groups, the Tiv of Nigeria and the Nuer of the Sudan (Sahlins 1961). Segmentary lineage structure organized more than 1 million Tiv, who believe that they all share the same remote ancestor, a man named Tiv who settled in their homeland many generations ago. They trace the line of descent leading from Tiv to the present, listing his male descendants in each generation.

Although the Nuer cannot demonstrate patrilineal descent that far back, they believe that they have a common ancestry separate from that of their neighbors. One of several **Nilotic populations** (populations that inhabit the Upper Nile region of eastern Africa), the Nuer (Evans-Pritchard 1940), numbering more than 200,000, live in Sudan. Cattle pastoralism is fundamental to their mixed economy, which also includes horticulture. The Nuer have many institutions that are typical of tribal societies, including patrilineal descent groups arranged into a segmentary structure. Their political organization is based on descent rules and genealogical reckoning.

Brothers are very close in segmentary societies, especially when the father is alive. He manages their joint property and stops them from quarreling too much. He also arranges their marriages. When he dies, the brothers usually keep on living in the same village, but one may take his share of the herds and start a settlement of his own. However, his brothers are still his closest allies. He will live as close as he can to them. Even if the brothers all stay in the same village, some of the grandchildren will move away in search of new pastures. However, each will try to remain as close to the home village as possible, settling nearest his brothers and nearer to his first cousins than to more distant relatives.

With SLO, the basic principle of solidarity is that the closer the descent-group relationship, the greater the mutual support. The more distant the shared ancestor, the greater the potential for hostility. This extends right up the genealogy; maximal lineages are more likely to fight each other than are major lineages.

Segmentary lineage organization seems to have been advantageous for the Tiv and the Nuer, allowing them to expand at their neighbors' expense. This sociopolitical organization confers a feeling of tribal identity. It provides an orderly way to mobilize temporarily against other societies. When the need arises, the Nuer or the

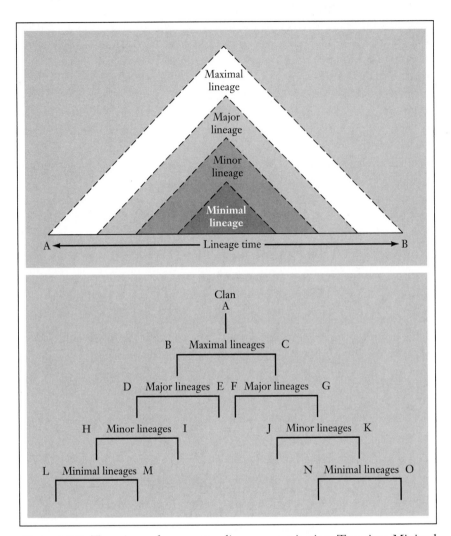

FIGURE 8-3 Two views of segmentary lineage organization. Top view: Minimal lineages nest within minor lineages, which nest within major lineages, which nest within maximal lineages, which may in turn belong to a clan (as in the view below). Common ancestry is most recent in the minimal lineage. Bottom view: Clan A is segmented into *maximal lineages* B and C. These have divided into *major lineages* D, E, F, and G. At the next level down, *minor lineages* H, I, J, and K are segments of major lineages D and G. L, M, N, and O are *minimal lineages* that are segments of H and K. For simplification, the minor lineages of E and F and the minimal lineages of I and J aren't shown.
(Reprinted by permission from E. E. Evans-Pritchard, *The Nuer: A Description of the Modes of Livelihood and Political Institutions of a Nilotic People* [Oxford: Clarendon Press, 1940].)

Tiv can easily present a common front against outsiders—people who claim different genealogical and ethnic identity (Sahlins 1961).

Segmentary descent also regulates disputes and their resolution. If a fight breaks out between men who share a living patrilineal ancestor, he intervenes to settle it. As head of the minimal descent group that includes the disputants, he backs his authority with the threat of banishment. However, when there is no common living ancestor, a blood feud may develop.

Disputes among the Nuer do not arise over land, which a person acquires as a member of a lineage. As a member of a minimal descent group, one has a right to its estate. A frequent cause of quarrels is adultery, and if a person injures or kills someone, a feud may develop. Conflicts also arise over divorce.

There is an alternative to a blood feud. The disputants may consult the leopard-skin man, so called because he customarily wears a leopard skin over his shoulders. Leopard-skin men conduct rituals, but their most important role is to mediate disputes. For instance, elders may ask a leopard-skin man to persuade a murder victim's kin to accept a certain number of cattle in recompense. While the mediator attempts to arrange a peaceful settlement, the murderer may take refuge in the leopard-skin man's village, which offers sanctuary until the mediator resolves the dispute or withdraws.

A leopard-skin man, mediator among the Nuer—tribal cattle herders and horticulturalists of Sudan. The Nuer mediator has recourse only to supernatural sanctions when arbitrating descent-group feuds in this segmentary society.

The leopard-skin man relies on persuasion and avoids blaming either side. He cannot enforce his decisions, but in theory he can use the threat of supernatural punishment. If one of the disputing groups is adamant, he may, in disgust, threaten to curse it. If, after seeking mediation, the disputants refuse to agree, the leopard-skin man may withdraw.

Negotiations involve the disputants, their elders, and other close kin. There is full and free discussion before a settlement is reached. The disputants may gradually come to accept the collective opinion of the mediator and the elders. However, although the peace-making abilities of the leopard-skin man are greater than anything found among the Yanomami and Eskimos, blood feuds still exist among the stateless Nuer.

With SLO, no one has a constant group of allies. One's allies change from one dispute to the next, depending on genealogical distance. Still, common descent does permit a temporary common front, as minimal lineages unite to form minor ones. Minor lineages form majors, and major lineages come together in a maximal lineage that, in the presence of an outside threat, unites all Nuer or Tiv society through its claim of common patrilineal descent.

Similarly, Arabs claim to demonstrate their segmentary descent patrilineally from the biblical Ishmael. There is an Arab adage, "I and my brother against my cousin [father's brother's son]. I, my brother, and my cousin against all other Arabs. I, my brother, my cousin, and all other Arabs against all the world" (Murphy and Kasdan 1959, p. 20). Jews believe themselves to be descended from Isaac, half-brother of Ishmael. The Jews and Arabs share a common ancestor, Abraham, the father of both Ishmael and Isaac. In the modern world, of course, political mechanisms other than SLO, including national governments and regional alliances, work to determine relations between Arabs and Jews.

Pantribal Sodalities, Associations, and Age Grades

We have seen that events initiated by big men temporarily unite people from different villages. Segmentary lineage organization permits short-term mobilization of an entire society against an outside threat. There are many other kinds of sociopolitical linkages between local groups in a region. Clans, for example, often span several villages.

Kinship and descent provide important social linkages in tribal societies. Principles other than kinship also may link local groups. A labor union, national sorority or fraternity, political party, or religious denomination may provide such a non-kin-based link in a modern nation. In tribes, nonkin groups called associations or **sodalities** may serve the same linking function. Often sodalities are based on common age or gender, with all-male sodalities more common than all-female ones.

Pantribal sodalities (those which extend across the whole tribe, spanning several villages) tend to be found in areas where two or more different cultures come into regular contact. They are especially likely to develop when there is warfare *be-*

tween tribes (as opposed to raiding between villages of the same tribe, as practiced by the Yanomami). Sodalities help organize the warfare that men wage against neighboring cultures. Since sodalities draw their members from different villages of the same tribe, they can mobilize men in many local groups for attack or retaliation against another tribe. Like SLO, pantribal sodalities have military value because they facilitate temporary regional mobilization. In particular, pantribal sodalities are common among pastoralists. One culture's sodality may organize raids to steal cattle or horses from another.

In the cross-cultural study of nonkin groups, we must distinguish between those which are confined to a single village and those which span several local groups. Only the latter, the *pantribal* groups, are important in general military mobilization and regional political organization. *Localized* men's houses and clubs, limited to particular villages, are found in many horticultural societies in tropical South America, Melanesia, and Papua-New Guinea. These groups may organize village activities and even intervillage raiding, but their leaders are similar to village heads and their political scope is mainly local. The following discussion, which continues our examination of the growth in scale of regional sociopolitical organization, concerns pantribal groups.

The best examples of pantribal sodalities come from the Central Plains of North America and from tropical Africa. During the eighteenth and nineteenth centuries, native populations of the Great Plains of the United States and Canada experienced a rapid growth of pantribal sodalities. This development reflected an economic change that followed the spread of horses, which had been brought to the New World by the Spanish, to the states between the Rocky Mountains and the Mississippi River. Many Plains Indian societies changed their adaptive strategies because of the horse. At first they had been foragers who hunted bison (buffalo) on foot. Later they adopted a mixed economy based on hunting, gathering, and horticulture. Finally they changed to a much more specialized economy based on horseback hunting of bison (eventually with rifles).

As the Plains tribes were undergoing these changes, other Indians also adopted horseback hunting and moved into the Plains. Attempting to occupy the same ecological niche, groups came into conflict. A pattern of warfare developed in which the members of one tribe raided another, usually for horses, as was portrayed in the movie *Dances with Wolves*. The new economy demanded that people follow the movement of the bison herds. During the winter, when the bison dispersed, a tribe fragmented into small bands and families. In the summer, as huge herds assembled on the Plains, members of the tribe reunited. They camped together for social, political, and religious activities, but mainly for communal bison hunting.

Only two activities in the new adaptive strategy demanded strong leadership: organizing and carrying out raids on enemy camps (to capture horses) and managing the summer bison hunt. All the Plains cultures developed pantribal sodalities, and leadership roles within them, to police the summer hunt. Leaders coordinated hunting efforts, making sure that people did not cause a stampede with an early shot or an ill-advised action. Leaders imposed severe penalties, including seizure of a culprit's wealth, for disobedience.

Some of the Plains sodalities were **age sets** of increasing rank. Each set included all the men—from that tribe's component bands—born during a certain time span. Each set had its distinctive dance, songs, possessions, and privileges. Members of each set had to pool their wealth to buy admission to the next higher level as they moved up the age hierarchy. Most Plains societies had pantribal warrior associations whose rituals celebrated militarism. As noted previously, the leaders of these associations organized bison hunting and raiding. They also arbitrated disputes during the summer, when large numbers of people came together.

Many of the tribes that adopted this Plains strategy of adaptation had once been foragers for whom hunting and gathering had been individual or small-group affairs. They had never come together previously as a single social unit. *Age and gender were available as social principles that could quickly and efficiently forge unrelated people into pantribal groups.*

Raiding of one tribe by another, this time for cattle rather than horses, was also common in eastern and southeastern Africa, where pantribal sodalities, including age sets, also developed. Among the pastoral Masai of Kenya, men born during the same four-year period were circumcised together and belonged to the same named group, an age set, throughout their lives. The sets moved through grades, the most important of which was the warrior grade. Members of the set who wished to enter

Among the pastoral Masai of Kenya, men born during the
same four-year period were circumcised together and
belonged to the same named group, an age set, throughout
their lives. The sets moved through grades, the most
important of which was the warrior grade.
Two Masai age sets are shown here.

the warrior grade were at first discouraged by its current occupants, who eventually vacated the warrior grade and married. Members of a set felt a strong allegiance to one another and eventually had sexual rights to each other's wives. Masai women lacked comparable set organization, but they also passed through culturally recognized age grades: initiate, married woman, and postmenopausal woman.

To understand the difference between an *age set* and an *age grade*, think of a college class, the Class of '96, for example, and its progress through the university. The age set would be the group of people constituting the Class of '96, while the first ("freshman"), sophomore, junior, and senior years would represent the age grades.

Not all cultures with age grades also have age sets. When there are no sets, men can enter or leave a particular grade individually or collectively, often by going through a predetermined ritual. The grades most commonly recognized in Africa are these:

1. Recently initiated youths
2. Warriors
3. One or more grades of mature men who play important roles in pantribal government
4. Elders, who may have special ritual responsibilities

In certain parts of West Africa and Central Africa, the pantribal sodalities are **secret societies,** made up exclusively of men or women. Like our college fraternities and sororities, these associations have secret initiation ceremonies. Among the Mende of Sierra Leone, men's and women's secret societies are very influential. The men's group, the Poro, trains boys in social conduct, ethics, and religion and supervises political and economic activities. Leadership roles in the Poro often overshadow village headship and play an important part in social control, dispute management, and tribal political regulation. Like descent, then, age, gender, and ritual can link members of different local groups into a single social collectivity in tribal society and thus create a sense of ethnic identity, of belonging to the same cultural tradition.

CHIEFDOMS

Having looked at bands and tribes, we turn to more complex forms of sociopolitical organization—chiefdoms and states. The first states (or *civilizations*, a near synonym) emerged in the Old World about 5,500 years ago. The first chiefdoms developed perhaps a thousand years earlier, but few survive today. The chiefdom was a transitional form of sociopolitical organization that emerged during the evolution of tribes into states. State formation began in Mesopotamia (currently Iran and Iraq) and then occurred in Egypt, the Indus Valley of Pakistan and India, and northern China. A few thousand years later states also arose in two parts of the Western Hemisphere—Mesoamerica (Mexico, Guatemala, Belize) and the central Andes (Peru and Bolivia). Early states are known as **archaic,** or nonindustrial, **states,** in contrast to modern industrial nation-states. Robert Carneiro defines the state as

> an autonomous political unit encompassing many communities within its territory, having a centralized government with the power to collect taxes, draft men for work or war, and decree and enforce laws. (Carneiro 1970, p. 733)

The chiefdom and the state, like many categories used by social scientists, are **ideal types.** That is, they are labels that make social contrasts seem more definite than they really are. In reality there is a continuum from tribe to chiefdom to state. Some societies have many attributes of chiefdoms but retain tribal features. Some advanced chiefdoms have many attributes of archaic states and thus are difficult to assign to either category. We see this when our sample of societies in time and space is large enough. Recognizing this "continuous change" (Johnson and Earle 1987), some anthropologists speak of "complex chiefdoms" (Earle 1987), which are almost states.

Political and Economic Systems in Chiefdoms

State formation remained incomplete and only chiefdoms emerged in several areas, including the circum-Caribbean (e.g., Caribbean islands, Panama, Colombia), lowland Amazonia, what is now the southeastern United States, and Polynesia. Chiefdoms created the megalithic cultures of Europe, such as the one that built Stonehenge. Indeed, between the emergence and spread of food production and the expansion of the Roman Empire, much of Europe was organized at the chiefdom level, to which it reverted after the fall of Rome. Some of those chiefdoms developed into states during the Dark Ages (Johnson and Earle 1987).

Much of our ethnographic knowledge about chiefdoms comes from Polynesia, where they were common at the time of European exploration. In chiefdoms, social relations are regulated by kinship, marriage, descent, age, generation, and gender—just as they are in bands and tribes. This is a fundamental difference between chiefdoms and states. States bring nonrelatives together and oblige them all to pledge allegiance to a government.

Unlike bands and tribes, chiefdoms are characterized by *permanent political regulation* of the territory they administer, which includes thousands of people living in many villages and/or hamlets. Regulation is carried out by the chief and his or her assistants, who occupy political offices. An **office** is a permanent position, which must be refilled when it is vacated by death or retirement. Because offices are systematically refilled, the structure of a chiefdom endures across the generations, ensuring permanent political regulation.

Social status in chiefdoms is based on seniority of descent. In the modern world system, seniority may still confer prestige, but the differences in wealth and power between chiefs and their juniors are often minor. Shown here is a contemporary chief (center) in the Marquesas Islands, Polynesia.

In the Polynesian chiefdoms, the chiefs were full-time political specialists in charge of regulating production, distribution, and consumption. Polynesian chiefs relied on religion to buttress their authority. They regulated production by commanding or prohibiting (using religious taboos) the cultivation of certain lands and crops. Chiefs also regulated distribution and consumption. At certain seasons—often on a ritualized occasion such as a first-fruit ceremony—people would offer part of their harvest to the chief through his or her representatives. Products moved up the hierarchy, eventually reaching the chief. Conversely, illustrating obligatory sharing with kin, chiefs sponsored feasts at which they gave back much of what they had received.

Such a flow of resources to and then from a central office is known as *chiefly redistribution*. Redistribution offers economic advantages. If different areas specialized in particular crops, goods, or services, chiefly redistribution made those products available to the whole society. Chiefly redistribution also played a role in risk management. It stimulated production beyond the immediate subsistence level and provided a central storehouse for goods that might become scarce at times of famine (Earle 1987, 1991). Chiefdoms and archaic states had similar economies, often based on intensive cultivation, and both administered systems of regional trade or exchange.

Social Status in Chiefdoms

Social status in chiefdoms was based on seniority of descent. Because rank, power, prestige, and resources came through kinship and descent, Polynesian chiefs kept extremely long genealogies. Some chiefs (without writing) managed to trace their ancestry back fifty generations. All the people in the chiefdom were thought to be related to each other. Presumably, all were descended from a group of founding ancestors.

The chief (usually a man) had to demonstrate seniority in descent. Degrees of seniority were calculated so intricately on some islands that there were as many ranks as people. For example, the third son would rank below the second, who in turn would rank below the first. The children of an eldest brother, however, would all rank above the children of the next brother, whose children would in turn outrank those of younger brothers. However, even the lowest-ranking person in a chiefdom was still the chief's relative. In such a kin-based context, everyone, even a chief, had to share with his or her relatives.

Because everyone had a slightly different status, it was difficult to draw a line between elites and common people. Although other chiefdoms calculated seniority differently and had shorter genealogies than did those in Polynesia, the concern for genealogy and seniority and the absence of sharp gaps between elites and commoners are features of all chiefdoms.

Status Systems in Chiefdoms and States

The status systems of chiefdoms and states are similar in that both are based on **differential access** to resources. This means that some men and women had privileged access to power, prestige, and wealth. They controlled strategic resources such as land, water, and other means of production. Earle characterizes chiefs as "an incipient aristocracy with advantages in wealth and lifestyle" (1987, p. 290). Nevertheless, differential access in chiefdoms was still very much tied to kinship. The people with privileged access were generally chiefs and their nearest relatives and assistants.

Compared with chiefdoms, archaic states drew a much firmer line between elites and masses, distinguishing at least between nobles and commoners. Kinship ties did not extend from the nobles to the commoners because of *stratum endogamy*—marriage within one's own group. Commoners married commoners; elites married elites. Such a division of society into socioeconomic strata contrasts strongly with the status systems of bands and tribes, which are based on prestige, not resources. The prestige differentials that do exist in bands reflect special qualities, talents, and abilities. Good hunters get respect from their fellows as long as they are generous. So does a skilled curer, dancer, storyteller—or anyone else with a talent or skill that others appreciate.

In tribes, some prestige goes to descent-group leaders, to village heads, and especially to the big man, a regional figure who commands the loyalty and labor of others. However, all these figures must be generous. If they accumulate more resources—that is, property or food—than others in the village, they must share them with the others. Since strategic resources are available to everyone, social classes based on the possession of unequal amounts of resources can never exist.

In many tribes, particularly those with patrilineal descent, men have much greater prestige and power than women do. The gender contrast in rights may diminish in chiefdoms, where prestige and access to resources are based on seniority of descent, so that some women are senior to some men. Unlike big men, chiefs are exempt from ordinary work and have rights and privileges that are unavailable to the masses. However, like big men, they still return much of the wealth they take in.

The status system in chiefdoms, although based on differential access, differed from the status system in states because the privileged few were always relatives and assistants of the chief. However, this type of status system didn't last very long. Chiefs would start acting like kings and try to erode the kinship basis of the chiefdom. In Madagascar they would do this by demoting their more distant relatives to commoner status and banning marriage between nobles and commoners (Kottak 1980). Such moves, *if accepted by the society*, created separate social strata—*unrelated* groups that differ in their access to wealth, prestige, and power. (A **stratum** is one of two or more groups that contrast in regard to social status and access to strategic resources. Each stratum includes people of both sexes and all ages.) The creation of separate social strata is called **stratification**, and its emergence signified the transition from chiefdom to state. *The presence and acceptance of stratification is one of the key distinguishing features of a state.*

The influential sociologist Max Weber (1962) defined three related dimensions of social stratification: (1) Economic status, or **wealth**, encompasses all a person's material assets, including income, land, and other types of property (Schaefer and Lamm 1992). (2) **Power**, the ability to exercise one's will over others—to do what one wants—is the basis of political status. (3) **Prestige**—the basis of social status—refers to esteem, respect, or approval for acts, deeds, or qualities considered exemplary. Prestige, or "cultural capital" (Bourdieu 1984), provides people with a sense of worth and respect, which they may often convert into economic advantage (Table 8-1).

These Weberian dimensions of stratification are present to varying degrees in chiefdoms. However, chiefdoms lack the sharp division into classes that characterizes states. Wealth, power, and prestige in chiefdoms are all tied to kinship factors.

In archaic states—for the first time in human evolution—there were contrasts in

---

TABLE 8-1 MAX WEBER'S THREE DIMENSIONS OF STRATIFICATION

wealth	→	economic status
power	→	political status
prestige	→	social status

wealth, power, and prestige between entire groups (social strata) of men and women. Each stratum included people of both sexes and all ages. The **superordinate** (the higher or elite) stratum had privileged access to wealth, power, and other valued resources. Access to resources by members of the **subordinate** (lower or underprivileged) stratum was limited by the privileged group.

Socioeconomic stratification continues as a defining feature of all states, archaic or industrial. The elites control a significant part of the means of production, for example, land, herds, water, capital, farms, or factories. Those born at the bottom of the hierarchy have reduced chances of social mobility. Because of elite ownership rights, ordinary people lack free access to resources. Only in states do the elites get to keep their differential wealth. Unlike big men and chiefs, they don't have to give it back to the people whose labor has built and increased it.

STATES

States, remember, are autonomous political units with social classes and a formal government, based on law. States tend to be large and populous, as compared with bands, tribes, and chiefdoms. Certain statuses, systems, and subsystems with specialized functions are found in all states. They include the following:

1. *Population control:* fixing of boundaries, establishment of citizenship categories, and the taking of a census
2. *Judiciary:* laws, legal procedure, and judges
3. *Enforcement:* permanent military and police forces
4. *Fiscal:* taxation

In archaic states, these subsystems were integrated by a ruling system or government composed of civil, military, and religious officials (Fried 1960).

Population Control

To know whom they govern, all states conduct censuses. States demarcate boundaries that separate them from other societies. Customs agents, immigration officers, navies, and coast guards patrol frontiers, regulating passage from one state to another. Even nonindustrial states have boundary-maintenance forces. In Buganda, an archaic state on the shores of Lake Victoria in Uganda, the king rewarded military officers with estates in outlying provinces. They became his guardians against foreign intrusion.

States also control population through administrative subdivision: provinces, districts, "states," counties, subcounties, and parishes. Lower-level officials manage the populations and territories of the subdivisions.

In nonstates, people work and relax with their relatives, in-laws, fictive kin, and agemates—people with whom they have a personal relationship. Such a personal social life existed throughout most of human history, but food production (plant cultivation and animal domestication) spelled its eventual decline. After millions of years of human evolution, it took a mere 4,000 years for the population increase and regulatory problems spawned by food production to lead from tribe to chiefdom to state. With state organization, kinship's pervasive role diminished. Descent groups may continue as kin groups within archaic states, but their importance in political organization declines, and their exclusive control over their members ends.

States—archaic and modern—foster geographic mobility and resettlement, severing longstanding ties between people, land, and kin. Population displacements have increased in the modern world. War, famine, and job seeking across national boundaries churn up migratory currents. People in states come to identify themselves by new statuses, both ascribed and achieved, including ethnic background, place of birth or residence, occupation, party, religion, and team or club affiliation, rather than as members of a descent group or extended family.

States also manage their populations by granting different rights and obligations to (making status distinctions between) citizens and noncitizens. Distinctions among citizens are also common. Many archaic states granted different rights to nobles, commoners, and slaves. Unequal rights within state-organized societies persist in today's world. In recent American history, before the Emancipation Proclamation, there were different laws for slaves and free people. In European colonies, separate courts judged cases involving only natives and those which involved Europeans. In contemporary America, a military code of justice and court system continue to coexist alongside the civil judiciary.

Judiciary

States have *laws* based on precedent and legislative proclamations. Without writing, laws may be preserved in oral tradition, with justices, elders, and other specialists responsible for remembering them. Oral traditions as repositories of legal wisdom have continued in some nations with writing, such as Great Britain. Laws regulate relations between individuals and groups.

Crimes are violations of the legal code, with specified types of punishment. However, a given act, such as killing someone, may be legally defined in different ways (e.g., as manslaughter, justifiable homicide, or first-degree murder). Furthermore, even in contemporary North America, where justice is supposed to be "blind" to social distinctions, the poor are prosecuted more often and more severely than are the rich.

To handle disputes and crimes, all states have courts and judges. Precolonial African states had subcounty, county, and district courts, plus a high court formed by the king or queen and his or her advisers. Most states allow appeals to higher courts, although people are encouraged to solve problems locally.

A striking contrast between states and nonstates is intervention in family affairs. In states, aspects of parenting and marriage enter the domain of public law. Governments step in to halt blood feuds and regulate previously private disputes. States attempt to curb *internal* conflict, but they aren't always successful. About 85 percent of the world's armed conflicts since 1945 have begun within states—in efforts to overthrow a ruling regime or as disputes over tribal, religious, or ethnic minority issues. Only 15 percent have been fights across national borders (Barnaby 1984). Rebellion, resistance, repression, terrorism, and warfare continue. Indeed, recent states have perpetrated some of history's bloodiest deeds.

Enforcement

All states have agents to enforce judicial decisions. Confinement requires jailers, and a death penalty calls for executioners. Agents of the state collect fines and confiscate property. These officials wield power that is much more effective than the curse of the Nuer leopard-skin man.

A major concern of government is to defend hierarchy, property, and the power of the law. The government suppresses (with the police) internal disorder and guards the nation (with the military) against external threats. As a relatively new form of sociopolitical organization, states have competed successfully with less complex societies throughout the world. Military organization helps states subdue neighboring nonstates, but this is not the only reason for the spread of state organization. Although states impose hardships, they also offer advantages. Most obviously, they provide protection from outsiders and preserve internal order. They curb the feuding that has plagued tribes such as the Yanomami and the Nuer. By promoting internal peace, states enhance production. Their economies support massive, dense populations, which supply armies and colonists to promote expansion.

Fiscal Systems

A financial, or **fiscal,** system is needed in states to support rulers, nobles, officials, judges, military personnel, and thousands of other specialists. As in the chiefdom, the state intervenes in production, distribution, and consumption. The state may decree that a certain area will produce certain things or forbid certain activities in particular places. Although, like chiefdoms, states also have redistribution (through taxation), generosity and sharing are played down. A smaller proportion of what comes in flows back to the people.

In nonstates, people customarily share with relatives, but residents of states face added obligations to bureaucrats and officials. Citizens must turn over a substantial portion of what they produce to the state. Of the resources that the state collects, it reallocates part for the general good and uses another part (often larger) for the elite.

The state does not bring more freedom or leisure to the common people, who usually work harder than do the people in nonstates. They may be called on to build monumental public works. Some of these projects, such as dams and irrigation systems, may be economically necessary. However, people also build temples, palaces, and tombs for the elites. Rulers may link themselves to godhood through divine right or claim to be deities or their earthly representatives. Rulers convoke peons or slaves to build magnificent castles or tombs, cementing the ruler's place in history or status in the afterlife. Monumental architecture survives as an enduring reminder of the exalted prestige of priests and kings.

Markets and trade are usually under at least some state control, with officials overseeing distribution and exchange, standardizing weights and measures, and collecting taxes on goods passing into or through the state. States also set standards for artisans, manufacturers, and members of other professions.

Taxes support government and the ruling class, which is clearly separated from the common people in regard to activities, privileges, rights, and obligations. Elites take no part in subsistence activities. Taxes also support the many specialists—administrators, tax collectors, judges, lawmakers, generals, scholars, and priests. As the state matures, the segment of the population freed from direct concern with subsistence grows.

The elites of archaic states revel in the consumption of **sumptuary goods**—jewelry, exotic food and drink, and stylish clothing reserved for, or affordable by, only the rich. Peasants' diets suffer as they struggle to meet government demands. Commoners perish in territorial wars that have little relevance to their own needs.

SUMMARY

Anthropologists may use a sociopolitical typology of bands, tribes, chiefdoms, and states, along with an economic typology based on adaptive strategy. Through these classification schemes we can compare the scale and effectiveness of social linkages and political regulation and of variations in power, authority, and legal systems cross-culturally. There are important cross-cultural contrasts in the kinds of groups that are significant, determinants of leadership, reasons for disputes, and means for resolving them.

Foragers usually have egalitarian societies, with bands and families as characteristic groups. Personal networks link individuals, families, and bands. There is little differential power. Band leaders are first among equals and have no means of enforcing decisions. Disputes rarely arise over strategic resources, because the resources are available to everyone. Among the Eskimos, disputes traditionally originated in adultery or wife stealing. Aggrieved individuals might kill offenders, but this could trigger a blood feud. Although no government existed to halt blood feuds, there were certain customary means of resolving disputes.

The descent group is a basic kin group in tribal societies. Unlike families, descent groups have perpetuity—they last for generations. There are several types of descent groups. Lineages are based on demonstrated descent; clans, on stipulated descent. Patrilineal and matrilineal descent are unilineal descent rules.

Political authority increases as population size and density and the scale of regulatory problems grow. Egalitarianism diminishes as village size increases. With more people, there are more interpersonal relationships to regulate. Increasingly complex economies pose further regulatory problems.

Horticultural villages generally have heads with limited authority. The heads lead by example and persuasion and have no sure means of enforcing their decisions. The Yanomami are tribal horticulturalists. Their sociopolitical organization has more varied groups than does the foraging society. There are villages and patrilineal descent groups. Authority is more developed than it is among foragers. However, village heads, the main Yanomami political figures, have no sure power. The Yanomami also illustrate a pattern of warfare that is widespread among tribal cultivators.

Big men are temporary regional regulators. Their influence extends beyond the village; they mobilize the labor of supporters in several villages. Big men have prestige, commanding the loyalty of many, but they must be generous. Sponsorship of feasts leaves them with little wealth but with a reputation for generosity, which must be maintained if the big man is to retain his influence.

Another form of temporary regional sociopolitical organization is segmentary lineage organization (SLO). The Nuer, tribal pastoralists of the Upper Nile, have SLO, as do the horticultural Tiv of Nigeria. The closest allies of the Tiv and the Nuer are their patrilineal relatives. The term *segmentary* describes the organization of descent groups into segments at different genealogical levels. Nuer belong to minimal lineages, which are residential units. Groups of minimal lineages constitute minor lineages, and groups of minor lineages make up major lineages. Groups of major lineages make up maximal lineages, and groups of maximal lineages make up clans. Although Nuer clans do not trace descent from the same ancestor, they believe that they share a common ethnic origin separate from that of their neighbors.

Among populations with segmentary descent organization, alliance is relative, depending on genealogical distance. Social solidarity is proportional to the closeness of patrilineal ancestry and geographic proximity. The Nuer have disputes over murder, injuries, and adultery. People support the disputant with whom they share the closest ancestor. Despite mediators, there is no sure way of halting feuds. Disputes can mobilize the entire segmentary lineage—that is, the entire society—against outsiders.

Age and gender are obvious social variables that, like SLO, can be used in regional political integration. The native Plains cultures of North America developed pantribal sodalities during the eighteenth and nineteenth centuries as they changed from generalized foraging and horticulture to horseback hunting of bison. Men's associations organized raiding parties and communal hunting and maintained order in the summer camp. Pantribal sodalities, often emphasizing the warrior/age grade, develop in areas where people from different cultures come into contact, particularly when there is intertribal raiding for domesticated animals.

The first states emerged in the Old World, in Mesopotamia, about 5,500 years ago. The first chiefdoms had developed a thousand years earlier, but few survive today. States also arose in two parts of the Western Hemisphere—Mesoamerica and the central Andes. The state is an autonomous political unit encompassing many communities; its central government has the power to collect taxes, draft people for work or war, and decree and enforce laws. The state is defined as a form of sociopolitical organization based on central government and socioeconomic stratification— a division of society into classes. Early states are known as archaic, or nonindustrial, states, in contrast to modern industrial nation-states.

The chiefdom is a form of sociopolitical organization intermediate and transitional between tribes and states. Like states and unlike tribes, chiefdoms are characterized by permanent regional regulation and differential access to strategic resources, but chiefdoms lack stratification. Unlike states but like bands and tribes, chiefdoms are organized by kinship, descent, and marriage.

State formation remained incomplete, and only chiefdoms emerged in several areas, including the circum-Caribbean, lowland Amazonia, the southeastern United States, and Polynesia. Between the rise of food production and the Roman Empire, much of Europe was organized at the chiefdom level, to which it reverted after Rome's collapse. Much of our ethnographic knowledge of chiefdoms comes from Polynesia, where they were common at the time of European exploration. Although other chiefdoms calculated seniority differently and had shorter genealogies, the concern for genealogy and seniority and the absence of sharp gaps between elites and commoners are features of all chiefdoms. Chiefdoms have redistribution, a flow of resources to and then from a central office.

The sociologist Max Weber defined three related dimensions of social stratification: wealth, power, and prestige. In archaic states—for the first time in human evolution—contrasts in wealth, power, and prestige between entire groups (social strata) of men and women came into being. A socioeconomic stratum includes people of both sexes and all ages. The superordinate—higher or elite—stratum enjoys privileged access to wealth, power, and other valued resources. The lower stratum is subordinate. Its members' access to resources is limited by the privileged group.

Certain systems and subsystems with specialized functions are found in all states. They include population control, judiciary, enforcement, and fiscal. In archaic states, these subsystems were integrated by a ruling system or government composed of civil, military, and religious officials. To know whom they govern, all states conduct censuses and demarcate boundaries. States have laws based on precedent and legislative proclamations. To handle disputes and crimes, all states have courts and judges. Governments intervene to preserve internal peace, halt blood feuds, and regulate previously private disputes. All states have agents to enforce judicial decisions.

The major concern of government is to defend hierarchy, property, and the power of the law. The government suppresses (with the police) internal disorder and defends the nation (with the military) against external threats. As a relatively new form of sociopolitical organization, states have competed successfully with less complex societies throughout the world.

A financial, or fiscal, subsystem is necessary to support rulers, nobles, officials, judges, military personnel, and other specialists. The state does not bring more freedom or leisure to the common people, who usually work harder than people do in nonstates.

CHAPTER NINE

Kinship, Descent, and Marriage

T he kinds of societies that anthropologists have traditionally studied have stimulated a strong interest in systems of kinship and marriage. Kinship—as vitally important in daily life in nonindustrial societies as work outside the home is in our own—has become an essential part of anthropology because of its importance to the people we study. We are ready to take a closer look at the systems of kinship, descent, and marriage that have organized human life for much of our history.

KIN GROUPS AND KINSHIP CALCULATION

Anthropologists study the *kin groups* that are significant in a society as well as **kinship calculation**—the system by which people in a society reckon kin relationships. Ethnographers quickly recognize social divisions (groups) within any society they study. During fieldwork, they learn about significant groups by observing their activities and composition. People often live in the same village or neighborhood or work, pray, or celebrate together because they are related in some way. To understand the social structure, an ethnographer must investigate such kin ties. For example, the most significant local groups may consist of descendants of the same grandfather. These people may live in neighboring houses, farm adjoining fields, and help each other in everyday tasks. Other groups, perhaps based on other kin links, get together less often.

To study kinship calculation, an ethnographer must first determine the word or words for different types of "relatives" used in a particular language and then ask questions such as, "Who are your relatives?" Kinship, like race and gender (discussed in other chapters), is culturally constructed. This means that some biological kin are considered to be relatives whereas others are not. Through questioning, the ethnographer discovers the specific genealogical relationships between "relatives" and the person who has named them—the **ego.** By posing the same questions to several informants, the ethnographer learns about the extent and direction of kinship calculation in that society. The ethnographer also begins to understand the relationship between kinship calculation and kin groups—how people use kinship to create and maintain personal ties and to join social groups. In one of the kinship charts that follow, the black square labeled "ego" (Latin for *I*) identifies the person whose kinship calculation is being examined.

Biological Kin Types and Kinship Calculation

At this point we may distinguish between **kin terms** (the words used for different relatives in a particular language) and **biological kin types.** We designate biological kin types with the letters and symbols shown in Figure 9-1. *Biological kin type* refers to an actual genealogical relationship (e.g., father's brother) as opposed to a kin term (e.g., *uncle*).

Kin terms reflect the social construction of kinship in a given culture. A kin term may (and usually does) lump together several genealogical relationships. In English, for instance, we use *father* primarily for one kin type—the genealogical father. However, *father* can be extended to an adoptive father or stepfather—and even to a priest. *Grandfather* includes mother's father and father's father. The term *cousin* lumps several kin types. Even the more specific *first cousin* includes mother's brother's son (MBS), mother's brother's daughter (MBD), mother's sister's son (MZS), mother's sister's daughter (MZD), father's brother's son (FBS), father's

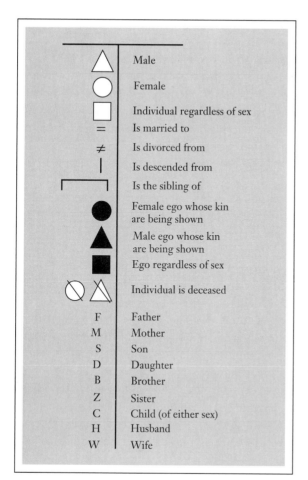

Figure 9-1 Kinship symbols and biological kin type notation.

△	Male
○	Female
□	Individual regardless of sex
=	Is married to
≠	Is divorced from
|	Is descended from
⌐¬	Is the sibling of
●	Female ego whose kin are being shown
▲	Male ego whose kin are being shown
■	Ego regardless of sex
⊘ △	Individual is deceased
F	Father
M	Mother
S	Son
D	Daughter
B	Brother
Z	Sister
C	Child (of either sex)
H	Husband
W	Wife

brother's daughter (FBD), father's sister's son (FZS), and father's sister's daughter (FZD). *First cousin* thus lumps together at least eight biological kin types.

Uncle encompasses mother's and father's brothers, and *aunt* includes mother's and father's sisters. We also use *uncle* and *aunt* for the spouses of our "blood" aunts and uncles. We use the same term for mother's brother and father's brother because we perceive them as being the same sort of relative. Calling them *uncles*, we distinguish between them and another kin type, F, whom we call *Father*, *Dad*, or *Pop*. In many societies, however, it is common to call a father and a father's brother by the same term.

In the United States and Canada, the *nuclear family* (a kin group composed of parents and children residing together) continues to be the most important group based on kinship. This is true despite an increased incidence of single parenthood, divorce, and remarriage. The nuclear family's relative isolation from other kin groups in modern nations reflects geographic mobility within an industrial economy with sale of labor for cash. (The nuclear family is also the most important kin group in many foraging societies, for reasons that will be discussed later.)

It's reasonable for North Americans to distinguish between relatives who belong to their nuclear families and those who don't. We are more likely to grow up with our parents than with our aunts or uncles. We tend to see our parents more often than we see our uncles and aunts, who may live in different towns and cities. We often inherit from our parents, but our cousins have first claim to inherit from our aunts and uncles. If our marriage is stable, we see our children daily as long as they remain at home. They are our heirs. We feel closer to them than to our nieces and nephews.

American kinship calculation and kin terminology reflect these social features. Thus the term *uncle* distinguishes between the kin types MB and FB on the one hand and the kin type F on the other. However, this term also lumps kin types together. We use the same term for MB and FB, two different kin types. We do this because American kinship calculation is **bilateral**—traced equally through males and females, for example, father and mother. Both kinds of uncle are brothers of one of our parents. We think of both as roughly the same kind of relative.

"No," you may object, "I'm closer to my mother's brother than to my father's brother." That may be. However, in a representative sample of American students, we would find a split, with some favoring one side and some favoring the other. We'd actually expect a bit of **matrilineal skewing**—a preference for relatives on the mother's side. This occurs because—for many reasons—when contemporary children are raised by just one parent, it's more likely to be the mother than the father. Thus, in the United States in 1993, 23 percent of all children lived in fatherless homes versus 3 percent residing in motherless homes and 71 percent living with both parents (*The American Almanac* 1994–1995, p. 66).

KIN GROUPS

The nuclear family is one kind of kin group that is widespread in human societies. Other kin groups include extended families (families consisting of three generations and/or of multiple adult siblings and their children) and descent groups—lineages and clans. *Descent groups,* which are composed of people claiming common ancestry, are basic units in the social organization of nonindustrial food producers.

There are important differences between nuclear families and descent groups. A descent group is *permanent;* a nuclear family lasts only as long as the parents and children remain together. Descent-group membership is often ascribed at birth (by a rule of patrilineal or matrilineal descent, as discussed in the last chapter) and is lifelong. In contrast, most people belong to at least two nuclear families at different times in their lives. They are born into a family consisting of their parents and siblings. When they reach adulthood, they may marry and establish a nuclear family that includes the spouse and eventually the children. Since most societies permit divorce, some people establish more than one family through marriage.

Anthropologists distinguish between the **family of orientation** (the family in which one is born and grows up) and the **family of procreation** (formed when one marries and has children). From the individual's point of view, the critical relationships are with parents and siblings in the family of orientation and with spouse and children in the family of procreation.

THE NUCLEAR FAMILY

Nuclear family organization is widespread but not universal. In certain societies, the nuclear family is rare or nonexistent. In other cultures, the nuclear family has no special role in social life. Other social units—most notably, descent groups and extended families—can assume most or all functions otherwise associated with the nuclear family. In other words, there are many alternatives to nuclear family organization.

One example is provided by the Nayars, who live on the Malabar Coast of southern India. Their kinship system is matrilineal (descent is traced only through females). Traditional Nayar marriages were mere formalities. Adolescent females went through a marriage ceremony with a man, after which the girl returned home, usually without having had sex with her husband. The man returned to his own household. Thereafter, Nayar women had many sexual partners. Children became members of the mother's household and kin group; they were not considered to be relatives of the biological father. Indeed, many Nayar children didn't even know who their father was. However, for children to be legitimate, a man, often neither the genitor nor the mother's original "husband," had to go through a ritual acknowledging paternity. Nayar society therefore reproduced itself biologically without the nuclear family.

Industrialism, Stratification, and Family Organization

For many Americans and Canadians, the nuclear family is the only well-defined kin group. Family isolation arises from geographic mobility, which is associated with industrialism, so that a nuclear family focus is characteristic of many modern nations. Born into a family of orientation, North Americans leave home for work or college, and the break with parents is underway. Eventually most North Americans marry and start a family of procreation. Because less than 3 percent of the American population now farms, most people aren't tied to the land. Selling our labor on the market, we often move to places where jobs are available.

Many married couples live hundreds of miles from their parents. Their jobs have determined where they live. Such a postmarital residence pattern is called

neolocality: Married couples are expected to establish a new place of residence—a "home of their own." Among middle-class North Americans, neolocal residence is both a cultural preference and a statistical norm. Most middle-class Americans eventually establish households and nuclear families of their own.

Recent Changes in North American Kinship Patterns

Although the nuclear family remains a cultural ideal for many Americans, Figure 9-2 shows that nuclear families accounted for just 25.6 percent of American households in 1993. *Nonnuclear family arrangements now outnumber the "traditional" American household by almost four to one.* Table 9-1, which compares American and Canadian households of the 1960s with households in those countries in 1993 and 1986, demonstrates substantial change. There are several reasons for changing household composition. North Americans leave home to work, often in a different community. Women are increasingly joining men in the workforce. This often removes them from the family of orientation while making it economically feasible to delay marriage. Furthermore, job demands compete with romantic attachments.

Single-parent families are increasing at a rapid rate. In 1960, 88 percent of American children lived with both parents versus 71 percent in 1993 (*The American Almanac* 1994–1995, p. 66). The percentage of American children living in fatherless households rose from 8 percent in 1960 to 23 percent in 1993. The percentage living in motherless households increased from 1 percent in 1960 to 3 percent in 1993 (Table 9-2).

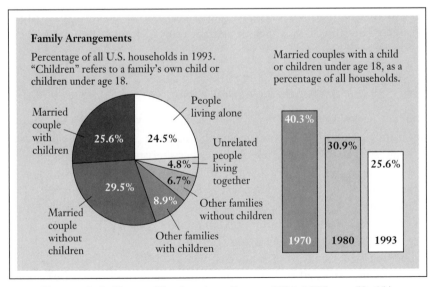

Family Arrangements

Percentage of all U.S. households in 1993. "Children" refers to a family's own child or children under age 18.

Married couple with children — 25.6%
People living alone — 24.5%
Unrelated people living together — 4.8%
Other families with children — 6.7%
Other families without children — 8.9%
Married couple without children — 29.5%

Married couples with a child or children under age 18, as a percentage of all households.

1970 — 40.3%
1980 — 30.9%
1993 — 25.6%

FIGURE 9-2 (*Source: The American Almanac* 1994–1995, pp. 59, 65.)

TABLE 9-1   CLASSIFICATION OF NORTH AMERICAN HOUSEHOLDS, UNITED STATES
(1960 AND 1993) AND CANADA (1961 AND 1986)

	Percentage of All Households			
	United States		Canada	
	1960	1993	1961	1986
Married with children	44	26	51	32
Married couple, no resident children	30	30	27	32
One adult	13	24	9	22
One parent and child(ren)	4	9	4	6
Other*	8	11	9	8

*Includes unrelated people living together, extended families, adult siblings, and so on.
Source: The American Almanac 1994–1995, p. 59.

The numbers in Table 9-1 suggest that life is growing increasingly lonely for many North Americans. The disappearance of extended families and descent groups reflects the mobility of industrialism. However, even nuclear families are breaking up. In the United States the unmarried population aged eighteen and over (single, widowed, and divorced) rose from 38 million in 1970 (28 percent of all adults) to 73 million in 1993 (39 percent of all adults) (*The American Almanac* 1994–1995, p. 56). To be sure, contemporary Americans maintain social lives through work, friendship, sports, clubs, religion, and organized social activities. However, the isolation from kin that these figures suggest is unprecedented in human history.

The Nuclear Family among Foragers

Populations with foraging economies are far removed from industrial societies in terms of social complexity. Here, again, however, the nuclear family is often the most significant kin group, although in no foraging culture is the nuclear family the

TABLE 9-2   PERCENTAGE OF AMERICAN CHILDREN RESIDING WITH ONE OR BOTH
PARENTS, 1960 AND 1993

	1960	1993
Both parents	88	71
Mother only	8	23
Father only	1	3
Neither parent	3	3

Source: The American Almanac 1994–1995, p. 66.

Brady Bunch Nirvana

he first-year students I teach at the University of Michigan belong to a generation raised after the almost total diffusion of television into the American home. Most young Americans have never known a world without TV. The tube is as familiar as Mom or Dad. Indeed, considering how common divorce has become, TV sets outlast the father in many homes. One habit I began about ten years ago, taking advantage of my students' familiarity with television, is to demonstrate changes in American kinship and marriage patterns by contrasting the programs of the fifties with more recent ones. Four decades ago, the usual TV family was a nuclear family made up of father (who often knew best), homemaker mother, and children. Examples include *Father Knows Best, Ozzie and Harriet,* and *Leave It to Beaver.* These programs were appropriate for the 1950s market, but they are out of sync with today's social and economic realities. Only 16 million American women worked outside the home in 1950, compared with three times that number today. Today less than 7 percent of American households fit the former ideal: breadwinner father, homemaker mother, and two children.

Virtually all my students have seen reruns of the more recent family series *The Brady Bunch.* The social organization of *The Brady Bunch* provides an instructive contrast with 1950s programs, because it illustrates what we call *blended family organization.* A new (blended) family forms when a widow with three daughters marries a widower with three sons. Blended families have been increasing in American society because of more frequent divorce and remarriage. During *The Brady Bunch*'s heyday, divorce remained controversial and could not give rise to a TV family. However, the first spouse's death may also lead to a blended family, as in *The Brady Bunch.*

The Brady husband-father was a successful architect. Even today, the average TV family tends to be more professional, successful, and rich than the average real-life family. The Bradys were wealthy enough to employ a housekeeper, Alice. Mirroring American culture when the program was produced, the wife's career was part-time and subsidiary. Women lucky enough to find wealthy husbands did not compete with other women—even professional housekeepers—in the workforce. (It is noteworthy that when *The Bradys* was revived as a weekly series in 1990, Mrs. Brady had a full-time job.)

Students enjoy learning about anthropological techniques through culturally familiar examples. Each time I begin my kinship lecture, a few people in the class immediately recognize (from reruns) the nuclear families of the 1950s. However, as soon as I begin diagramming the Brady characters (without saying what I'm doing), students start shouting out their names: "Jan," "Bobby," "Greg," "Cindy," "Marsha," "Peter," "Mike," "Carol," "Alice." The response mounts. As the cast of characters nears completion, almost everyone has joined in. Whenever I give my kinship lecture, Anthropology 101 is guaranteed to resemble a revival meeting, as hundreds of TV-enculturated American natives shout out in unison names made almost as familiar as their parents' through exposure to television reruns.

Furthermore, as the natives participate in this chant, based on common knowledge acquired by growing up in the post-1950s United States, there is an enthusiasm, a warm glow, that my course will not recapture until the next semester's rerun of my *Brady Bunch* lecture. My students seem to find *nirvana* (a feeling of religious ecstasy) through their collective remembrance of the Bradys and in the rituallike incantation of their names.

Some segments of our society stigmatize television as "trivial," yet the average American family owns 2.3 television sets (*World Almanac* 1992, p. 318). Given this massive penetration of the modern home (98 percent of all households), television's effects on our socialization and enculturation can hardly be trivial. Indeed, the common information and knowledge we acquire by watching the same TV programs is indisputably culture in the anthropological sense. Culture is collective, shared, meaningful. It is transmitted by conscious and unconscious learning experiences acquired by humans not through their genes but as a result of growing up in a particular society. Of the hundreds of culture bearers who have passed through the Anthropology 101 classroom over the past decade, many have been unable to recall the full names of their parents' first cousins. Some have forgotten their grandmother's maiden name. But most have absolutely no trouble identifying names and relationships in a family that exists only in television land.

only group based on kinship. The two basic social units of traditional foraging societies are the nuclear family and the band.

Unlike middle-class couples in industrial nations, foragers don't usually reside neolocally. Instead, they join a band in which either the husband or the wife has relatives. However, couples and families may move from one band to another several times. Although nuclear families are ultimately as impermanent among foragers as they are in any other society, they are usually more stable than bands are.

Many foraging societies lacked year-round band organization. The Native American Shoshone of the Great Basin in Utah and Nevada provide an example. The resources available to the Shoshone were so meager that for most of the year families traveled alone through the countryside hunting and gathering. In certain seasons families assembled to hunt cooperatively as a band; after a few months together they dispersed.

Industrial and foraging economies do have something in common. In neither type are people tied permanently to the land. The mobility and the emphasis on small, economically self-sufficient family units promote the nuclear family as a basic kin group in both types of societies.

TRIBAL SOCIAL ORGANIZATION

Lineages and Clans

We have seen that the nuclear family is important among foragers and in industrial nations. The analogous group among nonindustrial food producers is the descent group (described in the last chapter, where we distinguished between clans and lineages). Descent groups, unlike nuclear families, are permanent and enduring units, with new members added in every generation. Members have access to the lineage estate. Unlike the nuclear family, the descent group lives on even though specific members die.

Unilineal Descent Groups and Unilocal Residence

Most cultures have a prevailing opinion about where couples should live after they marry. Neolocality, which is the rule for most middle-class Americans, is not very common outside modern North America, Western Europe, and the European-derived cultures of Latin America. Much more common is **virilocality** (*vir* in Latin means "husband"): Married couples live with the husband's relatives. Often virilocality is associated with patrilineal descent. This makes sense. If the children of males are to become descent-group members, with rights in the father's estate, it's a good idea to raise them on that estate. This can be done if a wife moves to her husband's village rather than vice versa.

A less common postmarital residence rule that often is associated with matrilineal descent is **uxorilocality** (*uxor* in Latin means "wife"): Married couples live with the wife's relatives. Together, virilocality and uxorilocality are known as **unilocal** rules of postmarital residence.

MARRIAGE

No definition of marriage is broad enough to apply easily to all societies. A commonly quoted definition comes from *Notes and Queries in Anthropology:*

> Marriage is a union between a man and a woman such that the children born to the woman are recognized as legitimate offspring of both partners. (Royal Anthropological Institute 1951, p. 111)

This definition may describe marriage in contemporary North America, but it isn't universally valid for several reasons. For example, some nations recognize homosexual marriages. Also, in many societies marriages unite more than two spouses. Here we speak of *plural marriages*, as when a woman weds a group of brothers—an

Besides child rearing, several kinds of rights, obligations, and benefits (sexual, economic, property, and inheritance) may be allocated by forms of marriage. Here lesbian couples hold a mock wedding in front of the Internal Revenue Service in Washington, D.C., during a 1993 march for lesbian and gay rights. They are protesting the lack of income tax benefits for same-sex couples.

arrangement called *fraternal polyandry* that is characteristic of certain Himalayan cultures. In certain societies (usually patrilineal), a woman may marry another woman, in a nonsexual union. This can happen in West Africa when a successful market woman (perhaps already married to a man) wants a wife of her own to take care of her home and children while she works outside (Amadiume 1987).

In the African Sudan a Nuer woman can marry a woman if her father has only daughters but no male heirs, who are necessary if his patrilineage is to survive. He may ask his daughter to stand as a son in order to take a bride. This is a symbolic and social relationship rather than a sexual one. Indeed, the woman who serves as a man may already be living in another village as a man's wife!

The Nuer woman doesn't live with her "wife," who has sex with a man or men until she becomes pregnant. What's important here is *social* rather than *biological paternity*; we see again how kinship is socially constructed. The bride's children are considered the legitimate offspring of her "husband," who is biologically a woman but socially a man, and the descent line continues.

The British anthropologist Edmund Leach (1955) despaired of ever arriving at a universal definition of marriage. Instead, he suggested that depending on the society, several different kinds of rights are allocated by institutions classified as marriage. These rights vary from one culture to another, and no single one is widespread enough to provide a basis for defining marriage.

According to Leach, marriage can do the following:

1. Establish the legal father of a woman's children and the legal mother of a man's
2. Give either or both spouses a monopoly in the sexuality of the other
3. Give either or both spouses rights to the labor of the other
4. Give either or both spouses rights over the other's property
5. Establish a joint fund of property—a partnership—for the benefit of the children
6. Establish a socially significant "relationship of affinity" between spouses and their relatives

This list highlights particular aspects of marriage in different cultural contexts. However, I believe that we need some definition—even a loose one—to identify an institution found in some form in all human societies. I suggest the following:

Marriage is a socially approved relationship between a socially recognized male (the husband) and a socially recognized female (the wife) such that the children born to the wife are accepted as the offspring of both husband and wife. The husband may be the actual **genitor** (biological father) of the children or only the **pater** (socially recognized father).

THE INCEST TABOO AND EXOGAMY

In stateless societies a person's social world includes two main categories—friends and strangers. Strangers are potential or actual enemies. Marriage is one of the primary ways of converting strangers into friends, of creating and maintaining personal and political alliances. **Exogamy,** the practice of seeking a mate outside one's own group, has adaptive value because it links people into a wider social network that nurtures, helps, and protects them in times of need.

Incest refers to sexual relations with a close relative. All cultures have taboos against it. However, although the taboo is a cultural universal, people define their kin, and thus incest, differently in different societies. When unilineal descent is very strongly developed, the parent who does not belong to one's own descent group isn't considered a relative. Thus, with strict patrilineality, the mother is not a relative but a kind of in-law who has married a member of ego's group—ego's father. With strict matrilineality, the father isn't a relative, because he belongs to a different descent group.

The Lakher of Southeast Asia are strictly patrilineal (Leach 1961). Using the male ego in Figure 9-3, let's suppose that ego's father and mother get divorced. Each remarries and has a daughter by a second marriage. A Lakher always belongs to his or

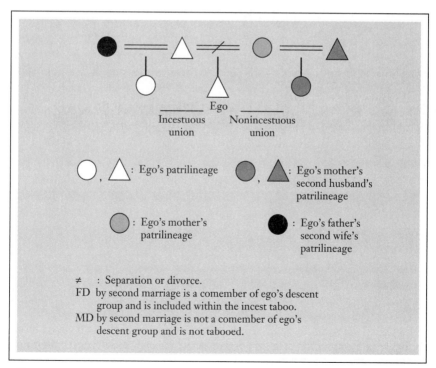

FIGURE 9-3 Patrilineal descent-group identity and incest among the Lakher.

her father's group, all the members of which (one's **agnates,** or patrikin) are considered too closely related to marry because they are members of the same patrilineal descent group. Therefore, ego can't marry his father's daughter by the second marriage; just as in contemporary North America it's illegal for half-siblings to marry.

However, unlike our society, where all half-siblings are tabooed, the Lakher permit ego to marry his mother's daughter by a different father. She is not ego's relative because she belongs to her own father's descent group rather than ego's. The Lakher illustrate very well that definitions of relatives, and therefore of incest, vary from culture to culture.

Marry Out or Die Out

One of the most accepted explanations for the incest taboo is that it arose in order to ensure exogamy, to force people to marry outside their kin groups (Tylor 1889; White 1959; Lévi-Strauss 1949/1969). In this view, the taboo originated early in human evolution because it was adaptively advantageous. Marrying a close relative, with whom one is already on peaceful terms, would be counterproductive. There is more to gain by extending peaceful relations to a wider network of groups.

In nonindustrial societies, marriage and exogamy play key roles in forming alliances between groups. One marries not just an individual, but an entire kin group. Here a groom's sister mimics her brother's role as husband, dressing as a man and embracing "their" bride.

This view emphasizes the role of marriage in creating and maintaining alliances. By forcing members to marry out, a group increases its allies. Marriage within the group, by contrast, would isolate that group from its neighbors and their resources and social networks and might ultimately lead to the group's extinction. Exogamy and the incest taboo that propels it help explain human adaptive success. Besides the sociopolitical function, exogamy also ensures genetic mixture between groups and thus maintains a successful human species.

ENDOGAMY

Exogamy pushes social organization outward, establishing and preserving alliances among groups. In contrast, rules of **endogamy** dictate mating or marriage within a group to which one belongs. Endogamic rules are less common but are still familiar to anthropologists. Indeed, most cultures *are* endogamous units, although they usually do not need a formal rule requiring people to marry someone from their own society. Members of the endogamic groups would never consider doing anything else.

Caste

An extreme example of endogamy is India's caste system. Castes are stratified groups in which membership is ascribed at birth and is lifelong. Castes are usually endogamous groups. Indian castes are grouped into five major categories, or *varna*. Each is ranked relative to the other four, and these categories extend throughout India. Each *varna* includes a large number of castes (*jati*), each of which includes people within a region who may intermarry. All the *jati* in a single *varna* in a given region are ranked, just as the *varna* themselves are ranked.

Occupational specialization often sets off one caste from another. A community may include castes of agricultural workers, merchants, artisans, priests, and sweepers. The untouchable *varna*, found throughout India, includes castes whose ancestry, ritual status, and occupations are considered so impure that higher-caste people consider even casual contact with untouchables to be defiling.

The belief that intercaste sexual unions lead to ritual impurity for the higher-caste partner is important in maintaining endogamy. A man who has sex with a lower-caste woman can restore his purity with a bath and a prayer. However, a woman who has intercourse with a man of a lower caste has no such recourse. Her defilement cannot be undone. Because the women have the babies, these differences protect the purity of the caste line, ensuring the pure ancestry of high-caste children. Although Indian castes are endogamous groups, many of them are internally subdivided into exogamous lineages. This means that Indians must marry a member of another descent group from the same caste.

MARRIAGE IN TRIBAL SOCIETIES

Outside of industrial societies, marriage is often more a relationship between groups than one between individuals. We think of marriage as an individual matter. Although the bride and groom usually seek their parents' approval, the final choice (to live together, to marry, to divorce) lies with the couple. The idea of romantic love symbolizes this individual relationship.

In nonindustrial societies, marriage is a group concern. People don't just take a spouse; they assume obligations to a group of in-laws. When residence is virilocal, for example, a woman must leave the community where she was born. She faces the prospect of spending the rest of her life in her husband's village, with his relatives. She may even have to transfer her major allegiance from her own group to her husband's.

Bridewealth

In societies with descent groups, people enter marriage not alone but with the help of the descent group. Descent-group members often have to contribute to **bridewealth,** a customary gift before, at, or after marriage from the husband and his kin to the wife and her kin. Another word for bridewealth is **brideprice,** but this term is inaccurate because people with the custom don't usually regard the exchange as a sale. They don't think of marriage as a commercial relationship between a man and an object that can be bought and sold.

Bridewealth compensates the bride's group for the loss of her companionship and labor. More important, it makes the children born to the woman full members of her husband's descent group. For this reason, the institution is also called **progeny price.** Rather than the woman herself, it is her children who are permanently transferred to the husband's group. Whatever we call it, such a transfer of wealth at marriage is common in patrilineal tribes. In matrilineal societies, children are members of the mother's group, and there is no reason to pay a progeny price.

Dowry is a marital exchange in which the wife's group provides substantial gifts to the husband's family. Dowry, best known from India, correlates with low female status. Women are perceived as burdens. When husbands and their families take a wife, they expect to be compensated for the added responsibility.

Bridewealth exists in many more cultures than dowry does, but the nature and quantity of transferred items differ. In many African societies, cattle constitute bridewealth, but the number of cattle given varies from society to society. *As the value of bridewealth increases, marriages become more stable.* Bridewealth is insurance against divorce.

Imagine a patrilineal society in which a marriage requires the transfer of about twenty-five cattle from the groom's descent group to the bride's. Michael, a member of descent group A, marries Sarah from group B. His relatives help him assemble the bridewealth. He gets the most help from his close agnates—his older brother, father, father's brother, and closest patrilineal cousins.

The distribution of the cattle once they reach Sarah's group mirrors the manner in which they were assembled. Sarah's father, or her oldest brother if the father is dead, receives her bridewealth. He keeps most of the cattle to use as bridewealth for his sons' marriages. However, a share also goes to everyone who will be expected to help when Sarah's brothers marry.

When Sarah's brother David gets married, many of the cattle go to a third group—C, which is David's wife's group. Thereafter, they may serve as bridewealth to still other groups. Men constantly use their sisters' bridewealth cattle to acquire their own wives. In a decade, the cattle given when Michael married Sarah will have been exchanged widely.

In tribal societies, marriage entails an agreement between descent groups. If Sarah and Michael try to make their marriage succeed but fail to do so, both groups may conclude that the marriage can't last. Here it becomes especially obvious that tribal marriages are relationships between groups as well as between individuals. If Sarah has a younger sister or niece (her older brother's daughter, for example), the concerned parties may agree to Sarah's replacement by a kinswoman.

However, incompatibility isn't the main problem that threatens marriage in societies with bridewealth. Infertility is a more important concern. If Sarah has no children, she and her group have not fulfilled their part of the marriage agreement. If the relationship is to endure, Sarah's group must furnish another woman, perhaps her younger sister, who can have children. If this happens, Sarah may choose to stay in her husband's village. Perhaps she will someday have a child. If she does stay on, her husband will have established a plural marriage.

Most nonindustrial food-producing societies, unlike most foraging societies and industrial nations, allow **plural marriages,** or **polygamy.** There are two varieties, one common and the other very rare. The more common variant is **polygyny,** in which a man has more than one wife. The rare variant is **polyandry,** in which a woman has more than one husband. If the infertile wife remains married to her husband after he has taken a substitute wife provided by her descent group, this is polygyny. I will discuss reasons for polygyny other than infertility shortly.

Durable Alliances

It is possible to exemplify the group-alliance nature of marriage in tribal societies by examining still another common practice—continuation of marital alliances when one spouse dies.

SORORATE What happens if Sarah dies young? Michael's group will ask Sarah's group for a substitute, often her sister. This custom is known as the **sororate** (Figure 9-4). If Sarah has no sister or if all her sisters are already married, another

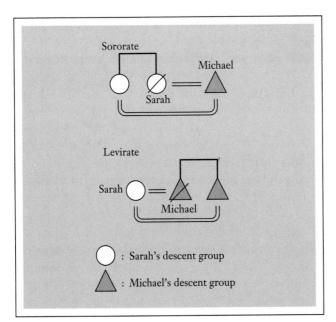

FIGURE 9-4 Sororate and levirate.

woman from her group may be available. Michael marries her; there is no need to return the bridewealth, and the alliance continues. The sororate exists in both matrilineal and patrilineal societies. In a matrilineal society with uxorilocal postmarital residence, a widower may remain with his wife's group by marrying her sister or another female member of her matrilineage (Figure 9-4).

LEVIRATE   What happens if the husband dies? In many societies, the widow may marry his brother. This custom is known as the **levirate** (Figure 9-4). Like the sororate, it is a continuation marriage that maintains the alliance between descent groups, in this case by replacing the husband with another member of his group. The implications of the levirate vary with age. A recent study found that in African societies the levirate, though widely permitted, rarely involves coresidence of the widow and her new husband. Furthermore, widows don't automatically marry the husband's brother just because they are allowed to. Often they prefer to make other arrangements (Potash 1986).

PLURAL MARRIAGES

In contemporary North America, where divorce is fairly easy and common, polygamy (marriage to more than one spouse at the same time) is against the law. Marriage in industrial nations joins individuals, and relationships between individuals can be severed more easily than can those between groups. As divorce grows more common, North Americans practice **serial monogamy:** Individuals have more than one spouse but never, legally, more than one at the same time. As stated earlier, the two forms of polygamy are polygyny and polyandry. Polyandry is practiced in only a few cultures, notably among certain groups in Tibet, Nepal, and India (Berreman 1962, 1975). Polygyny is much more common.

Polygyny

We must distinguish between the social approval of plural marriage and its actual frequency in a particular society. Many cultures approve of a man's having more than one wife. However, even when polygyny is encouraged, most people are monogamous, and polygyny characterizes only a fraction of the marriages. Why?

One reason is equal sex ratios. In the United States, about 105 males are born for every 100 females. In adulthood the ratio of men to women equalizes, and eventually it reverses. The average North American woman outlives the average man. In many nonindustrial societies as well, a male-biased sex ratio among children also reverses in adulthood.

The custom of men marrying later than women can also promote polygyny. Among Nigeria's Kanuri people (Cohen 1967), men get married between the ages of eighteen and thirty; women, between twelve and fourteen. The age difference between spouses means that there are more widows than widowers. Most of the widows remarry, some in polygynous unions. Among the Kanuri and in other polygynous societies, widows make up a large number of the women involved in plural marriages (Hart and Pilling 1960).

In certain societies, the first wife requests a second wife to help with household chores. The second wife's status is lower than that of the first; they are senior and junior wives. The senior wife sometimes chooses the junior one from among her close kinswomen. Among the Betsileo of Madagascar, the different wives always lived in different villages. A man's first and senior wife, called "Big Wife," lived in the village where he cultivated his best rice field and spent most of his time. High-status men with several rice fields had households near each field. They spent most of their time with the senior wife but visited the others occasionally throughout the year.

Plural wives can also play important political roles in nonindustrial states. The king of the Merina, a society with more than 1 million people in the highlands of Madagascar, had palaces for each of his twelve wives in different provinces. He stayed with them when he traveled through the kingdom. They were his local agents, overseeing and reporting on provincial matters. The king of Buganda, the major precolonial state of Uganda, took hundreds of wives, representing all the clans in his nation. Everyone in the kingdom became the king's in-law, and all the clans had a chance to provide the next ruler. This was a way of giving the common people a stake in the government.

These examples show that there is no single explanation for polygyny. Its context and function vary from society to society and even within the same society. Some men are polygynous because they have inherited a widow from a brother.

Others have plural wives because they seek prestige or want to increase household productivity. Still others use marriage as a political tool or a means of economic advancement. Men and women with political and economic ambitions cultivate marital alliances that serve their aims. In many societies, including the Betsileo of Madagascar and the Igbo of Nigeria, women arrange the marriages.

Polyandry

Polyandry is very rare and is practiced under very specific conditions. Most of the world's polyandrous peoples live in South Asia—Tibet, Nepal, India, and Sri Lanka. In some of these areas, polyandry seems to be a cultural adaptation to mobility associated with customary male travel for trade, commerce, and military operations. Polyandry ensures that there will be at least one man at home to accomplish male activities within a gender-based division of labor. Fraternal polyandry is also an effective strategy when resources are scarce. Brothers with limited resources (in land) pool their resources in expanded (polyandrous) households. They take just one wife. Polyandry restricts the number of wives and heirs. Less competition among heirs means that land can be transmitted with minimal fragmentation.

Polyandry in northwest Nepal. The seated young woman is Terribal, age fifteen. She holds her youngest husband, age five. To her left is another husband, age twelve. Standing directly behind her is her third husband, age nine. The two older standing men are brothers who are married to the same woman, standing to the right. These are Terribal's "fathers" and mother.

SUMMARY

In nonindustrial societies, kinship, descent, and marriage are the basis of social life and political organization. We must distinguish between kin groups, whose composition and activities can be observed, and kinship calculation, the manner in which people identify and designate their relatives.

One widespread but nonuniversal kin group is the nuclear family, consisting of a married couple and their children. The nuclear family is a variable form of social organization, which is most important in foraging and industrial societies. Food producers have kin-based ties to estates, and other kinds of kin and descent groups often overshadow the nuclear family. In contemporary North America, the nuclear family is the characteristic kin group for the middle class, but even in that class, nuclear family households are declining as single-person households and other domestic arrangements increase.

The descent group is the basic kin group among nonindustrial food producers. Unlike nuclear families, descent groups have perpetuity—they last for several generations. Descent-group members share and manage a common estate. Unilineal (patrilineal and matrilineal) descent is associated with unilocal (respectively, virilocal and uxorilocal) postmarital residence rules.

All cultures have incest taboos, but different cultures taboo different biological kin types. The taboo promotes exogamy, thereby increasing networks of friends and allies. The main adaptive advantage of exogamy is the extension of social and political ties outward. This is confirmed by a consideration of endogamy—marriage within the group. Endogamic rules are common in stratified societies. One example is India, where castes are the endogamous units. However, castes are subdivided into exogamous descent groups. The same culture, therefore, can have both endogamic and exogamic rules.

In societies with descent groups, marriages are relationships between groups as well as between spouses. With the custom of bridewealth, the groom and his relatives transmit wealth to the bride and her relatives. As the bridewealth's value increases, the divorce rate declines. Bridewealth customs show that marriages among nonindustrial food producers create and maintain group alliances. So do the sororate, by which a man marries the sister of his deceased wife, and the levirate, by which a woman marries the brother of her deceased husband. Replacement marriages in cases of spousal incompatibility also confirm the importance of group alliances.

Many cultures permit plural marriages. The two kinds of polygamy are polygyny and polyandry. The former involves multiple wives; the latter, multiple husbands. Polygyny and polyandry are found in varied social and cultural contexts and occur for many reasons. Polygyny is much more common than is polyandry.

CHAPTER TEN

Gender

GENDER ISSUES AMONG FORAGERS
BOX: Hidden Women, Public Men—Public Women, Hidden Men

GENDER ISSUES AMONG HORTICULTURALISTS
Reduced Gender Stratification—Matrilineal, Uxorilocal Societies   ~
Reduced Gender Stratification—Matrifocal Societies   ~   Increased Gender
Stratification—Patrilineal-Virilocal Societies   ~   Etoro Homosexuality   ~
BOX: Varieties of Human Sexuality

GENDER ISSUES AMONG AGRICULTURALISTS

GENDER ISSUES AND INDUSTRIALISM
The Feminization of Poverty

WHAT DETERMINES VARIATION IN GENDER ISSUES?

B ecause anthropologists study biology, society, and culture, they are in a unique position to comment on nature (biological predispositions) and nurture (environment) as determinants of human behavior. Human attitudes, values, and behavior are limited not only by our genetic predispositions—which are difficult to identify—but also by our experiences during enculturation. Our attributes as adults are determined both by our genes and by our environment during growth and development.

Debate about the effects of nature and nurture proceeds today in scientific and public arenas. **Naturists** assume that some—they differ about how much—human behavior and social organization is biologically determined. **Nurturists, or environmentalists,** do not deny that some universal aspects of human behavior may have a genetic base. However, they find most attempts to link behavior to genes unconvincing. The basic environmentalist assumption is that human evolutionary success rests on flexibility, or the ability to adapt in various ways. Because human adaptation relies so strongly on cultural learning, we can change our behavior more readily than members of other species can.

The nature-nurture debate emerges in the discussion of human sex-gender roles and sexuality. Men and women differ genetically. Women have two X chromosomes, and men have an X and a Y. The father determines a baby's sex because only he has the Y chromosome to transmit. The mother always provides an X chromosome.

The chromosomal difference is expressed in hormonal and physiological contrasts. Humans are sexually dimorphic. **Sexual dimorphism** refers to marked differences in male and female biology besides the contrasts in breasts and genitals. Men and women differ not just in primary (genitalia and reproductive organs) and secondary (breasts, voice, hair distribution) sexual characteristics but in average weight, height, and strength.

Just how far, however, do these genetically and physiologically determined differences go? What effect do they have on the way men and women act and are treated in different cultures? On the environmentalist side, anthropologists have discovered substantial variability in the roles of men and women in different cultures. The anthropological position on sex-gender roles and biology may be stated as follows:

> The biological nature of men and women [should be seen] not as a narrow enclosure limiting the human organism, but rather as a broad base upon which a variety of structures can be built. (Friedl 1975, p. 6)

Although in most cultures men tend to be somewhat more aggressive than women, many of the behavioral and attitudinal differences between the sexes emerge from culture rather than biology. *Sex* differences are biological, but *gender* encompasses all the traits that a culture assigns to and inculcates in males and females. "Gender," in other words, refers to the cultural construction of male and female characteristics (Rosaldo 1980b).

Given "rich and various constructions of gender" within the realm of cultural diversity, Susan Bourque and Kay Warren (1987) note that the same images of masculinity and femininity do not always apply. Margaret Mead did an early ethnographic study of variation in gender roles. Her book *Sex and Temperament in Three Primitive Societies* (1935/1950) was based on fieldwork in three societies in Papua-New Guinea: Arapesh, Mundugumor, and Tchambuli. The extent of personality variation in men and women in these three societies on the same island amazed Mead. She found that Arapesh men and women acted as Americans have traditionally expected women to act—in a mild, parental, responsive way. Mundugumor men and women, in contrast, acted as she believed we expect men to act—fiercely and aggressively. Tchambuli men were "catty," wore curls, and went shopping, but Tchambuli women were energetic and managerial and placed less emphasis on personal adornment than did the men. [Drawing on their recent case study of the Tchambuli, whom they call the Chambri, Errington and Gewertz (1987), while recognizing gender malleability, have disputed the specifics of Mead's account.]

There is a growing field of feminist scholarship within anthropology (di Leonardo, ed. 1991; Nash and Safa 1986; Rosaldo 1980b; Strathern 1988), and in recent years ethnographers have been gathering systematic ethnographic data about gender in many cultural settings (Morgen, ed. 1989; Mukhopadhyay and Higgins 1988). We can see that gender roles vary with environment, economy, adaptive strategy, and type of political system. Before we examine the cross-cultural data, some definitions are in order.

Gender roles are the tasks and activities that a culture assigns to the sexes. Related to gender roles are **gender stereotypes,** which are oversimplified but strongly held ideas about the characteristics of males and females. **Gender stratification** describes an unequal distribution of rewards (socially valued resources, power, prestige, and personal freedom) between men and women, reflecting their different positions in a social hierarchy (Light, Keller, and Calhoun 1994). According to Ann Stoler (1977), the "economic determinants of female status" include freedom or autonomy (in disposing of one's labor and its fruits) and social power (control over the lives, labor, and produce of others).

In stateless societies, gender stratification is often more obvious in regard to prestige than it is in regard to wealth. In her study of the Ilongots of northern Luzon in the Philippines, Michelle Rosaldo (1980a) described gender differences related to the positive cultural value placed on adventure, travel, and knowledge of the external world. More often than women, Ilongot men, as headhunters, visited distant places. They acquired knowledge of the external world, amassed experiences there, and returned to express their knowledge, adventures, and feelings in public oratory. They received acclaim as a result. Ilongot women had inferior prestige because they lacked external experiences on which to base knowledge and dramatic expression. On the basis of Rosaldo's study and findings in other stateless societies, Ong (1989) argues that we must distinguish between prestige systems and actual power in a given society. High male prestige may not entail economic or political power held by men over their families.

GENDER ISSUES AMONG FORAGERS

Several studies have shown that economic roles affect gender stratification. In one cross-cultural study Peggy Sanday (1974) found that gender stratification decreased when men and women made roughly equal contributions to subsistence. She found that gender stratification was *greatest* when the women contributed either *much more* or *much less* than the men did.

This finding applied mainly to food producers, not to foragers. In foraging societies gender stratification was most marked when men contributed much *more* to the diet than women did. This was true among the Inuit and other northern hunters and fishers. Among tropical and semitropical foragers, by contrast, gathering usually supplies more food than hunting and fishing do. Gathering is generally women's work; men usually hunt and fish. With gathering prominent, gender status tends to be more equal than it is when hunting and fishing are the main subsistence activities.

Gender status is also more equal when the domestic and public spheres aren't sharply separated. (**Domestic** means within or pertaining to the home.) Strong differentiation between the home and the outside world is called the **domestic-public dichotomy** or the *private-public contrast.* The outside world can include politics, trade, warfare, or work. Often when domestic and public spheres are clearly separated, public activities have greater prestige than domestic ones do. This can promote gender stratification, because men are more likely to be active in the public domain than women are. Cross-culturally, women's activities tend to be closer to home than men's are. Thus, another reason hunter-gatherers have less gender stratification than food producers do is that the domestic-public dichotomy is more developed among food producers.

A division of labor linked to gender has been found in all cultures. However, the particular tasks assigned to men and women don't always reflect differences in strength and endurance. Food producers often assign the arduous tasks of carrying water and firewood and pounding grain to women. In 1967, in the Soviet Union, women filled 47 percent of factory positions, including many unmechanized jobs requiring hard physical labor. Most Soviet sanitation workers, physicians, and nurses were women (Martin and Voorhies 1975). Many jobs that men do in some societies are done by women in others, and vice versa.

Certain roles are more sex-linked than others. Men are the usual hunters and warriors. Given such weapons as spears, knives, and bows, men make better fighters because they are bigger and stronger on the average than are women in the same population (Divale and Harris 1976). The male hunter-fighter role also reflects a tendency toward greater male mobility.

In foraging societies, women are either pregnant or lactating during most of their childbearing period. Late in pregnancy and after childbirth, carrying a baby limits a woman's movements, even her gathering. Given the effects of pregnancy and lactation on mobility, it is rarely feasible for women to be the primary hunters (Friedl 1975). Warfare, which also requires mobility, is not found in most foraging societies, nor is interregional trade well developed. Warfare and trade are two public arenas that contribute to status inequality of males and females among food producers.

The !Kung San illustrate the extent to which the activities and spheres of influence of men and women may overlap among foragers (Draper 1975). Traditional !Kung gender roles were interdependent. During gathering, women discovered information about game animals, which they passed on to the men. Men and women spent about the same amount of time away from camp, but neither worked more than three days a week. Between one-third and one-half of the band stayed home while the others worked.

The !Kung saw nothing wrong in doing the work of the other gender. Men often gathered food and collected water. A general sharing ethos dictated that men distribute meat and that women share the fruits of gathering. Boys and girls of all ages played together. Fathers took an active role in raising children. Resources were

Hidden Women, Public Men—Public Women, Hidden Men

For the past few years, one of Brazil's top sex symbols has been Roberta Close, whom I first saw in a furniture commercial. Roberta, whose looks reminded me of those of the young Natalie Wood, ended her pitch with an admonition to prospective furniture buyers to accept no substitute for the advertised product. "Things," she warned, "are not always what they seem."

Nor was Roberta. This petite and incredibly feminine creature was actually a man. Nevertheless, despite the fact that he—or she (speaking as Brazilians do)—is a man posing as a woman, Roberta has won a secure place in Brazilian mass culture. Her photos decorate magazines. She has been a panelist on a TV variety show and has starred in a stage play in Rio with an actor known for his super-macho image. Roberta

Things aren't always what they seem. Roberta Close, a known transvestite (a transsexual as of 1989) who for years has been one of Brazil's top sex symbols, is genetically male.

even inspired a well-known, apparently heterosexual, pop singer to make a video honoring her. In it she pranced around Rio's Ipanema Beach in a bikini, showing off her ample hips and buttocks.

The video depicted widespread male appreciation of Roberta's beauty. As confirmation, one heterosexual man told me that he had recently been on the same plane as Roberta and had been struck by her looks. Another man said he wanted to have sex with her. These comments, it seemed to me, illustrated striking cultural contrasts about gender and sexuality. In Brazil, a Latin American country noted for its *machismo*, heterosexual men do not feel that attraction toward a transvestite blemishes their masculine identities.

Roberta Close exists in relation to a gender-identity scale that jumps from extreme femininity to extreme masculinity, with little in between. Masculinity is stereotyped as active and public, femininity as passive and domestic. The male-female contrast in rights and behavior is much stronger in Brazil than it is in North America. Brazilians confront a more rigidly defined masculine role than North Americans do.

The active-passive dichotomy also provides a stereotypical model for male homosexuality: One man is supposed to be the active, masculine (inserting) partner, whereas the other is the passive, effeminate one. The latter is derided as a *bicha* (intestinal worm), but little stigma attaches to the inserter. However, for Brazilian men who are unhappy with active masculinity or passive effeminacy there is one other choice—active femininity. For Roberta Close and others like her, the cultural demand of ultramasculinity has yielded to a performance of ultrafemininity. These men-women form a third gender in relation to Brazil's more polarized male-female identity scale.

Transvestites such as Roberta are particularly prominent in Rio's annual Carnival, when an ambience of inversion rules the city. In the culturally accurate words of the American popular novelist Gregory McDonald, who sets one of his books in Brazil at Carnival time:

> Everything goes topsy-turvy. . . . Men become women; women become men; grown-ups become children; rich people pretend they're poor; poor people, rich; sober people become drunkards; thieves become generous. Very topsy-turvy. (McDonald 1984, p. 154)

Most notable in this costumed inversion (DaMatta 1991), men dress as women. Carnival reveals and expresses normally hidden tensions and conflicts as social life is turned upside down. Reality is illuminated through a dramatic presentation of its opposite.

This is the final key to Roberta's cultural meaning. She emerged in a setting in which male-female inversion is part of the year's most popular festival. Transvestites are the pièces de résistance at Rio's Carnival balls, where they dress as scantily as the real women do. They wear postage-stamp bikinis, sometimes with no tops. Photos of real women and transformed ones vie for space in the magazines. It is often impossible to tell the born women from the hidden men. Roberta Close is a permanent incarnation of Carnival—a year-round reminder of the spirit of Carnivals past, present, and yet to come.

Roberta emerges from a Latin culture whose gender roles contrast strongly with those of the United States. From small village to massive city, Brazilian males are public and Brazilian females are private creatures. Streets, beaches, and bars belong to the men. Although bikinis adorn Rio's beaches on weekends and holidays, there are many more men than women there on weekdays. The men revel in their ostentatiously sexual displays. As they sun themselves and play soccer and volleyball, they regularly stroke their genitals to keep them firm. They are living publicly, assertively, and sexually in a world of men.

Brazilian men must work hard at this public image, constantly acting out their culture's definition of masculine behavior. Public life is a play whose strong roles go to men. Roberta Close, of course, is a public figure. Given that Brazilian culture defines the public world as male, we can perhaps better understand now why the nation's number one sex symbol is a man who excels at performing in public as a woman.

adequate, and competition and aggression were discouraged. Exchangeability and interdependence of roles are adaptive in small groups.

Patricia Draper's fieldwork among the !Kung is especially useful in showing the relationships among economy, gender roles, and stratification because she studied both foragers and a group of former foragers who had become sedentary. Just a few thousand !Kung continue their culture's traditional foraging pattern. Most are now sedentary, living near food producers or ranchers (see Kent 1992; Solway and Lee 1990; Wilmsen 1989).

Draper studied sedentary !Kung at Mahopa, a village where they herded, grew crops, worked for wages, and did a small amount of gathering. Their gender roles were becoming more rigidly defined. A domestic-public dichotomy was developing as men traveled farther than women did. With less gathering, women were confined more to the home. Boys could gain mobility through herding, but girls' movements were more limited. The equal and communal world of the bush was yielding to the social features of sedentary life. A differential ranking of men according to their herds, houses, and sons began to replace sharing. Males came to be seen as the more valuable producers.

If there is some degree of male dominance in every contemporary society, it may be because of changes such as those which have drawn the !Kung into wage work, market sales, and thus the world capitalist economy. A historical interplay among local, national, and international forces influences systems of gender stratification (Ong 1989). In traditional foraging cultures, however, egalitarianism extended to the relations between the sexes. The social spheres, activities, rights, and obligations of men and women overlapped. Foragers' kinship systems tend to be bilateral (calculated equally through males and females) rather than favoring either the mother's side or the father's side. Foragers may live with either the husband's or the wife's kin and often shift between one group and the other.

One last observation about foragers: It is among them that the public and private spheres are least separate, hierarchy is least marked, aggression and competition are most discouraged, and the rights, activities, and spheres of influence of men and women overlap the most. Our ancestors lived entirely by foraging until 10,000 years ago. If there is any most "natural" form of human society, it is best (although imperfectly—see the box in Chapter 7) represented by foragers. Despite the popular stereotype of the club-wielding caveman dragging his mate by the hair, relative gender equality is a much more likely ancestral pattern.

GENDER ISSUES AMONG HORTICULTURALISTS

Gender roles and stratification among cultivators vary widely, depending on specific features of the economy and social structure. Demonstrating this, Martin and Voorhies (1975) studied a sample of 515 horticultural societies, representing all parts of the world. They looked at several variables, including descent and postmarital residence, the percentage of the diet derived from cultivation, and the productivity of men and women.

Women were found to be the main producers in horticultural societies. In 50 percent of those societies, women did most of the cultivating. In 33 percent, contributions to cultivation by men and women were equal. In only 17 percent did men do most of the work. Women tended to do a bit more cultivating in matrilineal compared with patrilineal societies. They dominated horticulture in 64 percent of the matrilineal societies versus 50 percent of the patrilineal ones.

Reduced Gender Stratification—Matrilineal, Uxorilocal Societies

Cross-cultural variation in gender status is related to rules of descent and postmarital residence (Martin and Voorhies 1975; Friedl 1975). Among horticulturalists with matrilineal descent and uxorilocality (residence after marriage with the wife's relatives), female status tends to be high. Matriliny and uxorilocality disperse related males, rather than consolidating them. By contrast, patriliny and virilocality (residence after marriage with the husband's kin) keep male relatives together.

Women have high status in matrilineal, uxorilocal societies because
descent-group membership, succession to political positions, allocation
of land, and overall social identity come through female links. Among
these Minangkabau of Negeri Sembilan (Malaysia), matriliny gave
women sole inheritance of ancestral rice fields and
promoted clusters of female kin.

Women tend to have high status in matrilineal, uxorilocal societies for several reasons. Descent-group membership, succession to political positions, allocation of land, and overall social identity all come through female links. Among the Minangkabau in Malaysia (Peletz 1988), matriliny gave women sole inheritance of ancestral rice fields. Uxorilocality created solidary clusters of female kin. Minangkabau women had considerable influence beyond the household (Swift 1963). In such matrilineal contexts, women are the basis of the entire social structure. Although public authority may be (or may appear to be) assigned to the men, much of the power and decision making may actually belong to the senior women.

Anthropologists have never discovered a **matriarchy,** a society ruled by women. Still, some matrilineal societies, including the **Iroquois** (Brown 1975), a confederation of tribes in aboriginal New York, show that women's political and ritual influence can rival that of the men.

We saw that among foragers gender status was most equal when there was no sharp separation of male and female activities and of public and domestic spheres. However, gender stratification can also be reduced by roles that remove men from the local community. We now refine our generalizations: It is the sharp contrast between male and female roles *within the local community* that promotes gender stratification. Gender stratification may be reduced when women play prominent local roles, while men pursue activities in a wider, regional system. Iroquois women, for example, played a major subsistence role, while men left home for long periods. As is usual in matrilineal societies, *internal* warfare was uncommon. Iroquois men waged war only on distant groups; this could keep them away for years.

Iroquois men hunted and fished, but women controlled the local economy. Women did some fishing and occasional hunting, but their major productive role was in horticulture. Women owned the land, which they inherited from matrilineal kinswomen. Women controlled the production and distribution of food.

Iroquois women lived with their husbands and children in the family compartments of a communal longhouse. Women born in a longhouse remained there for life. Senior women, or **matrons,** decided which men could join the longhouse as husbands, and they could evict incompatible men. Women therefore controlled alliances between descent groups, an important political job in tribal society.

Iroquois women thus managed production and distribution. Social identity, succession to office and titles, and property all came through the female line, and women were prominent in ritual and politics. Related tribes made up a confederacy, the League of the Iroquois, with chiefs and councils.

A council of male chiefs managed military operations, but chiefly succession was matrilineal. The matrons of each longhouse nominated a man as their representative. If the council rejected their first nominee, the women proposed others until one was accepted. Matrons constantly monitored the chiefs and could impeach them. Women could veto war declarations, withhold provisions for war, and initiate peace efforts. In religion, too, women shared power. Half the tribe's religious practitioners were women, and the matrons helped select the others.

Reduced Gender Stratification—Matrifocal Societies

Nancy Tanner (1974) also found that the combination of male travel and a prominent female economic role reduced gender stratification and promoted high female status. She based this finding on a survey of the **matrifocal** (mother-centered, often with no resident husband-father) organization of certain societies in Indonesia, West Africa, and the Caribbean. Matrifocal societies are not necessarily matrilineal. A few are even patrilineal.

For example, Tanner (1974) found matrifocality among the Igbo of eastern Nigeria, who are patrilineal, virilocal, and polygynous (men have multiple wives). Each wife had her own house, where she lived with her children. Women planted crops next to their houses and traded surpluses. Women's associations ran the local markets, while men did the long-distance trading.

In a case study of the Igbo, Ifi Amadiume (1987) noted that either sex could fill male gender roles. Before Christian influence, successful Igbo women and men used wealth to take titles and acquire wives. Wives freed husbands (male and female) from domestic work and helped them accumulate wealth. Female husbands were not considered masculine but preserved their femininity. Igbo women asserted themselves in women's groups, including those of lineage daughters, lineage wives, and a community-wide women's council led by titled women. The high status and influence of Igbo women rested on the separation of males from local subsistence and on a marketing system that allowed women to leave home and gain prominence in distribution and—through these accomplishments—in politics.

Increased Gender Stratification—Patrilineal-Virilocal Societies

The Igbo are unusual among patrilineal-virilocal societies, many of which have marked gender stratification. Martin and Voorhies (1975) link the decline of matriliny and the spread of the **patrilineal-virilocal** complex (consisting of patrilineality, virilocality, warfare, and male supremacy) to pressure on resources. Faced with scarce resources, patrilineal-virilocal cultivators such as the Yanomami often wage warfare against other villages. This favors virilocality and patriliny, customs that keep related men together in the same village, where they make strong allies in battle. Such societies tend to have a sharp domestic-public dichotomy, and men tend to dominate the prestige hierarchy. Men may use their public roles in warfare and trade and their greater prestige to symbolize and reinforce the devaluation or oppression of women.

The patrilineal-virilocal complex characterizes many societies in highland Papua-New Guinea. Women work hard growing and processing subsistence crops, raising and tending pigs (the main domesticated animal and a favorite food), and doing domestic cooking, but they are isolated from the public domain, which men control. Men grow and distribute prestige crops, prepare food for feasts, and arrange marriages. The men even get to trade the pigs and control their use in ritual.

In densely populated areas of the Papua-New Guinea highlands, male-female avoidance is associated with strong pressure on resources (Lindenbaum 1972). Men fear all female contacts, including sex. They think that sexual contact with women will weaken them. Indeed, men see everything female as dangerous and polluting. They segregate themselves in men's houses and hide their precious ritual objects from women. They delay marriage, and some never marry.

By contrast, the sparsely populated areas of Papua-New Guinea, such as recently settled areas, lack taboos on male-female contacts. The image of woman as polluter fades, heterosexual intercourse is valued, men and women live together, and reproductive rates are high.

Etoro Homosexuality

One of the most extreme examples of male-female sexual antagonism in Papua-New Guinea comes from the **Etoro** (Kelly 1976), a group of 400 people who subsist by hunting and horticulture in the Trans-Fly region. The Etoro also illustrate the power of culture in molding human sexuality. The following account applies only to Etoro males and their beliefs. Etoro culture norms prevented the male anthropologist who studied them from gathering comparable information about female attitudes. Etoro opinions about sexuality are linked to their beliefs about the cycle of birth, physical growth, maturity, old age, and death.

The Etoro believe that semen is necessary to give life force to a fetus, which is said to be placed within a woman by an ancestral spirit. Because men are believed to have a limited supply of semen, sexuality saps male vitality. The birth of children, nurtured by semen, symbolizes a necessary (and unpleasant) sacrifice that will lead to the husband's eventual death. Heterosexual intercourse, which is needed only for reproduction, is discouraged. Women who want too much sex are viewed as witches, hazardous to their husbands' health. Etoro culture permits heterosexual intercourse only about 100 days a year. The rest of the time it is tabooed. Seasonal birth clustering shows that the taboo is respected.

So objectionable is heterosexuality that it is removed from community life. It can occur neither in sleeping quarters nor in the fields. Coitus can happen only in the woods, where it is risky because poisonous snakes, the Etoro say, are attracted by the sounds and smells of sex.

Although coitus is discouraged, homosexual acts are viewed as essential. Etoro believe that boys cannot produce semen on their own. To grow into men and eventually give life force to their children, boys must acquire semen orally from older men. From the age of ten until adulthood, boys are inseminated by older men. No taboos are attached to this. Homosexual activity can go on in the sleeping area or garden. Every three years a group of boys around the age of twenty are formally initiated into manhood. They go to a secluded mountain lodge, where they are visited and inseminated by several older men.

Etoro homosexuality is governed by a code of propriety. Although homosexual

In some parts of Papua-New Guinea, the patrilineal-virilocal complex has extreme social repercussions. Regarding females as dangerous and polluting, men may segregate themselves in men's houses (such as this one, located near the Sepik River), where they hide their precious ritual objects from women.

relationships between older and younger males are culturally essential, those between boys of the same age are discouraged. A boy who gets semen from other youths is believed to be sapping their life force and stunting their growth. When a boy develops very rapidly, this suggests that he is ingesting semen from other boys. Like a sex-hungry wife, he is shunned as a witch.

Etoro homosexuality rests not on hormones or genes but on cultural traditions. The Etoro represent one extreme of a male-female avoidance pattern that is widespread in Papua-New Guinea and in patrilineal-virilocal societies.

Varieties of Human Sexuality

argaret Mead called attention to the fact that sexual behavior varies from culture to culture. A later, more systematic cross-cultural study (Ford and Beach 1951) found wide variation in attitudes about masturbation, bestiality (sex with animals), and homosexuality. Even in a single culture, such as the United States, attitudes about sex differ with socioeconomic status, region, and rural versus urban residence. However, even in the 1950s, before the "age of sexual permissiveness" (the late 1960s and 1970s) began, research showed that almost all American men (92 percent) and more than half of American women (54 percent) admitted to masturbation. Between 40 and 50 percent of American farm boys had sex with animals. In the famous Kinsey report (Kinsey, Pomeroy, and Martin 1948), 37 percent of the men surveyed admitted having had at least one homosexual experience leading to orgasm. In a later study of 1,200 unmarried women, 26 percent reported homosexual activities.

Attitudes toward homosexuality, masturbation, and bestiality in other cultures differ strikingly, as I find when I contrast the cultures I know best—the United States, urban and rural Brazil, and Madagascar. During my first stay in Arembepe, Brazil, when I was nineteen years old and unmarried, young men told me details of their experiences with prostitutes in the city. In Arembepe, a rural community, sex with animals was common. Targets of the male sex drive included cattle, horses, sheep, goats, and turkeys. Arembepe's women were also more open about their sex lives than their North American counterparts were.

Arembepeiros talked about sex so willingly that I wasn't prepared for the silence and avoidance of sexual subjects that I encountered in Madagascar. My wife's and my discreet attempts to get the Betsileo to tell us at least the basics of their culture's sexual practices led nowhere. I did discover from city folk that, as in many non-Western cultures, traditional ceremonies were times of ritual license, when normal taboos lapsed and Betsileo men and women engaged in what Christian missionaries described as "wanton" sexuality. Only during my last week in Madagascar did a young man in the village of Ivato, where I had spent a year, take me aside and offer to write down the words for genitals and sexual intercourse. He could not say these tabooed words, but he wanted me to know them so that my knowledge of Betsileo culture would be as complete as possible.

I have never worked in a culture with institutionalized homosexuality of the sort that exists among several tribes in Papua-New Guinea, such as the Kaluli

(Schieffelin 1976) or Sambia (Herdt 1981, 1987). The Kaluli believe that semen has a magical quality that promotes knowledge and growth. Before traveling into alien territory, boys must eat a mixture of ginger, salt, and semen to enhance their ability to learn a foreign language. At age eleven or twelve, a Kaluli boy forms a homosexual relationship with an older man chosen by his father. (This man cannot be a relative, because that would violate their incest taboo.) The older man has anal intercourse with the boy. The Kaluli cite the boy's peach-fuzz beard, which appears thereafter, as evidence that semen promotes growth. Young Kaluli men also have homosexual intercourse at hunting lodges, where they spend an extended period learning the lore of the forest and the hunt from older bachelors.

Homosexual activities were absent, rare, or secret in only 37 percent of seventy-six societies for which data were available (Ford and Beach 1951). In the others, various forms of homosexuality were considered normal and acceptable. Sometimes sexual relations between people of the same sex involved transvestism on the part of one of the partners. However, this was not true of homosexuality among the Sudanese Azande, who valued the warrior role (Evans-Pritchard 1970). Prospective warriors—boys aged twelve to twenty—left their families and shared quarters with adult fighting men, who paid bridewealth for, and had sex with, them. During this apprenticeship, the boys performed the domestic duties of women. Upon reaching warrior status, young men took their own boy brides. Later, retiring from the warrior role, Azande men married women. Flexible in their sexual expression, Azande men had no difficulty shifting to heterosexual coitus.

There appears to be greater cross-cultural acceptance of homosexuality than of bestiality or masturbation. Most societies in the Ford and Beach (1951) study discouraged masturbation, and only five allowed human-animal sex. However, these figures measure only the social approval of sexual practices, not their actual frequency. As in our own society, socially disapproved sex acts are more widespread than people admit.

We see nevertheless that flexibility in human sexual expression is an aspect of our primate heritage. Both masturbation and homosexual behavior exist among chimpanzees and other primates (White 1989). Primate sexual potential is molded both by the environment and by reproductive necessity. Heterosexuality is practiced in all human societies—which, after all, must reproduce themselves—but alternatives are also widespread (Davis and Whitten 1987). The sexual component of personality—just how humans express their "natural" sexual urges—is a matter that culture and environment determine and limit.

GENDER ISSUES AMONG AGRICULTURALISTS

As horticulture developed into agriculture, women lost their role as primary cultivators. Certain agricultural techniques, particularly plowing, were assigned to men because of their greater average size and strength (Martin and Voorhies 1975). Except when irrigation was used, plowing eliminated the need for constant weeding, an activity usually done by women.

Cross-cultural data illustrate these changes in productive roles. Women were the main workers in 50 percent of the horticultural societies surveyed but in only 15 percent of the agricultural groups. Male subsistence labor dominated 81 percent of the agricultural societies but only 17 percent of the horticultural ones (Martin and Voorhies 1975) (see Table 10-1).

With agriculture, women were cut off from production for the first time in human history. Belief systems started contrasting men's valuable extradomestic labor with women's domestic role, now viewed as inferior. (**Extradomestic** means outside the home; within or pertaining to the public domain.) Changes in kinship and postmarital residence patterns also hurt women. Descent groups and polygyny declined with agriculture, and the nuclear family became more common. Living with her husband and children, a woman was isolated from her kinswomen and cowives. Female sexuality is carefully supervised in agricultural economies; men have easier access to divorce and extramarital sex, reflecting a "double standard."

Still, female status in agricultural societies is not inevitably bleak. Gender stratification is associated with plow agriculture rather than with intensive cultivation per se. Studies of peasant gender roles and stratification in France and Spain (Harding 1975; Reiter 1975), which have plow agriculture, show that people think of the house as the female sphere and the fields as the male domain. However, such a dichotomy is not inevitable, as my own research among Betsileo agriculturalists in Madagascar shows.

Betsileo women play a prominent role in agriculture, contributing a third of the

TABLE 10-1 MALE AND FEMALE CONTRIBUTIONS TO PRODUCTION IN CULTIVATING SOCIETIES

	Horticulture (Percentage of 104 Societies)	Agriculture (Percentage of 93 Societies)
Women are primary cultivators	50	15
Men are primary cultivators	17	81
Equal contributions to cultivation	33	3

Source: Martin and Voorhies 1975, p. 283.

hours invested in rice production. They have their customary tasks in the division of labor, but their work is more seasonal than men's is.

No one has much to do during the ceremonial season, between mid-June and mid-September. Men work in the rice fields almost daily the rest of the year. Women's cooperative work occurs during transplanting (mid-September through November) and harvesting (mid-March through early May). Along with other members of the household, women do daily weeding in December and January. After the harvest, all family members work together winnowing the rice and transporting it to the granary.

If we consider the strenuous daily task of husking rice by pounding (a part of food preparation rather than production per se), women actually contribute slightly more than 50 percent of the labor devoted to producing and preparing rice before cooking.

Not just women's prominent economic role but traditional social organization enhances female status among the Betsileo. Although postmarital residence is mainly virilocal, descent rules permit married women to keep membership in and a strong allegiance to their own descent groups. Kinship is broadly and bilaterally (on both sides—as in contemporary North America) calculated. The Betsileo exemplify

Bilateral kinship systems, combined with subsistence economies in which the sexes have complementary roles in food production and distribution, have reduced gender stratification. Such features are common among Asian rice cultivators (the Ifugao of the Philippines are shown here).

Aihwa Ong's (1989) generalization that bilateral (and matrilineal) kinship systems, combined with subsistence economies in which the sexes have complementary roles in food production and distribution, are characterized by reduced gender stratification. Such societies are common among South Asian peasants (Ong 1989).

The Betsileo woman has obligations to her husband and his kin, but they are also obligated to her and her relatives. Often accompanied by their husbands and children, women pay regular visits to their home villages. The husband and his relatives help the wife's kin in agriculture and attend ceremonials hosted by them. When a woman dies, she is normally buried in her husband's ancestral tomb. However, a delegation from her own village always comes to request that she be buried at home. Women often marry into villages where some of their kinswomen have previously married; thus, even after marriage a woman lives near some of her own relatives.

Betsileo men do not have exclusive control over the means of production. Women can inherit rice fields, but most women, on marrying, relinquish their shares to their brothers. Sometimes a woman and her husband cultivate her field, eventually passing it on to their children.

Traditionally, Betsileo men participate more in politics, but women also hold political office. Women sell their produce and products in markets, invest in cattle, sponsor ceremonials, and are mentioned during offerings to ancestors. Arranging marriages, an important extradomestic activity, is more women's concern than men's. Sometimes Betsileo women seek their own kinswomen as wives for their sons, reinforcing their own prominence in village life and continuing kin-based female solidarity in the village.

The Betsileo illustrate the idea that intensive cultivation does not necessarily entail sharp gender stratification. We can see that gender roles and stratification reflect not just the type of adaptive strategy but also specific environmental variables and cultural attributes. Betsileo women continue to play a significant role in their society's major economic activity, rice production.

Plowing has become prominent in Betsileo agriculture only recently, but irrigation makes weeding, in which women participate, a continued necessity. If new tools and techniques eventually reduce women's roles in transplanting, harvesting, and weeding, gender stratification may develop. In the meantime, several features of the economy and social organization continue to shield the Betsileo from the gender hierarchies found in many agricultural and virilocal societies.

We have seen that virilocality is usually associated with gender stratification. However, some cultures with these institutions, including the Betsileo and the matrifocal Igbo of eastern Nigeria, offer contrasts to the generalization. The Igbo and Betsileo are not alone in allowing women a role in trade. Many patrilineal, polygynous societies in West Africa also allow women to have careers in commerce. Polygyny may even help an aspiring woman trader, who can leave her children with her cowives while she pursues a business career. She repays them with cash and other forms of assistance.

and Capitalism, 15th–18th Century (1981, 1982, 1984), Braudel argues that society consists of parts assembled into an interrelated system. Societies are subsystems of bigger systems, with the world system as the largest.

THE EMERGENCE OF THE WORLD SYSTEM

As Europeans took to ships, developing a transoceanic trade-oriented economy, people throughout the world entered Europe's sphere of influence. In the fifteenth century, Europe established regular contact with Asia, Africa, and eventually the New World (the Caribbean and the Americas). Christopher Columbus's first voyage from Spain to the Bahamas and the Caribbean in 1492 was soon followed by additional voyages. These journeys opened the way for a major exchange of people, resources, diseases, and ideas, as the Old and New Worlds were forever linked (Crosby 1972, 1986; Viola and Margolis 1991). Led by Spain and Portugal, Europeans extracted silver and gold, conquered the natives (taking some as slaves), and colonized their lands.

Previously in Europe, as throughout the world, rural people had produced mainly for their own needs, growing their own food and making clothing, furniture, and tools from local products. Production beyond immediate needs was undertaken to pay taxes and purchase trade items such as salt and iron. As late as 1650 the English diet, like diets in most of the world today, was based on locally grown starches (Mintz 1985). However, in the 200 years that followed, the English became extraordinary consumers of imported goods. One of the earliest and most popular of those goods was sugar (Mintz 1985).

Sugar was originally domesticated in Papua-New Guinea and was first processed in India. Reaching Europe via the Middle East and the eastern Mediterranean, it was carried to the New World by Columbus (Mintz 1985). The climate of Brazil and the Caribbean proved ideal for growing sugarcane, and Europeans built plantations there to supply the growing demand for sugar. This led to the development in the seventeenth century of a plantation economy based on a single cash crop—a system known as **monocrop production.**

The demand for sugar in a growing international market spurred the development of the transatlantic slave trade and of New World plantation economies based on slave labor. By the eighteenth century an increased English demand for raw cotton led to the rapid settlement of what is now the southeastern United States and the emergence there of another slave-based monocrop production system. Like sugar, cotton was a key trade item that fueled the growth of the world system.

The increasing dominance of international trade led to the capitalist world economy (Wallerstein 1982)—a single world system committed to production for sale or exchange, with the object of maximizing profits rather than supplying domestic needs. **Capital** refers to wealth or resources invested in business, with the intent of producing a profit, and the defining attribute of capitalism is economic orientation to the world market for profit.

The key claim of world-system theory is that an identifiable social system extends beyond individual states and nations. That system is formed by a set of economic and political relations that has characterized much of the globe since the sixteenth century, when the Old World established regular contact with the New World.

According to Wallerstein (1982), the nations within the world system occupy three different positions: core, periphery, and semiperiphery. There is a geographic center or **core,** the dominant position in the world system, which consists of the strongest and most powerful nations, with advanced systems of production. In core nations, "the complexity of economic activities and the level of capital accumulation is the greatest" (Thompson 1983, p. 12). Core countries specialize in producing the most "advanced" goods, using the most sophisticated technologies and mechanized means of production. The core produces capital-intensive high-technology goods and exports some of them to the semiperiphery and periphery.

Semiperiphery and **periphery** nations, which roughly correspond to what is usually called the Third World, have less power, wealth, and influence. The semiperiphery is intermediate between the core and the periphery. Contemporary nations of the semiperiphery are industrialized. Like core nations, they export both industrial goods and commodities, but they lack the power and economic dominance of core nations. Thus Brazil, a semiperiphery nation, exports automobiles to Nigeria and auto engines, orange juice extract, and coffee to the United States.

Economic activities in the periphery are less mechanized and use human labor more intensively than do those in the semiperiphery. The periphery produces raw materials and agricultural commodities for export to the core and the semiperiphery. However, in the modern world, industrialization is invading even peripheral nations. The relationship between the core and the periphery is fundamentally exploitative. Trade and other forms of economic relations between core and periphery tend to benefit capitalists in the core at the expense of the periphery (Shannon 1989).

INDUSTRIALIZATION

By the eighteenth century the stage had been set for the **Industrial Revolution**—the historical transformation (in Europe, after 1750) of "traditional" into "modern" societies through industrialization of the economy. Industrialization required capital for investment. The established system of transoceanic trade and commerce supplied this capital from the enormous profits it generated. Wealthy people sought investment opportunities and eventually found them in machines and engines to drive living standards are much lower. The current *world stratification system* features a substantial contrast between both capitalists and workers in core nations and workers on the periphery.

With the expansion of the world capitalist economy, people on the periphery have been removed from the land by large landowners and multinational agribusiness interests. One result is increased poverty, including food shortages. Displaced people can't earn enough to buy the food they can no longer grow. The effects of the world economy can also create peripheral regions within core nations, such as areas of the rural South in the United States (see the box "The American Periphery" in this chapter).

INDUSTRIAL AND NONINDUSTRIAL SOCIETIES IN THE WORLD SYSTEM TODAY

World-system theory stresses the existence of a global culture. It emphasizes historical contacts and linkages between local people and international forces. The major forces influencing cultural interaction during the past 500 years have been commercial expansion and industrial capitalism (Wolf 1982; Wallerstein 1982). As state formation had done previously, industrialization accelerated local participation in larger networks. According to Bodley (1985), perpetual expansion (whether in population or consumption) is the distinguishing feature of industrial economic systems. Unlike bands and tribes, which are small, self-sufficient, subsistence-based systems, industrial economies are large, highly specialized systems in which local areas don't consume the products they produce and in which market exchanges occur with profit as the primary motive (Bodley 1985).

After 1870 European business began a concerted search for more secure markets in Asia, Africa, and other less developed areas. This process, which led to European imperialism in Africa, Asia, and Oceania, was aided by improved transportation, which brought huge new areas within easy reach. Europeans also colonized vast areas of previously unsettled or sparsely settled lands in the interior of North and South America and Australia. The new colonies purchased masses of goods from the industrial centers and shipped back wheat, cotton, wool, mutton, beef, and leather. Thus began the second phase of colonialism (the first had been in the New World after Columbus) as European nations competed for colonies between 1875 and 1914, a process that helped cause World War I.

Industrialization spread to many other nations and continues today (Table 11-1). By 1900 the United States had become a core nation within the world system (Figure 11-1) and had overtaken Great Britain in iron, coal, and cotton production. In a few decades (1868–1900) Japan changed from a medieval handicraft country to an industrial one, joining the semiperiphery by 1900 and moving to the core between 1945 and 1970.

Table 11-1 Ascent and Decline of Nations Within the World System

Periphery to Semiperiphery	Semiperiphery to Core	Core to Semiperiphery
United States (1800–1860)	United States (1860–1900)	Spain (1620–1700)
Japan (1868–1900)	Japan (1945–1970)	
Taiwan (1949–1980)	Germany (1870–1900)	
South Korea (1953–1980)		

Source: Reprinted by permission of Westview Press from *An Introduction to the World-System Perspective* by Thomas Richard Shannon. Copyright Westview Press 1989, Boulder, Colorado.

Twentieth-century industrialization has added hundreds of new industries and millions of new jobs. Production has increased, often beyond immediate demand, and this has spurred strategies such as advertising to sell everything that industry could churn out. Mass production gave rise to a culture of overconsumption, which valued acquisitiveness and conspicuous consumption. Bodley defines overconsumption as "consumption in a given area that exceeds the rates at which natural resources are produced by natural processes, to such an extent that the long-run stability of the culture involved is threatened" (1985, p. 39). Industrialization entailed a shift from reliance on renewable resources to the use of fossil fuels. Fossil fuel energy, stored over millions of years, is being rapidly depleted to support a previously unknown and probably unsustainable level of consumption (Bodley 1985). Table 11-2 compares energy consumption in various types of cultures. Americans are the world's foremost consumers of nonrenewable resources. Since becoming a core nation in 1900, the United States has tripled its per capita energy use while increasing its total energy consumption thirtyfold.

The Effects of Industrialization on the World System

How has industrialization affected the Third World—Latin America, Africa, the Pacific, and the less developed parts of Asia? One effect is the destruction of indigenous economies, ecologies, and populations. Two centuries ago, as industrialization was developing, 50 million people still lived beyond the periphery in politically independent bands, tribes, and chiefdoms. Occupying vast areas, those nonstate societies, although not totally isolated, were only marginally affected by nation-states and the world capitalist economy. Bands, tribes, and chiefdoms controlled half the globe and 20 percent of its population in 1800 (Bodley, ed. 1988). Industrialization then tipped the balance in favor of states.

Industrialization is "a global process that has destroyed or transformed all previous cultural adaptations and has given humanity the power not only to bring about its own extinction as a species, but also to speed the extinction of many other species and to alter biological and geological processes as well" (Bodley 1985, p. 4). The

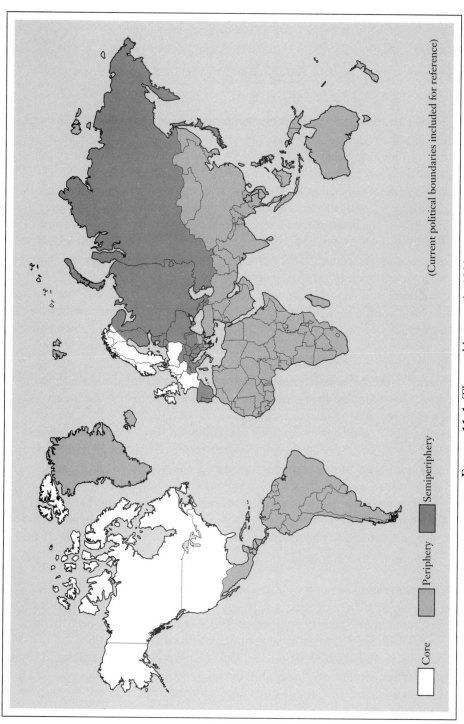

FIGURE 11-1 The world system in 1900.

(Reprinted by permission of Westview Press from *An Introduction to the World-System Perspective* by Thomas Richard Shannon. Copyright Westview Press 1989, Boulder, Colorado.)

The American Periphery

I n a comparative study of two counties at opposite ends of Tennessee, Thomas Collins (1989) reviews the effects of industrialization on poverty and unemployment. Hill County, with an Appalachian white population, is on the Cumberland Plateau in eastern Tennessee. Delta County, predominantly African-American, is 60 miles from Memphis in western Tennessee's lower Mississippi region. Both counties once had economies based on agriculture and timber, but jobs in those sectors declined sharply with the advent of mechanization. Both counties have unemployment rates more than twice that of Tennessee as a whole. More than a third of the people in each county live below the poverty level. Such poverty pockets represent a slice of the world periphery within modern America. Given very restricted job opportunities, the best-educated local youths have migrated to northern cities for three generations.

To increase jobs, local officials and business leaders have tried to attract industries from outside. Their efforts exemplify a more general rural southern strategy, which began during the 1950s, of courting industry by advertising "a good business climate"—which means low rents, cheap utilities, and a nonunion labor pool. However, few firms are attracted to an impoverished and poorly educated workforce. All the industries that have come to such areas have very limited market power and a narrow profit margin. Such firms survive by offering low wages and minimal benefits, with frequent layoffs. These industries tend to emphasize traditional female skills such as sewing and mostly attract women.

The garment industry, which is highly mobile, is Hill County's main employer. The knowledge that a garment plant can be moved to another site very rapidly tends to reduce employee demands. Management can be as arbitrary and authoritarian as it wishes. The unemployment rate and low educational level ensure that many women will accept sewing jobs for a bit more than the minimum wage.

In neither county has new industry brought many jobs for men, who have a higher unemployment rate than do women (as do blacks, compared with whites). Collins found that many men in Hill County had never been permanently employed; they had just done temporary jobs, always for cash.

The effects of industrialization in Delta County have been similar. That county's recruitment efforts have also drawn only marginal industries. The largest is a bicycle seat and toy manufacturer, whose employees are 60 percent women. Three other large plants, which make clothing and auto seat covers, employ 95 percent women. Egg production was once significant in Delta

County but folded when the market for eggs fell in response to rising national concern over the effects of cholesterol.

In both counties the men, ignored by industrialization, maintain an informal economy. They sell and trade used goods through personal networks. They take casual jobs, such as operating farm equipment on a daily or seasonal basis. Collins found that maintaining an automobile was the most important and prestigious contribution these men made to their families. Neither county has public transportation; Hill County even lacks school buses. Families need cars to get women to work and kids to school. Men who keep an old car running longest get special respect.

Reduced opportunities for men to do well at work—to which American culture attributes great importance—lead to a feeling of lowered self-worth, which is expressed in physical violence. The rate of domestic violence in Hill County exceeds the state average. Spousal abuse arises from men's demands to control women's paychecks. (Men regard the cash they earn themselves as their own, to spend on male activities.)

One important difference between the two counties involves unionization. In Delta County, organizers have waged campaigns for unionization. There is just one unionized plant in Delta County now, but recent campaigns in two other factories failed in close votes. Attitudes toward workers' rights in Tennessee correlate with race. Rural southern whites usually don't vote for unions when they have a chance to do so, whereas African Americans are more likely to challenge management about pay and work rules. Local blacks view their work situation in terms of black against white rather than from a position of working-class solidarity. They are attracted to unions because they see only whites in managerial positions and resent differential advancement of white factory workers. One manager told Collins that "once the workforce of a plant becomes more than one-third black, you can expect to have union representation within a year" (Collins 1989, p. 10). Responding to the probability of unionization, canny core capitalists from Japan don't build plants in the primarily African-American counties of the lower Mississippi. The state's Japanese factories cluster in eastern and central Tennessee.

Poverty pockets of the rural South (and other regions) represent a slice of the world periphery within modern America. Through mechanization, industrialization, and other changes promoted by larger systems, local people have been deprived of land and jobs. After years of industrial development, a third of the people of Hill and Delta counties remain below the poverty level. Emigration of educated and talented locals continues as opportunities shrink. Collins concludes that rural poverty won't be reduced by attracting additional peripheral industries because these firms lack the market power to improve wages and benefits. Different development schemes are needed for these counties and the rural South generally.

TABLE 11-2   ENERGY CONSUMPTION IN VARIOUS CONTEXTS

Type of Society	Daily Kilocalories per Person
Bands and tribes	4,000–12,000
Preindustrial states	26,000 (maximum)
Early industrial states	70,000
Americans in 1970	230,000
Americans in 1990	275,000

Source: From John H. Bodley, *Anthropology and Contemporary Human Problems*, 1985. Reprinted by permission of Mayfield Publishing.

negative effects of an expanding industrial world system include genocide, ethno-cide, and ecocide. **Genocide** is the physical destruction of ethnic groups by murder, warfare, and introduced diseases. When ethnic groups survive but lose or severely modify their ancestral cultures, we speak of **ethnocide.** The term for the destruc-tion of local ecosystems is **ecocide.**

As industrial states have conquered, annexed, and "developed" nonstates, there has been genocide on a grand scale. Bodley (1988) estimates that an average of 250,000 indigenous people perished annually between 1800 and 1950. Foreign dis-eases (to which natives had no resistance), warfare, slavery, land grabbing, and other forms of dispossession and impoverishment contributed to this genocide. Fortu-nately, many native groups, having been incorporated as ethnic minorities within nation-states, recouped their population. Many indigenous peoples survive and maintain their ethnic identity despite having lost their ancestral cultures to varying degrees (partial ethnocide).

Today's world contains some 200 million people who are members of con-quered tribes or of still autonomous tribal nations, of which, however, only a handful survive. Compare this with 75 million people living in perhaps 150,000 independent bands and tribes 10,000 years ago at the dawn of food production (Bodley 1988). Many descendants of tribespeople live on as culturally distinct colonized peoples, many of whom aspire to autonomy. As the original inhabitants of their territories, they are called **indigenous peoples.** They become *peasants* when their dependency and integration within states are complete and they remain on the land. When they move to urban areas, they are often called **ethnic minorities.** Bodley (1988) argues that indigenous peoples have consistently resisted integration within nation-states because such integration—usually into the impoverished classes—is likely to lead to a decline in their quality of life.

Many contemporary nations are repeating—at an accelerated rate—the process of resource depletion that occurred in Europe and the United States during the In-dustrial Revolution. Fortunately, however, today's world has some environmental watchdogs that were absent during the first centuries of the Industrial Revolution.

Given national and international cooperation and sanctions, the modern world may benefit from the lessons of the past.

SUMMARY

Local societies increasingly participate in wider systems—regional, national, and global. Columbus's voyages opened the way for a major and continuing exchange between the Old and New Worlds. The first plantation economies based on a single cash crop (most notably sugar) appeared in the seventeenth century. In the eighteenth century a monocrop economy based on slave labor also emerged in the cotton plantations of the southeastern United States.

The capitalist world economy is based on production for sale, with the goal of maximizing profits. The capitalist world economy has political and economic specialization based on three positions. Core, semiperiphery, and periphery have existed within the world system since the sixteenth century, although the particular countries filling these niches have changed.

The Industrial Revolution—the historical transformation of "traditional" into "modern" societies through industrialization of the economy—began around 1760. Transoceanic trade and commerce supplied capital for industrial investment. Industrialization developed from the domestic system of manufacture and from increased production in farming and manufacturing. Industrialization began in industries that produced goods that were widely used already. This illustrates Romer's rule: An innovation that evolves to maintain an existing system can play a major role in changing that system. The Industrial Revolution started in England rather than France because French industry could grow through expansion of the domestic system. England, with fewer people, had to industrialize.

Marx saw socioeconomic stratification as a sharp and simple division between the bourgeoisie (capitalists) and the proletariat (propertyless workers). Industrialization hastened the separation of workers from the means of production. Class consciousness was a vital part of Marx's view of class, whereas Weber believed that social solidarity based on ethnicity, religion, race, or nationality could take priority over class.

The modern capitalist world system maintains the distinction between those who own the means of production and those who don't, but the division is now worldwide. Modern stratification systems also include a middle class of skilled and professional workers. Besides class contrasts, the modern world system is cross-cut by status groups, of which nations are the most important. Class conflicts tend to occur within nations, and nationalism has prevented global class solidarity. World stratification features a substantial contrast between capitalists and workers in core nations and workers on the periphery. With the expansion of world capitalism, Third World peoples have been removed from the land by large landowners and multinational agribusiness interests.

The major forces influencing cultural interaction during the past 500 years have been commercial expansion and industrial capitalism. Perpetual expansion is a distinguishing feature of industrial economic systems. After 1870 businesses began a concerted search for more secure markets. This process led to European imperialism in Africa, Asia, and Oceania. Europeans also colonized vast areas of previously unsettled or sparsely settled lands in the interior of North and South America and Australia.

By 1900 the United States had become a core nation within the world system. Mass production gave rise to a culture of overconsumption, which valued acquisitiveness and conspicuous consumption. Industrialization shifted reliance from renewable resources to fossil fuels. One effect of industrialization is the destruction of indigenous economies, ecologies, and populations. Two centuries ago, 50 million people still lived in politically independent bands, tribes, and chiefdoms, which controlled half the globe and 20 percent of its population. Industrialization tipped the balance in favor of states. The negative effects of the industrial world system include genocide, ethnocide, and ecocide.

CHAPTER TWELVE

Applied Anthropology

nthropology can reduce ethnocentrism by instilling an appreciation of cultural diversity. This broadening, educational role affects the knowledge, values, and attitudes of people exposed to anthropology. Now we focus on the question: What contributions can anthropology make in identifying and solving problems stirred up by contemporary currents of economic, social, and cultural change, including industrialization and the spread of the world system?

Applied anthropology refers to the application of anthropological data, perspectives, theory, and methods to identify, assess, and solve social problems. There are two important professional groups of applied anthropologists (also called *practicing anthropologists*). The older is the independent Society for Applied Anthropology, founded in 1941. The second, the National Association for the Practice of Anthropology, was established as a unit of the American Anthropological Association in 1983. (Many people belong to both groups.) Practicing anthropologists work, regularly or occasionally, for nonacademic clients: governments, **nongovernmental organizations (NGOs),** tribal and ethnic associations, interest groups, businesses, and social service, medical, and educational agencies. Practicing anthropologists make it their business to apply their specialized knowledge and skills to problem solving.

THEORY AND PRACTICE

One of the applied anthropologist's most valuable research tools is the ethnographic method. Ethnographers study societies firsthand, living with and learning from ordinary people. Ethnographers are participant-observers, taking part in the events they study in order to understand native thought and behavior. Ethnographic techniques guide applied anthropologists in both foreign and domestic settings.

Other "expert" participants in social change programs may be content to converse with officials, read reports, and copy statistics. However, the applied anthropologist's likely early request is some variant of "take me to your villagers." We know that local people must play an active role in the changes that affect them and that "the people" have information that "the experts" lack.

Anthropological theory—the body of findings, perspectives, and generalizations of the subdisciplines—also guides applied anthropology. Anthropology's holistic perspective—its interest in biology, society, culture, and language—permits the evaluation of many issues that affect people. Anthropology's **systemic perspective** recognizes that changes don't occur in a vacuum. A project, policy, or program always has multiple effects, some unforeseen. For example, dozens of economic development projects intended to increase productivity through irrigation have worsened public health by creating waterways where diseases thrive. In an American example of unintended consequences, a program aimed at enhancing teachers' appreciation of cultural differences led to ethnic stereotyping (Kleinfeld 1975). Specifically, Native American students did not welcome teachers' frequent comments about their Indian heritage. The students felt set apart from their classmates and saw this attention to their ethnicity as patronizing and demeaning.

Theory aids practice, and application fuels theory. As we compare social change policy and projects, our understanding of cause and effect increases. We add new generalizations about culture change to those discovered in traditional and ancient cultures.

URBAN ANTHROPOLOGY

By the twenty-first century, most people will be descendants of the non-Western groups that anthropologists have traditionally studied. By 2025 the developing countries will account for 85 percent of the world's population, compared with 77 percent in 1992 (Stevens 1992). Solutions to future problems will depend increasingly on understanding non-Western cultural backgrounds. The Southern Hemisphere is steadily increasing its share of world population, and the fastest population growth rates are in Third World cities. The world had only 16 cities with more than a million people in 1900, but there were 276 such cities in 1990. By 2025, 60 percent of the global population will be urban, compared with 37 percent in 1990 (Stevens 1992). Rural migrants usually move to slums, where they live in hovels, without utilities and public sanitation facilities.

If current trends continue, urban population increase and the concentration of people in slums will be accompanied by rising rates of crime and water, air, and noise pollution. These problems will be most severe in the less developed countries. Almost all (97 percent) of the projected world population increase will occur in developing countries, 34 percent in Africa alone (Lewis 1992). Still, global population growth will also affect the Northern Hemisphere, through international migration.

As social complexity, industrialization, and urbanization spread globally, anthropologists increasingly study these processes and the social problems they create. Urban anthropology, which has theoretical (basic research) and applied dimensions, is the cross-cultural and ethnographic study of global urbanization and life in cities. The United States and Canada have also become popular arenas for urban anthropological research on topics such as ethnicity, poverty, class, and subcultural variations (Mullings, ed. 1987).

Urban versus Rural

Recognizing that a city is a social context that is very different from a tribal or peasant village, an early student of Third World urbanization, the anthropologist Robert Redfield, focused on contrasts between rural and urban life. He contrasted rural communities, whose social relations are on a face-to-face basis, with cities, where impersonality characterizes many aspects of life. Redfield (1941) proposed that urbanization be studied along a rural-urban continuum. He described differences in values and social relations in four sites that spanned such a continuum. In Mexico's Yucatán peninsula, Redfield compared an isolated Maya-speaking Indian community, a rural peasant village, a small provincial city, and a large capital. Several studies in Africa (Little 1971) and Asia were influenced by Redfield's view that cities are centers through which cultural innovations spread to rural and tribal areas.

In any nation, urban and rural represent different social systems. However, cultural diffusion occurs as people, products, and messages move from one to the other. Migrants bring rural practices and beliefs to town and take urban patterns back home. The experiences and social forms of the rural area affect adaptation to city life. For example, principles of tribal organization, including descent, provide migrants to African cities with coping mechanisms that Latin American peasants lack. City folk also develop new institutions to meet specific urban needs (Mitchell 1966).

African urban groups include ethnic associations, occupational groups, social clubs, religious groups, and burial societies. Through membership in these groups, urban Africans have networks of personal support. Ethnic or "tribal" associations, which build a bridge between one social system and another (rural and urban), are common both in West and East Africa (Little 1965; Banton 1957).

The ideology of such associations is that of a gigantic kin group. Members call one another "brother" and "sister." As in an extended family, rich members help their poor relatives. When members fight among themselves, the group acts as judge. A member's improper behavior can lead to expulsion—an unhappy fate for a migrant in an ethnically heterogeneous city.

Modern North American cities also have kin-based ethnic associations. One example comes from Los Angeles, which has the largest Samoan immigrant community (12,000 people) in the United States. Samoans in Los Angeles draw on their tra-

Most African cities have ethnic associations that link rural
and urban social systems. In Kampala, Uganda, shown here,
urban members of the Luo tribe are organized by
traditional clan ties and rural areas of origin.
Luo associations provide economic and
moral support, including transportation of
destitute people back to the country.

ditional system of *matai* (respect for elders) to deal with modern urban problems. For example, in 1992, a white policeman shot and killed two unarmed Samoan brothers. When a judge dismissed charges against the officer, local leaders used the *matai* system to calm angry youths (who have formed gangs, like other ethnic groups in the Los Angeles area). Clan leaders and elders organized a well-attended community meeting, in which they urged young members to be patient. Los Angeles Samoans aren't just traditionalists; they also use the American judicial system. They brought a civil case against the officer in question and pressed the U.S. Justice Department to initiate a civil-rights case in the matter (Mydans 1992*b*).

Urban Poverty and Homelessness

In 1992, 14.5 percent of the American population (37 million people) lived below the official poverty level (*American Almanac* 1994–1995, p. 476). (The comparable

Poverty is particularly obvious in big cities throughout the world.
Millions of rural Brazilians have settled in burgeoning urban shanty
towns (*favelas*), such as this one in Rio de Janeiro.

figures were 11.4 percent and 24.5 million people in 1978.) Poverty and homelessness are obvious on the streets of big cities in North America and worldwide. For example, millions of rural Brazilians have migrated to burgeoning urban shanty towns (*favelas*). Abandoned children camp in the streets, bathe in fountains, beg, rob, and scavenge like their homeless counterparts in North America.

Homelessness in North America is an extreme form of downward mobility, which may follow job loss, layoffs, or situations in which women and children flee from domestic abuse. The causes of homelessness are varied—psychological, economic, and social. They include inability to pay rent, eviction, sale of urban real estate to developers, and mental illness. In New York City many of the urban poor sleep in cardboard cartons and at train stations, on sidewalks and near warm-air gratings. They feed themselves by begging, scavenging, and raiding garbage (particularly that of restaurants) for food. The homeless are the foragers of modern society. They are poorly clad urban nomads, shaggy men and bag ladies who carry their meager possessions with them as they move.

Today's most extreme socioeconomic contrasts within the world capitalist economy are between the richest people in core nations and the poorest people on the periphery. However, as the gap between rich and poor has widened in North America, the social distance between the underclasses of core and periphery has shrunk. The road to Bangladesh passes through Times Square.

MEDICAL ANTHROPOLOGY

Both biological and cultural, both academic and applied, anthropologists work in **medical anthropology.** This growing field considers the sociocultural context and implications of disease and illness. **Disease** refers to an etic or scientifically identified health threat caused by a bacterium, virus, fungus, parasite, or other pathogen. **Illness** is an emic condition of poor health felt by an individual (Inhorn and Brown 1990). Cross-cultural research shows that perceptions of good and bad health, along with health threats and problems, are culturally constructed. Different ethnic groups and cultures recognize different illnesses, symptoms, and causes and have developed different health care systems and treatment strategies.

Disease also varies among cultures. Traditional and ancient foragers, because of their small numbers, mobility, and relative isolation from other groups, lacked most of the epidemic infectious diseases that affect agrarian and urban societies (Inhorn and Brown 1990; Cohen and Armelagos, eds. 1984). Epidemic diseases like cholera, typhoid, and bubonic plague thrive in dense populations, and thus among farmers and city dwellers. The spread of malaria has been linked to population growth and deforestation associated with food production.

Certain diseases have spread with economic development. **Schistosomiasis** (liver flukes) is probably the fastest-spreading and most dangerous parasitic infection now known (Heyneman 1984). It is propagated by snails that live in ponds, lakes, and waterways, usually ones created by irrigation projects. A study done in a Nile Delta village in Egypt (Farooq 1966) illustrated the role of culture (religion) in the spread of schistosomiasis. The disease was more common among Muslims than among Christians because of an Islamic practice called *wudu,* ritual ablution (bathing) before prayer. In eastern Africa, AIDS and other sexually transmitted diseases (STDs) have spread along highways, via encounters between male truckers and female prostitutes. STDs are also spread through prostitution as young men from rural areas seek wage work in cities, labor camps, and mines. When the men return to their natal villages, they infect their wives (Larson 1989; Miller and Rockwell, eds. 1988). Cities have also been prime sites of STD transmission in Europe, Asia, and North and South America.

We see that the incidence of particular diseases varies between societies, and cultures interpret and treat illness differently. Standards for sick and healthy bodies are cultural constructions that vary in time and space (Martin 1992). Still, all societies have what George Foster and Barbara Anderson (1978) call "disease-theory systems" to identify, classify, and explain illness. According to Foster and Anderson (1978), there are three basic theories about the causes of illness: personalistic, naturalistic, and emotionalistic. **Personalistic disease theories** blame illness on agents (often malicious), such as sorcerers, witches, ghosts, or spirits (see box). **Naturalistic disease theories** explain illness in impersonal terms. One example is Western medicine or **biomedicine,** which links illness to scientifically demonstrated agents, which bear no personal malice toward their victims. Thus Western medicine attributes illness to organisms (e.g., bacteria, viruses, fungi, parasites) or toxic materials. Other naturalistic ethnomedical systems blame poor health on unbalanced body fluids. Many Latin cultures classify food, drink, and environmental conditions as "hot" or "cold." People believe their health suffers when they eat or drink hot or cold substances together or under inappropriate conditions. One shouldn't drink something cold after a hot bath or eat a pineapple (a "cold" fruit) when one is menstruating (a "hot" condition).

Emotionalistic disease theories assume that emotional experiences cause illness. For example, Latin Americans may develop *susto*, an illness caused by anxiety or fright (Bolton 1981; Finkler 1985). Its symptoms (lethargy, vagueness, distraction) are similar to those of "soul loss," a diagnosis of similar symptoms made by people in Madagascar. Modern psychoanalysis also focuses on the role of the emotions in physical and psychological well-being.

All societies have **health care systems**—beliefs, customs, specialists, and techniques aimed at ensuring health and preventing, diagnosing, and curing illness. A society's illness-causation theory is important for treatment. When illness has a personalistic cause, shamans and other magicoreligious specialists may be good curers. They draw on varied techniques (occult and practical), which comprise their special expertise. A shaman may cure soul loss by enticing the spirit back into the body. Shamans may ease difficult childbirths by asking spirits to travel up the vagina and guide the baby out (Lévi-Strauss 1967). A shaman may cure a cough by counteracting a curse or removing a substance introduced by a sorcerer.

If there is a "world's oldest profession" besides hunter and gatherer, it is **curer,** or shaman. The curer's role has some universal features (Foster and Anderson 1978). Thus curers emerge through a culturally defined process of selection (parental prodding, inheritance, visions, dream instructions) and training (apprenticeship shamanship, medical school). Eventually, the curer is certified by older practitioners and acquires a professional image. Patients believe in the skills of the curer, whom they consult and compensate.

We should not lose sight, ethnocentrically, of the difference between **scientific medicine** and Western medicine per se (Lieban 1977). Despite advances in pathology, microbiology, biochemistry, surgery, diagnostic technology, and applications, many Western medical procedures have little justification in logic or fact. Overprescription of tranquilizers and drugs, unnecessary surgery, and the impersonality and inequality of the physician-patient relationship are questionable features of Western medical systems.

Still, biomedicine surpasses tribal treatment in many ways. Although medicines like quinine, coca, opium, ephedrine, and rauwolfia were discovered in nonindustrial societies, traditional medicines aren't as effective against bacteria as antibiotics are. Preventive health care has improved during the twentieth century. Today's surgical procedures are safer and more effective than those of traditional societies.

But industrialization has spawned its own health problems. Modern stressors include noise, air, and water pollution; poor nutrition; dangerous machinery; imper-

Spirit Possession in
Malaysian Factories

Successive waves of integration into the world system have washed over Malaysia, a former British colony. The Malays have witnessed sea trade, conquest, the influx of British and Chinese capital, and immigration from China and India. For centuries Malaysia has been part of the world system, but the immediate effects of industrialization, including effects on mental health, are recent. The Malaysian government has promoted export-oriented industry to bring rural Malays into the capitalist system. This has been done in response to rural discontent over poverty and landlessness as some 10,000 families per year are pushed off the land. Since 1970 transnational companies have been installing labor-intensive manufacturing operations in rural Malaysia. Between 1970 and 1980 agriculture's contribution to the national labor force fell from 53 to 41 percent as manufacturing jobs proliferated.

The industrialization of Malaysia is part of a global strategy. To escape mounting labor costs in the core, corporations headquartered in Japan, Western Europe, and the United States have been moving labor-intensive factories to the periphery. Malaysia now has hundreds of Japanese and American subsidiaries, which mainly produce garments, foodstuffs, and electronics components. In electronics plants in rural Malaysia, thousands of young women from peasant families now assemble microchips and microcomponents for transistors and capacitors. Aihwa Ong (1987) did a study of electronics assembly workers in an area where 85 percent of the workers were young unmarried females from nearby villages.

Ong found that factory discipline and social relations contrast strongly with traditional community life. Previously, agricultural cycles and daily Islamic prayers, rather than production quotas and work shifts, had framed the rural economy and social life. Villagers had planned and done their own work, without bosses. In factories, however, village women had to cope with a rigid work routine and constant supervision by men.

Factory relations of production featured a hierarchy, pay scale, and division of labor based on ethnicity and gender. Japanese men filled top management, while Chinese men were the engineers and production supervisors. Malay men also worked as supervisors of the factory workforce, which consisted of nonunion female semiskilled workers from poor Malay peasant families.

The Japanese firms in rural Malaysia were paternalistic. Managers assured village parents that they would care for their daughters as though they were their own. Unlike the American firms, the Japanese subsidiaries worked hard at maintaining good relations with rural elders. Management gave money for village events, visited workers' home communities, and invited parents to the plant for receptions. In return, village elders accorded high status to the Japanese managers. The elders colluded with the managers to urge young women to accept and stay with factory work.

The discipline, diligence, and obedience that factories value are learned in local schools, where uniforms help prepare girls for the factory dress code. Peasant women wear loose, flowing tunics, sarongs, and sandals, but factory workers must don tight overalls and heavy rubber gloves, in which they feel constrained and controlled.

Assembling electronics components requires precise, concentrated labor. Demanding, exhausting, depleting, and dehumanizing, labor in these factories illustrates the separation of intellectual and manual activity that Marx considered the defining feature of industrial work. One woman said about her bosses, "They exhaust us very much, as if they do not think that we too are human beings" (Ong 1987, p. 202). Nor does factory work bring women a substantial financial reward, given low wages, job uncertainty, and family claims on wages. Young women typically work just a few years. Production quotas, three daily shifts, overtime, and surveillance take their toll in mental and physical exhaustion.

One response to factory discipline and relations of production is spirit possession, which Ong interprets as an unconscious protest against labor discipline and male control of the industrial setting. Sometimes possession takes the form of mass hysteria. Spirits have simultaneously invaded as many as 120 factory workers. Weretigers (the Malay equivalent of the werewolf) arrive to avenge the construction of a factory on aboriginal burial grounds. Disturbed earth and grave spirits swarm on the shop floor. First the women see the spirits; then their bodies are invaded. The women become violent and scream abuses. Vengeful weretigers send the women into sobbing, laughing, and shrieking fits. To deal with possession, factories employ local medicine men, who sacrifice chickens and goats to fend off the spirits. This solution works only some of the time; possession still goes on. Factory women continue to act as vehicles to express the anger of avenging ghosts and their own frustrations.

Ong argues that spirit possession expresses anguish caused by, and resistance to, capitalist relations of production. However, she also notes that by engaging in this form of rebellion, factory women avoid a direct confrontation with the source of their distress. Ong concludes that spirit possession, while expressing repressed resentment, doesn't do much to modify factory conditions. (Unionization would do more.) Spirit possession may even help maintain the current conditions of inequality and dehumanization by operating as a safety valve for accumulated tensions.

Western medicine and scientific medicine are not the same thing. Many Western medical procedures have no clear justification, but scientific medicine surpasses tribal health care systems in several ways. Clinics such as this one bring antibiotics, minor surgery, and preventive medicine to the Masai of Kenya.

sonal work; isolation; poverty; homelessness; and substance abuse. Health problems in industrial nations are due as much to economic, social, political, and cultural factors as to pathogens. In modern North America, for example, poverty contributes to many illnesses, including arthritis, heart conditions, back problems, and hearing and vision impairment. Poverty is even a factor in the differential spread of infectious diseases.

Medical anthropology, which is based on biological, sociocultural, and cross-cultural research, has theoretical and applied dimensions. Anthropologists have served as cultural interpreters in public health programs, which must pay attention to native theories about the nature, causes, and treatment of illness. Successful health interventions are not forced on communities; they must fit into local cultures and be accepted by local people. When Western medicine is introduced, people usually retain many of their old methods while also accepting new ones (see Green 1992). Native curers may go on treating certain conditions (like *susto* or spirit possession), whereas M.D.s may deal with others. If both modern and traditional specialists are consulted and the patient is cured, the native curer may get more credit than the physician.

A more personal treatment of illness that emulates the non-Western curer-patient-community relationship could help Western systems. Western medicine tends to draw a rigid line between biological and psychological causation. Non-Western theories usually lack this sharp distinction, recognizing that poor health has intertwined physical, emotional, and social causes. The mind-body opposition is part of Western folk taxonomy, not of science.

ANTHROPOLOGY AND EDUCATION

Anthropology and education refers to anthropological research in classrooms, homes, and neighborhoods. Some of the most interesting research has been done in classrooms, where anthropologists observe interactions between teachers, students, parents, and visitors. Jules Henry's classic account of the American elementary school classroom (1955) shows how students learn to conform to and compete with their peers. Anthropologists also follow students from classrooms into their homes and neighborhoods, viewing children as total cultural creatures whose enculturation and attitudes toward education belong to a context that includes family and peers.

Sociolinguists and cultural anthropologists work side by side in education research, for example, in a study of Puerto Rican seventh-graders in the urban Midwest (Hill-Burnett 1978). In classrooms, neighborhoods, and homes, anthropologists uncovered some misconceptions by teachers. For example, the teachers had mistakenly assumed that Puerto Rican parents valued education less than did non-Hispanics. However, in-depth interviews revealed that the Puerto Rican parents valued it more.

Researchers also found that certain practices were preventing Hispanics from being adequately educated. For example, the teachers' union and the board of education had agreed to teach "English as a foreign language." However, they had not provided bilingual teachers to work with Spanish-speaking students. The school started assigning all students (including non-Hispanics) with low reading scores and behavior problems to the English-as-a-foreign-language classroom.

This educational disaster brought together a teacher who spoke no Spanish, children who barely spoke English, and a group of English-speaking students with reading and behavior problems. The Spanish speakers were falling behind not just in reading but in all subjects. They could at least have kept up in the other subjects if a Spanish speaker had been teaching them science, social studies, and math until they were ready for English-language instruction in those areas.

CAREERS IN ANTHROPOLOGY

Many college students find anthropology interesting and consider majoring in it. However, their parents or friends may discourage them by asking, "What kind of job are you going to get with an anthropology major?" The purpose of this section is to answer that question.

The first step in answering "What do you do with an anthropology major?" is to consider the more general question "What do you do with any college major?" The answer is "Not much, without a good bit of effort, thought, and planning." A survey of graduates of the literary college of the University of Michigan showed that few had jobs that were clearly linked to their majors. Medicine, law, and many other professions require advanced degrees. Although many colleges offer bachelor's degrees in engineering, business, accounting, and social work, master's degrees are often needed to get the best jobs in those fields.

A broad college education, and even a major in anthropology, can be an excellent basis for success in many fields. A recent survey of women executives showed that most had not majored in business but in the social sciences or humanities. Only after graduating did they study business, obtaining a master's degree in business administration. These executives felt that the breadth of their college educations had contributed to their success in business careers. Anthropology majors go on to medical, law, and business schools and find success in many professions that often have little explicit connection to anthropology.

Anthropology's breadth provides knowledge and an outlook on the world that are useful in many kinds of work. For example, an anthropology major combined with a master's degree in business is excellent preparation for work in international business and economic development. However, job seekers must convince employers that they have a special and valuable "skillset."

Breadth is anthropology's hallmark. Anthropologists study people biologically, culturally, socially, and linguistically, in time and space, in developed and underdeveloped nations, in simple and complex settings. Most colleges have anthropology courses that compare cultures and others that focus on particular world areas, such as Latin America, Asia, and Native North America. The knowledge of foreign areas acquired in such courses can be useful in many jobs. Anthropology's comparative outlook, its long-standing Third World focus, and its appreciation of diverse lifestyles combine to provide an excellent foundation for overseas employment.

Even for work in North America, the focus on culture is valuable. Every day we hear about cultural differences, about social problems whose solutions require a multicultural viewpoint—an ability to recognize and reconcile ethnic differences. Government, schools, and private firms constantly deal with people from different social classes, ethnic groups, and tribal backgrounds. Physicians, attorneys, social workers, police officers, judges, teachers, and students can all do a better job if they understand social differences in a part of the world that is one of the most ethnically diverse in history.

Anthropologists also work to help natives threatened by external systems. As highways and power-supply systems cross tribal boundaries, the "modern" world comes into conflict with historic land claims and traditions. An anthropological study is often considered necessary before permission is granted to extend a public system across native lands.

Knowledge about the traditions and beliefs of subgroups within a nation is important in planning and carrying out programs that affect those subgroups. Attention to social background and cultural categories helps ensure the welfare of affected ethnic groups, communities, and neighborhoods. Experience in planned social changes—whether community organization in North America or economic development overseas—shows that a proper social study should be done before a project begins. When local people want the change and it fits their lifestyle and traditions, it will be more successful, beneficial, and cost-effective. There will be not only a more humane but a more economical solution to a real social problem.

People with anthropology backgrounds are doing well in many fields. Furthermore, even if the job has little or nothing to do with anthropology in a formal or obvious sense, anthropology is always useful when we work with fellow human beings. For most of us, this means every day of our lives.

SUMMARY

Applied anthropology is the application of anthropological data, perspectives, theory, and methods to identify, assess, and solve contemporary social problems. Applied (or practicing) anthropologists work for governments; nongovernmental organizations; tribal, ethnic, and interest groups; businesses; social services; and educational agencies.

Ethnography has become one of applied anthropology's most valuable research tools, along with the comparative, cross-cultural perspective. Holism allows applied anthropologists to perceive the biological, social, cultural, and linguistic dimensions of policy issues. A systemic perspective helps anthropologists recognize that all changes have multiple consequences, some unintended.

In the face of globalization and urbanization, both academic and applied anthropologists have turned their attention to migration from rural areas to cities and across national boundaries. Urban anthropology includes the study of life in cities and the process of urbanization that affects people throughout the world. The United States has become a popular arena for urban anthropological research on such topics as ethnicity, poverty, class, and subcultural variation. Rural social relations are personal and face to face, but impersonality characterizes many aspects of life in cities. Although urban and rural are different social systems, there is cultural diffusion from one to the other. Rural and tribal social forms affect adjustment to the city. For example, principles of tribal organization, including descent, provide migrants to African cities with adaptive mechanisms.

Medical anthropology unites biological and cultural, theoretical and applied, anthropologists in the cross-cultural study of health problems and conditions, disease, illness, disease theories, and health care systems. Characteristic diseases reflect diet, population density, economy, and social complexity. The three main native theories of illness are personalistic, naturalistic, and emotionalistic. Personalistic causes refer to such agents as witches and sorcerers. In this context, shamans can be effective curers. Western medicine or biomedicine is not the same as scientific medicine. The latter has made many advances, particularly in bacterial diseases and surgery.

Anthropology and education researchers work in classrooms, homes, neighborhoods, and other settings relevant to education. Some of their research leads to policy recommendations. Courses in cultural anthropology and sociolinguistics are making teachers more aware of how linguistic and ethnic differences should be handled in the classroom.

A broad college education, including anthropology and foreign-area courses, offers excellent preparation for many fields. Anthropology's comparative outlook, long-standing Third World focus, and cultural relativism provide an excellent basis for overseas employment. Even for work in North America, a focus on culture is valuable. Anthropological training is useful in dealing with issues that reflect cultural contrasts and problems whose solutions require an ability to recognize and reconcile social or ethnic differences. Anthropologists have worked for and with natives threatened by external systems. Anthropology majors attend medical, law, and business schools and succeed in many fields, some of which have little explicit connection with anthropology.

Experience with social change programs, whether community organization in North America or economic development abroad, offers a common lesson. If local people want the change and it fits their lifestyle and traditions, the change will be more successful, beneficial, and cost-effective.

CHAPTER THIRTEEN

Development and Innovation

DEVELOPMENT
The Greening of Java ~ Equity
STRATEGIES FOR INNOVATION
Overinnovation ~ Underdifferentiation ~ Third World Models and
Culturally Appropriate Development ~ BOX: Culturally Appropriate Marketing

D uring the Industrial Revolution, a strong current of thought viewed industrialization as a beneficial process of organic development and progress. Many economists still assume that industrialization increases production and income. They seek to create in Third World ("developing") countries a process like the one that first occurred spontaneously in eighteenth-century Great Britain.

DEVELOPMENT

Economic development plans usually are guided by some kind of **intervention philosophy,** an ideological justification for outsiders to guide native peoples in specific directions. Bodley (1988) argues that the basic belief behind interventions—whether by colonialists, missionaries, governments, or development planners—has been the same for more than 100 years. This belief is that industrialization, modernization, westernization, and individualism are desirable evolutionary advances and that development schemes that promote them will bring long-term benefits to natives. In a more extreme form, intervention philosophy may pit the assumed wisdom of enlightened colonial or other First World planners against the purported conservatism, ignorance, or "obsolescence" of "inferior" natives.

Anthropologists dispute such views. We know that for thousands of years bands and tribes have done "a reasonable job of taking care of themselves" (Bodley 1988, p. 93). Indeed, because of their low energy needs, they have managed their resources better than we manage our own. Many problems that people face today are due to their position within nation-states and their increasing dependence on the world cash economy.

Sometimes when natives are reluctant to change, it isn't because they have unduly conservative attitudes but because powerful interest groups oppose reform. Many Third World governments are reluctant to tamper with existing socioeconomic conditions in their countries (Manners 1956/1973). The attempt to bring the "green revolution" to Java that is analyzed below illustrates this situation. Resistance by elites to land reform is a reality throughout the Third World. Millions of people in colonies and underdeveloped nations have learned from bitter experience that if they increase their incomes, their taxes and rents also rise.

Conflicts between governments (colonial or postcolonial) and natives often arise when outside interests exploit resources on tribal lands. Driven by deficits and debts, governments seek to wrest as much wealth as possible from the territory they administer. This goal helps explain the worldwide intrusion on indigenous peoples and their local ecosystems by highway construction, mining, hydroelectric projects, ranching, lumbering, agribusiness, and planned colonization (Bodley 1988).

Studying people at the local level, ethnographers have a unique view of the impact of national and international planning on intended "beneficiaries." Local-level research often reveals inadequacies in the measures that economists use to assess development and a nation's economic health. For example, per capita income and gross national product don't measure the distribution of wealth. Because the first is an average and the second is a total, they may rise as the rich get richer and the poor get poorer.

Today, many government agencies, international groups, and private foundations encourage attention to local-level social factors and the cultural dimension of development. Anthropological expertise is important because social problems can doom projects to failure. A study of fifty development projects (Lance and McKenna 1975) judged only twenty-one to be successes. Social and cultural incompatibilities had doomed most of the failed projects.

For example, a 1981 anthropological study of a multimillion-dollar development project in Madagascar uncovered several reasons for its failure. The project had been planned and funded by the World Bank in the late 1960s. The planners (no anthropologists among them) anticipated none of the problems that emerged. The project was aimed at draining and irrigating a large plain to increase rice production. Its goal was to raise production through machinery and double cropping—growing two crops annually on the same plot. However, the planners disregarded several things, including the unavailability of spare parts and fuel for the machines. The designers also ignored the fact, well known to anthropologists, that cross-culturally, intensive cultivation is associated with dense populations. If there are no machines to do the work, there have to be people around to do it. However, population densities in the project area (15 per square kilometer) were much too low to support intensive cultivation without modern machinery.

Planners should have known that labor and machinery for the project were unavailable. Furthermore, many local people were understandably hostile toward the project because it gave their ancestral land away to outsiders. (Unfortunately, this is a common occurrence in development projects.) Many land-grant recipients were members of regional and national elites who used their influence to get fields that were intended for poor farmers. The project also suffered from technical problems. The foreign firm hired to dig the irrigation canals dug them lower than the land they had to irrigate, and so the water couldn't flow up into the fields.

Hundreds of millions of dollars of development funds could have produced greater human benefits if anthropologists had helped plan, supervise, and evaluate the projects. Planners who are familiar with the language and customs of a country can make better forecasts about project success than can those who are not. Accordingly, anthropologists increasingly work in organizations that promote, manage, and assess programs that influence human life in the United States and abroad.

However, ethical dilemmas often confront applied anthropologists (Escobar 1991). Our respect for cultural diversity is often offended because efforts to extend industry and technology may entail profound cultural changes. Foreign aid doesn't usually go where need and suffering are greatest. It is spent on political, economic, and strategic priorities as national leaders and powerful interest groups perceive them. Planners' interests don't always coincide with the best interests of the local people. Although the aim of most development projects is to enhance the quality of life, living standards often decline in the target area (Bodley 1988).

The Greening of Java

Anthropologist Richard Franke (1977) conducted an independent study of discrepancies between goals and results in a scheme to promote social and economic change in Java, Indonesia. Experts and planners of the 1960s and 1970s assumed that as small-scale farmers got modern technology and more productive crop varieties, their lives would improve. The media publicized new, high-yielding varieties of wheat, maize, and rice. These new crops, along with chemical fertilizers, pesticides, and new cultivation techniques, were hailed as the basis of a **green revolution.** This "revolution" was expected to increase the world's food supply and thus improve the diets and living conditions of victims of poverty, particularly in land-scarce, overcrowded regions.

The green revolution was an economic success. It did increase the global food supply. New strains of wheat and rice doubled or tripled food supplies in many Third World countries (except for sub-Saharan Africa). Thanks to the green revolution, world food prices declined by more than 20 percent during the 1980s (Stevens 1992). But its social effects were not what its advocates had intended, as we learn from Javanese experience.

Java received a genetic cross between rice strains from Taiwan and Indonesia—a high-yielding "miracle" rice known as IR-8. This hybrid could raise the productivity of a given plot by at least half. Governments throughout southern Asia, including Indonesia, encouraged the cultivation of IR-8, along with the use of chemical fertilizers and pesticides.

Governments throughout southern Asia, including Indonesia, have encouraged cultivation of new rice varieties and use of chemical fertilizers and pesticides. Shown here are experimental seedlings at Java's Rice Research Center.

The Indonesian island of Java, one of the most densely populated places in the world (over 700 people per square kilometer), was a prime target for the green revolution. Java's total crop was insufficient to supply its people with minimal daily requirements of calories (2,150) and protein (55 grams). In 1960 Javanese agriculture supplied 1,950 calories and 38 grams of protein per capita. By 1967 these already inadequate figures had fallen to 1,750 calories and 33 grams. Could miracle rice, by increasing crop yields 50 percent, reverse the trend?

Java shares with many other underdeveloped nations a history of socioeconomic stratification and colonialism. Indigenous contrasts in wealth and power were intensified by Dutch colonialism. Although Indonesia gained political independence from the Netherlands in 1949, internal stratification continued. Today, contrasts between the wealthy (government employees, businesspeople, large landowners) and the poor (small-scale peasants) exist even in small farming communities. Stratification led to problems during Java's green revolution.

In 1963 the University of Indonesia's College of Agriculture launched a program in which students went to live in villages. They worked with peasants in the fields and shared their knowledge of new agricultural techniques while learning from the peasants. The program was a success. Yields in the affected villages increased by half. The program, directed by the Department of Agriculture, was expanded in 1964; nine universities and 400 students joined. These intervention programs succeeded where others had failed because the outside agents recognized that economic development rests not only on technological change but on political change as well. Students could observe firsthand how interest groups resisted attempts by peasants to improve their lot. Once, when local officials stole fertilizer destined for peasant fields, students got it back by threatening in a letter to turn evidence of the crime over to higher-level officials.

The combination of new work patterns and political action was achieving promising results when, in 1965–1966, there was an insurrection against the government. In the eventual military takeover, Indonesia's President Sukarno was ousted and replaced by President Suharto. Efforts to increase agricultural production resumed soon after Suharto took control. However, the new government assigned the task to multinational corporations based in Japan, West Germany, and Switzerland rather than to students and peasants. These industrial firms were to supply miracle rice and other high-yielding seeds, fertilizers, and pesticides. Peasants adopting the whole green revolution kit were eligible for loans that would allow them to buy food and other essentials in the lean period just before harvesting.

Java's green revolution soon encountered problems. One pesticide, which had never been tested in Java, killed the fish in the irrigation canals and thus destroyed an important protein resource. One development agency turned out to be a fraud, set up to benefit the military and government officials.

Java's green revolution also encountered problems at the village level because of entrenched interests. Traditionally, peasants had fed their families by taking temporary jobs, or borrowing, from wealthier villagers before the harvest. However, having accepted loans, the peasants were obliged to work for wages lower than those paid on the open market. Low-interest loans would have made peasants less dependent on wealthy villagers, thus depriving local patrons of cheap labor.

Local officials were put in charge of spreading information about how the program worked. Instead they limited peasant participation by withholding information. Wealthy villagers also discouraged peasant participation more subtly: They raised doubts about the effectiveness of the new techniques and about the wisdom of taking government loans when familiar patrons were nearby. Faced with the thought that starvation might follow if innovation failed, peasants were reluctant to take risks—an understandable reaction.

Production increased, but wealthy villagers rather than small-scale farmers reaped the benefits of the green revolution. Just 20 percent of one village's 151 households participated in the program. However, because they were the wealthiest households, headed by people who owned the most land, 40 percent of the land was being cultivated by means of the new system. Some large-scale landowners used their green revolution profits at the peasants' expense. They bought up peasants' small plots and purchased labor-saving machinery, including rice-milling machines and tractors. As a result, the poorest peasants lost both their means of subsistence— land—and local work opportunities. Their only recourse was to move to cities, where a growing pool of unskilled laborers depressed already low wages.

In a complementary view of the green revolution's social effects, Ann Stoler (1977) focused on gender and stratification. She took issue with Esther Boserup's (1970) contention that colonialism and development inevitably hurt Third World women more than men by favoring commercial agriculture and excluding women from it. Stoler found that the green revolution had permitted some women to gain power over other women and men. Javanese women were not a homogeneous group but varied by class. Stoler found that whether the green revolution helped or harmed Javanese women depended on their position in the class structure. The status of landholding women rose as they gained control over more land and the labor of more poor women. The new economy offered wealthier women higher profits, which they used in trading. However, poor women suffered along with poor men as traditional economic opportunities declined. Nevertheless, the poor women fared better than did the poor men, who had no access at all to off-farm work.

These studies of the local effects of the green revolution reveal results different from those foreseen by policy makers, planners, and the media. Again we see the unintended and undesirable effects of development programs that ignore traditional social, political, and economic divisions. New technology, no matter how promising, does not inevitably help the intended beneficiaries. It may very well hurt them if vested interests interfere. The Javanese student-peasant projects of the 1960s worked because peasants need not just technology but also political clout. But Java's green revolution program, although designed to alleviate poverty, actually increased it. Peasants stopped relying on their own subsistence production and started depending on a more volatile pursuit—cash sale of labor. Agricultural production became profit-oriented, machine-based, and chemical-dependent. Local autonomy diminished as linkages with the world system increased. Production rose, as the rich got richer and poverty increased.

Equity

A common goal, in theory at least, of development policy is to promote equity. **Increased equity** means reduced poverty and a more even distribution of wealth. However, if projects are to increase equity, they must have the support of reform-minded governments. Peasants oppose projects that interfere too much with their basic economic activities. Similarly, wealthy and powerful people resist projects that threaten their vested interests, and their resistance is usually more difficult to combat.

Some types of projects, particularly irrigation schemes, are more likely than others to widen wealth disparities, that is, to have a negative equity impact. An initial uneven distribution of resources (particularly land) often becomes the basis for greater skewing after the project. The social impact of new technology tends to be more severe, contributing negatively to quality of life and to equity, when inputs are channeled to or through the rich, as in Java's green revolution.

Many fisheries projects have also had negative equity results. In Bahia, Brazil (Kottak 1992), sailboat owners (but not nonowners) got loans to buy motors for their boats. To repay the loans, the owners increased the percentage of the catch they took from the men who fished in their boats. Over the years, they used the rising profits to buy larger and more expensive boats. The result was stratification—the creation of a group of wealthy people within a formerly egalitarian community. These events hampered individual initiative and interfered with further development of the fishing industry. With new boats so expensive, ambitious young men who once would have sought careers in fishing no longer had any way to obtain their own boats. To avoid such results, credit-granting agencies must seek out enterprising young fishers rather than giving loans only to owners and established businesspeople.

STRATEGIES FOR INNOVATION

Too many true local needs cry out for a solution to waste money by funding projects that are inappropriate in area A but needed in area B or unnecessary anywhere. Social expertise can sort out the A's and B's and fit the projects accordingly. Projects that put people first by responding to the needs for change they perceive must be identified. After that, social expertise is needed to ensure efficient and socially compatible ways of carrying out the projects.

In a comparative study of sixty-eight development projects from all over the world, I found the **culturally compatible economic development projects** to be twice as successful financially as the incompatible ones (Kottak 1990a, 1991). This finding shows that using anthropological expertise in planning, to ensure cultural compatibility, is cost-effective. To maximize social and economic benefits, projects must (1) be culturally compatible, (2) respond to locally perceived needs, (3) involve people in planning and carrying out the changes that affect them, (4) harness traditional organizations, and (5) be flexible. Applied anthropologists should not just implement (carry out) development policies; they are as qualified as economists are to make policy.

Overinnovation

In my comparative study, the compatible and successful projects avoided the fallacy of **overinnovation** (too much change). Instead, they (intuitively) applied Romer's rule, which was used in the chapter "The World System, Industrialism, and Stratification," to explain why the Industrial Revolution took place in England. Recall that Romer (1960) developed his rule to explain the evolution of land-dwelling vertebrates from fish. The ancestors of land animals lived in pools of water that dried up seasonally. Fins evolved into legs to enable those animals to get back to water when particular pools dried up. Thus an innovation (legs) that later proved essential to land life originated to maintain life in the water.

Romer's lesson is that an innovation that evolves to *maintain* a system can play a major role in *changing* that system. Evolution occurs in increments. Systems take a series of small steps to maintain themselves, and they gradually change. Romer's rule can be applied to economic development, which, after all, is a process of (planned) socioeconomic evolution. Applying Romer's rule to development, we would expect people to resist projects that require major changes in their daily lives, especially ones that interfere with subsistence pursuits. People usually want to change just enough to keep what they have. Motives for modifying behavior come from the traditional culture and the small concerns of ordinary life. Peasants' values are not such abstract ones as "learning a better way," "progressing," "increasing technical know-how," "improving efficiency," or "adopting modern techniques." (Those phrases exemplify intervention philosophy.) Instead, their objectives are down-to-earth and specific ones. People want to improve yields in a rice field, amass resources for a ceremony, get a child through school, or pay taxes. The goals and values of subsistence producers differ from those of people who produce for cash, just as they differ from the intervention philosophy of development planners. Different value systems must be considered during planning.

Project problems often arise from inadequate attention to, and consequent lack of fit with, local culture. In Ethiopia, overinnovative planners wanted to convert nomadic herders into sedentary farmers. The planners naively expected free-ranging herders to give up a generations-old way of life to work three times harder plowing, growing rice, and picking cotton.

Note that development guided by Romer's rule can even be compatible with social "revolutions" that reallocate land in highly stratified nations. If land reform permits peasants to go on farming their fields and get more of the product, it can be very successful.

Failed projects usually work in opposition to Romer's rule. For example, one South Asian project promoted the cultivation of onions and peppers, expecting this practice to fit into a preexisting labor-intensive system of rice growing. Cultivation of these cash crops wasn't traditional in the area. It conflicted with existing crop priorities and other interests of farmers. The labor peaks for pepper and onion production coincided with those for rice, to which farmers gave priority.

Throughout the world, project problems have arisen from inadequate attention to, and consequent lack of fit with, local culture. Another naive and incompatible project was an overinnovative scheme in Ethiopia. Its major fallacy was to try to convert nomadic herders into sedentary cultivators. It ignored traditional land rights. Outsiders—commercial farmers—were to get much of the herders' territory. The pastoralists were expected to settle down and start farming. This project neglected social and cultural issues. It helped wealthy outsiders instead of the natives. The planners naively expected free-ranging herders to give up a generations-old way of life to work three times harder growing rice and picking cotton.

Underdifferentiation

The fallacy of **underdifferentiation** is the tendency to view the less developed countries as more alike than they are. Development agencies have often ignored cultural diversity (e.g., between Brazil and Burundi) and adopted a uniform approach to deal with very different sets of people. Neglecting cultural diversity, many projects also have tried to impose incompatible property notions and social units. Most often, the faulty social design assumes either (1) individualistic productive units that are privately owned by an individual or couple and worked by a nuclear family or (2) cooperatives that are at least partially based on models from the former Eastern bloc and Socialist countries.

Often development aims at generating *individual* cash wealth through exports. This goal contrasts with the tendency of bands and tribes to share resources and depend on local ecosystems and renewable resources (Bodley 1988). Development planners commonly emphasize benefits that will accrue to individuals; more concern with the effects on communities is needed (Bodley 1988).

One example of faulty Euro-American models (the individual and the nuclear family) was a West African project designed for an area where the extended family was the basic social unit. The project succeeded despite its faulty social design because the participants used their traditional extended family networks to attract additional settlers. Eventually, twice as many people as planned benefitted as extended family members flocked to the project area. This case shows that local people are not helpless victims of the world system. Settlers modified the project design that had been imposed on them by using the principles of their traditional society.

The second dubious foreign social model that is common in development strategy is the cooperative. In my comparative study of development projects, new cooperatives fared badly. Cooperatives succeeded only when they harnessed preexisting local-level communal institutions. This is a corollary of a more general rule: Participants' groups are most effective when they are based on traditional social organization or on a socioeconomic similarity among members.

Neither foreign social model—the nuclear family farm or the cooperative—has an unblemished record in development. An alternative is needed: greater use of Third World social models for Third World development. These are traditional social units, such as the clans, lineages, and other extended kinship groups of Africa, Oceania, and many nations, with their communally held estates and resources. The most humane and productive strategy for change is to base the social design for innovation on traditional social forms in each target area.

Third World Models and Culturally Appropriate Development

Many governments lack a genuine commitment to improving the lives of their citizens. Interference by major powers has also kept governments from enacting needed

Third World models for Third World development include traditional
cultural and social units, such as the extended kinship groups of Africa
and Oceania. The social design for innovation should be based on
existing groups and institutions in each target area. A traditional system
of planning and management by Hindu temples has been harnessed for
culturally appropriate agricultural development in Bali, Indonesia.

reforms. In many highly stratified societies, particularly in Latin America, the class structure is very rigid. Movement of individuals into the middle class is difficult. It is equally hard to raise the living standards of the lower class as a whole. These nations have a long history of control of government by powerful interest groups that tend to oppose reform.

In some nations, however, the government acts more as an agent of the people. Madagascar provides an example. As in many areas of Africa, precolonial states had developed in Madagascar before its conquest by the French in 1895. The people of Madagascar, the Malagasy, had been organized into descent groups before the origin of the state. Imerina, the major precolonial state of Madagascar, wove descent groups into its structure, making members of important groups advisers to the king and thus giving them authority in government. Imerina made provisions for the people it ruled. It collected taxes and organized labor for public works projects. In return, it redistributed resources to peasants in need. It also granted them some protection against war and slave raids and allowed them to cultivate their rice fields in peace. The government maintained the waterworks for rice cultivation. It opened to ambitious peasant boys the chance of becoming, through hard work and study, state bureaucrats.

Throughout the history of Imerina—and continuing in modern Madagascar—there have been strong relationships between the individual, the descent group, and the state. Local Malagasy communities, where residence is based on descent, are more cohesive and homogeneous than are communities in Java or Latin America. Madagascar gained political independence from France in 1960. Although it was still economically dependent on France when I first did research there in 1966–1967, the new government was committed to a form of socialist development. Its economic development schemes were increasing the ability of the Malagasy to feed themselves. Government policy emphasized increased production of rice, a subsistence crop, rather than cash crops. Furthermore, local communities, with their traditional cooperative patterns and solidarity based on kinship and descent, were treated as partners in, not obstacles to, the development process.

In a sense, the descent group is preadapted to equitable national development. In Madagascar, members of local descent groups have customarily pooled their resources to educate their ambitious members. Once educated, these men and women gain economically secure positions in the nation. They then share the advantages of their new positions with their kin. For example, they give room and board to rural cousins attending school and help them find jobs.

Malagasy administrators appear generally to have shared a commitment to democratic economic development. Perhaps this is because government officials are of the peasantry or have strong personal ties to it. By contrast, in Latin American countries, the elites and the lower class have different origins and no strong connections through kinship, descent, or marriage.

Furthermore, societies with descent-group organization contradict an assumption that many social scientists and economists seem to make. It is not inevitable that

Culturally Appropriate Marketing

Innovation succeeds best when it is culturally appropriate. This axiom of applied anthropology could guide the international spread not only of development projects but also of businesses, such as fast food. Each time McDonald's or Burger King expands to a new nation, it must devise a culturally appropriate strategy for fitting into the new setting.

McDonald's has been successful internationally, with a quarter of its sales outside the United States. One area where McDonald's is expanding successfully is Brazil, where 30 to 40 million middle-class people, most living in densely packed cities, provide a concentrated market for a fast-food chain. Still, it took McDonald's some time to find the right marketing strategy for Brazil.

In 1980 I visited Brazil after a seven-year absence. One manifestation of Brazil's growing participation in the world economy was the appearance of two McDonald's restaurants in Rio de Janeiro. There wasn't much difference between Brazilian and American McDonald's. The restaurants looked alike. The menu was more or less the same, as was the taste of the quarter-pounders. I picked up an artifact, a white paper bag with yellow lettering, exactly like the take-out bags then used in American McDonald's. An advertising device, it carried several messages about how Brazilians could bring McDonald's into their lives. However, it seemed to me that McDonald's Brazilian ad campaign was missing some important points about how fast food should be marketed in a culture that values large, leisurely lunches.

The bag proclaimed, "You're going to enjoy the [McDonald's] difference," and listed several "favorite places where you can enjoy McDonald's products." This list confirmed that the marketing people were trying to adapt to Brazilian middle-class culture, but they were making some mistakes. "When you go out in the car with the kids" transferred the uniquely developed North American cultural combination of highways, affordable cars, and suburban living to the very different context of urban Brazil. A similar suggestion was "traveling to the country place." Even Brazilians who own country places can't find McDonald's, still confined to the cities, on the road. The ad creator had apparently never attempted to drive up to a fast-food restaurant in a neighborhood with no parking spaces.

Several other suggestions pointed customers toward the beach, where *cariocas* (Rio natives) do spend much of their leisure time. One could eat McDonald's products "after a dip in the ocean," "at a picnic at the beach," or "watching the surfers." These suggestions ignored the Brazilian custom of consuming cold things, such as beer, soft drinks, ice cream, and ham and cheese sandwiches, at the beach. Brazilians don't consider a hot, greasy hamburger proper beach food. They view the sea as "cold" and hamburgers as "hot"; they avoid "hot" foods at the beach.

Also culturally dubious was the suggestion to eat McDonald's hamburgers "lunching at the office." Brazilians prefer their main meal at midday, often eating at a leisurely pace with business associates. Many firms serve ample lunches to their employees. Other workers take advantage of a two-hour lunch break to go home to eat with the spouse and children. Nor did it make sense to suggest that children should eat hamburgers for lunch, since most kids attend school for half-day sessions and have lunch at home. Two other suggestions—"waiting for the bus" and "in the beauty parlor"—did describe common aspects of daily life in a Brazilian city. However, these settings have not proved especially inviting to hamburgers or fish filets.

The homes of Brazilians who can afford McDonald's products have cooks and maids to do many of the things that fast-food restaurants do in the United States. The suggestion that McDonald's products be eaten "while watching your favorite television program" is culturally appropriate, because Brazilians watch TV a lot. However, Brazil's consuming classes can ask the cook to make a snack when hunger strikes. Indeed, much televiewing occurs during the light dinner served when the husband gets home from the office.

Most appropriate to the Brazilian lifestyle was the suggestion to enjoy McDonald's "on the cook's day off." Throughout Brazil, Sunday is that day. The Sunday pattern for middle-class families is a trip to the beach, liters of beer, a full midday meal around 3 P.M., and a light evening snack. McDonald's has found its niche in the Sunday evening meal, when families flock to the fast-food restaurant, and it is to this market that its advertising is now appropriately geared.

McDonald's is expanding rapidly in Brazilian cities, and in Brazil as in North America, teenage appetites are fueling the fast-food explosion. As McDonald's outlets appeared in urban neighborhoods, Brazilian teenagers used them for after-school snacks, while families had evening meals there. As an anthropologist could have predicted, the fast-food industry has not revolutionized Brazilian food and meal customs. Rather, McDonald's is succeeding because it has adapted to preexisting Brazilian cultural patterns.

The main contrast with North America is that the Brazilian evening meal is lighter. McDonald's now caters to the evening meal rather than to lunch. Once McDonald's realized that more money could be made by fitting in with, rather than trying to Americanize, Brazilian meal habits, it started aiming its advertising at that goal.

as nations become more tied to the world capitalist economy, native forms of social organization will break down into nuclear family organization, impersonality, and alienation. Descent groups, with their traditional communalism and corporate solidarity, have important roles to play in economic development.

The use of descent groups in Malagasy rice production exemplifies culturally appropriate innovation. So does a successful Papua-New Guinea resettlement project. Here, participants used their profits just as (in Romer's study) the ancestors of land vertebrates had used their finlike legs. They changed (began producing palm oil for sale) not to forge a brand-new lifestyle but to keep their ties with home. The settlers constantly revisited their homelands and invested in its social life and ceremonies. This cash-crop project fit Oceanian values and customs involving competition for wealth and capital, such as big-man systems. The settlers came from different tribes, but intertribal mingling was already part of local experience. Marriage between people who speak different dialects and languages is common in Papua-New Guinea, as is participation in common religious movements.

Realistic development promotes change but not overinnovation. Many changes are possible if the aim is to preserve local systems while making them work better. Successful projects respect, or at least don't attack, local cultural patterns. Effective development draws on indigenous cultural practices and social structures.

SUMMARY

Development plans are usually guided by some kind of intervention philosophy, an ideological justification for outsiders to direct native peoples toward particular goals. Development is usually justified by the belief that industrialization, modernization, westernization, and individualism are desirable and beneficial evolutionary advances. However, bands and tribes, with their low-energy adaptations, usually manage resources better than industrial states do. Many problems that Third World people face today are due to their position within nation-states and their increasing dependence on the world cash economy.

Conflicts between governments and natives may arise when outsiders claim resources on tribal lands. There has been worldwide intrusion on indigenous peoples and their local ecosystems by roads, mining, hydroelectric projects, ranching, lumbering, agribusiness, and planned colonization.

Increasingly, government agencies, international groups, and private foundations are encouraging attention to local-level social factors and the cultural dimension of social change and economic development. Anthropologists work in organizations that promote, manage, and assess programs that affect human life in the United States and abroad.

Development projects that replace subsistence pursuits with economies dependent on the unpredictable alternations of the world capitalist economy can be especially damaging. Research in Java found that the green revolution was failing because it stressed new technology rather than a combination of technology and peasant political organization. Java's green revolution was increasing poverty rather than ending it, although women were not as hard hit by the new economy as men were. Because so many projects have failed for social and political reasons, development organizations are increasingly using anthropologists in planning, supervision, and evaluation.

Governments are not equally committed to eradicating poverty and increasing equity. Local interest groups often oppose reform, and resistance by elites is especially hard to combat. Culturally compatible projects tend to be more financially successful than incompatible ones are. This means that the use of anthropological expertise in development not only promotes more humane changes but is also cost-effective.

Compatible and successful projects avoid the fallacy of overinnovation and apply Romer's rule: An innovation that evolves to maintain a system can play a major role in changing that system. Natives are unlikely to cooperate with projects that require major changes in their daily lives, especially ones that interfere too much with customary subsistence pursuits. People usually want to change just enough to keep what they have. Peasants' motives to change come from their traditional culture and the small concerns of everyday existence. Peasant values are not abstract and long-term and thus differ from those of development planners.

The fallacy of underdifferentiation refers to the tendency to see less developed countries as an undifferentiated group. Neglecting cultural diversity and the local context, many projects impose culturally biased and incompatible property notions and social units on the intended beneficiaries. The most common flawed social models are the nuclear family farm and the cooperative, neither of which has an unblemished record in development. A more promising alternative is to harness Third World social units for purposes of development. These traditional social forms include the clans, lineages, and other extended kinship groups of Africa and Oceania, with their communally held resources. The most productive strategy for change is to base the social design for innovation on traditional social forms in each target area.

CHAPTER FOURTEEN

Cultural Exchange and Survival

PEOPLE IN MOTION

DOMINATION
Development and Environmentalism ~ BOX: Voices of the Rainforest ~
Religious Domination

RESISTANCE AND SURVIVAL
Weapons of the Weak ~ Cultural Imperialism, Stimulus Diffusion, and
Creative Opposition

MAKING AND REMAKING CULTURE
Popular Culture ~ Indigenizing Popular Culture ~ A World System
of Images ~ A Transnational Culture of Consumption

THE CONTINUANCE OF DIVERSITY

I n a global culture that heralds diversity, the linkages in the modern world system have both enlarged and erased old boundaries and distinctions. Arjun Appadurai (1990, p. 1) characterizes today's world as a "translocal" "interactive system" that is "strikingly new." Whether as refugees, migrants, tourists, pilgrims, proselytizers, laborers, businesspeople, development workers, employees of nongovernmental organizations (NGOs), politicians, soldiers, sports figures, or media-borne images, people travel more than ever.

So important is transnational migration that many Mexican villagers find "their most important kin and friends are as likely to be living hundreds or thousands of miles away as immediately around them" (Rouse 1991). Most migrants maintain their ties with their native land (phoning, visiting, sending money, watching "ethnic TV"), so that, in a sense, they live multilocally—in different places at once. Dominicans in New York City, for example, have been characterized as living "between two islands"—Manhattan and the Dominican Republic (Grasmuck and Pessar 1991). Many Dominicans—like migrants from other countries—migrate to the United States temporarily, seeking cash to transform their lifestyles when they return to the Caribbean.

PEOPLE IN MOTION

With so many people "in motion," the unit of anthropological study expands from the local community to the **diaspora**—the offspring of an area who have spread to many lands. Anthropologists increasingly follow descendants of the villages we have studied as they move from rural to urban areas and across national boundaries. For the 1991 annual meeting of the American Anthropological Association in Chicago, the anthropologist Robert Van Kemper organized a session of presentations about long-term ethnographic fieldwork. Kemper's own longtime research focus has been the Mexican village of Tzintzuntzan, which, with his mentor George Foster, Kemper has studied for decades. However, their database now includes not just Tzintzuntzan but its descendants all over the world (one of whom reached Alaska in 1990). Given the Tzintzuntzan diaspora, Kemper was even able to use some of his time in Chicago to visit people from Tzintzuntzan who had established a colony there. In today's world, as people move, they take their traditions, and their anthropologists, along with them.

Postmodernity describes our time and situation—today's world in flux, these people on the move who have learned to manage multiple identities depending on place and context. In its most general sense, **postmodern** refers to the blurring and breakdown of established canons (rules or standards), categories, distinctions, and boundaries. The word is taken from **postmodernism**—a style and movement in architecture that succeeded modernism, beginning in the 1970s. Postmodern architecture rejected the rules, geometric order, and austerity of modernism. Modernist buildings were expected to have a clear and functional design. Postmodern design is "messier" and more playful. It draws on a diversity of styles from different times and places—including popular, ethnic, and non-Western cultures. Postmodernism extends "value" well beyond classic, elite, and Western cultural forms. *Postmodern* is now used to describe comparable developments in music, literature, and visual art. From this origin, *postmodernity* describes a world in which traditional standards, contrasts, groups, boundaries, and identities are opening up, reaching out, and breaking down.

Globalization describes the accelerating links between nations and people in a world system connected economically, politically, and by modern media and transportation. Globalization promotes intercultural communication, including travel and migration, which bring people from different cultures into direct contact. The world is more integrated than ever. Yet *dis*integration also surrounds us. Nations dissolve (Yugoslavia, Czechoslovakia, the Soviet Union), as do political blocs (the Warsaw Pact nations) and ideologies (communism). The notion of a "Free World" collapses because it existed mainly in opposition to a group of "Captive Nations"—a label that has lost much of its meaning.

Simultaneously new kinds of political and ethnic units are emerging. Ethnicity, "once a genie contained in the bottle of some sort of locality . . . has now become a global force, forever slipping in and through the cracks between states and borders"

(Appadurai 1990, p. 15). For example, not only do Native American cultures survive, there is a growing Panindian identity, and an international Pantribal movement as well. Thus, in June 1992, the World Conference of Indigenous Peoples met in Rio de Janeiro concurrently with UNCED (the United Nations Conference on the Environment and Development). Along with diplomats, journalists, and environmentalists came 300 representatives of the tribal diversity that survives in the modern world—from Lapland to Mali (Brooke 1992).

DOMINATION

Different degrees of destruction, domination, resistance, survival, adaptation, and modification of native cultures may follow interethnic contact. In the most destructive encounters native and subordinate cultures face obliteration. Yet in many modern arenas the contact leads to cultural exchange. Today many non-Western cultures are making important contributions to an emerging world culture.

In cases where contact between indigenous cultures and more powerful outsiders leads to destruction—a situation most characteristic of colonialist and expansionist eras—a "shock phase" often follows the initial encounter (Bodley, ed. 1988). Traders and settlers may exploit the native people. Such exploitation may increase mortality, disrupt subsistence, fragment kin groups, damage social support systems, and inspire new religious movements (Bodley, ed. 1988). There may be civil repression backed by military force. Such factors may lead to the tribe's cultural collapse (*ethnocide*) or its physical extinction (*genocide*).

More recently, in the development/modernization era, native landscapes and their traditional management systems have been attacked and often destroyed. Outsiders often attempt to remake native landscapes and cultures in their own image. A name for this process—"terraforming"—can be borrowed from science fiction. Anticipating space exploration and planetary colonization, science fiction writers have imagined a policy of **terraforming.** This refers to the use of technology to make other worlds as much like earth (*terra*) as possible—so that earth colonists can feel at home.

By analogy, we can say that dominant nations and cultures have "terraformed" right here on earth. Political and economic colonialists have tried to redesign conquered and dependent lands, peoples, and cultures, imposing their cultural standards on others. The aim of many agricultural development projects, for example, seems to have been to make the world as much like Iowa as possible, complete with mechanized farming and nuclear family ownership—despite the fact that these models may be inappropriate for settings outside the North American heartland.

Development and Environmentalism

Today it is often multinational corporations, usually based in core nations, rather than the governments of those nations, that are changing the nature of Third World economies. However, nations do tend to support the predatory enterprises that seek cheap labor and raw materials in countries outside the core, such as Brazil, where economic development has contributed to ecological devastation.

Simultaneously, environmentalists from core nations increasingly preach ecological morality to the rest of the world. This doesn't play very well in Brazil, whose Amazon is a focus of environmentalist attention. Brazilians complain that northerners talk about global needs and saving the Amazon after having destroyed their own forests for First World economic growth. Akbar Ahmed (1992) finds the non-Western world to be cynical about Western ecological morality, seeing it as yet another imperialist message. "The Chinese have cause to snigger at the Western suggestion that they forgo the convenience of the fridge to save the ozone layer" (Ahmed 1992, p. 120).

In the last chapter we saw that development projects usually fail if they try to replace native forms with culturally alien property concepts and productive units. A strategy that incorporates the native forms is more effective than the fallacies of overinnovation and underdifferentiation. To those fallacies in promoting cultural diffusion, we may add "the fallacy of the noble global." This refers to a modern intervention philosophy that seeks to impose global ecological morality without due attention to cultural variation and autonomy. Countries and cultures may resist interventionist philosophies aimed at either development or globally oriented environmentalism.

A clash of cultures related to environmental change may occur when *development threatens indigenous peoples and their environments.* Native groups like the Kayapó Indians of Brazil and the Kaluli of Papua-New Guinea (see box) may be threatened by regional, national, and international development plans (such as a dam or commercially driven deforestation) that would *destroy* their homelands.

A second clash of cultures related to environmental change occurs when *external regulation threatens indigenous peoples.* Native groups may be harmed by regional, national, and international environmental plans that seek to *save* their homelands. Sometimes outsiders expect local people to give up many of their customary economic and cultural activities without clear substitutes, alternatives, or incentives. The traditional approach to conservation has been to restrict access to protected areas, hire park guards, and punish violators.

Problems often arise when external regulation replaces the native system. Like development projects, conservation schemes may ask people to change the way they have been doing things for generations to satisfy planners' goals rather than local goals. In locales as different as Madagascar, Brazil, and the Pacific Northwest of North America people are being asked, told, or forced to change or abandon basic economic activities because to do so is good for "nature" or "the globe." Ironically, well-meaning conservation efforts can be as insensitive as development schemes that promote radical changes without involving local people in planning and carrying out the policies that affect them. When people are asked to give up the basis of their livelihood, they usually resist.

Voices of the Rainforest

T he government of Papua-New Guinea has approved oil exploration by American, British, Australian, and Japanese companies in the rainforest habitat of the Kaluli and other indigenous peoples. The forest degradation that usually accompanies logging, ranching, road building, and drilling endangers plants, animals, peoples, and cultures. Lost along with trees are songs, myths, words, ideas, artifacts, and techniques—the cultural knowledge and practices of rainforest people like the Kaluli, whom the anthropologist and ethnomusicologist Steven Feld has been studying for more than fifteen years.

Feld teamed up with Mickey Hart of the Grateful Dead in a project designed to promote the cultural survival of the Kaluli through their music. For years Hart has worked to preserve musical diversity through educational funding, concert promotion, and recording, including a successful series called "The World" on the Rykodisc label. *Voices of the Rainforest*, released in that series in April 1991, is the first CD completely devoted to indigenous music from Papua-New Guinea. In one hour it encapsulates twenty-four hours of a day in Kaluli life in Bosavi village. The recording permits a form of cultural survival and diffusion in a high-quality commercial product. Bosavi is presented as a "soundscape" of blended music and natural environmental sounds. Kaluli weave the natural sounds of birds, frogs, rivers, and streams into their texts, melodies, and rhythms. They sing and whistle with birds and waterfalls. They compose instrumental duets with birds and cicadas.

The rock star Sting, known for his support of the Amazon rainforest and the Kayapó Indians, isn't the only media figure working to save endangered habitats, peoples, and cultures. The Kaluli project was launched on Earth Day 1991 at *Star Wars* creator George Lucas's Skywalker Ranch. There Randy Hayes, the executive director of the Rainforest Action Network, and musician Mickey Hart spoke about the linked issues of rainforest destruction and musical survival. Next came a San Francisco benefit dinner for the Bosavi People's Fund. This is the trust established to receive royalties from the Kaluli recording—a financial prong in Steven Feld's strategy to foster Kaluli cultural survival.

Voices of the Rainforest is being marketed as "world music." This term is intended to point up musical diversity, the fact that music originates from all world regions and cultures. Our postmodern world recognizes more than one canon (standard for excellence). In the postmodern view, "tribal" music joins Western "classical" music as a form of artistic expression worth performing, hearing, and preserving. Hart's series offers music of non-Western origin as well as that of ethnically dominated groups of the Western world. Like Paul Simon's recordings *Graceland* and *Rhythm of the Saints*, which draw on African and Brazilian music, a "world music" record series helps blur the boundaries between the exotic and the familiar. The local and the global unite in a transnational popular culture.

Hart's record series aims at preserving "endangered music" against the artistic loss suffered by indigenous peoples. Its intent is to give a "world voice" to people who are being silenced by the dominant world system. In 1993, Hart launched a new series, *The Library of Congress Endangered Music Project*, which will include digitally remastered field recordings collected by the American Folklife Center. The first of this series, "The Spirit Cries," concentrates on music from a broad range of cultures in South and Central America and the Caribbean. Proceeds from this project will be used to support the performers and their cultural traditions.

In *Voices of the Rainforest*, Feld and Hart excised all "modern" and "dominant" sounds from their recording. Gone are the world-system sounds that Kaluli villagers now hear every day. The recording temporarily silences "machine voices": the tractor that cuts the grass on the local airstrip, the gas generator, the sawmill, the helicopters and light planes buzzing to and from the oil-drilling areas. Gone, too, are the village church bells, Bible readings, evangelical prayers and hymns, and the voices of teachers and students at an English-only school.

Initially, Feld anticipated criticism for attempting to create an idealized Kaluli "soundscape" insulated from invasive forces and sounds. Among the Kaluli he expected varied opinions about the value of his project:

> It is a soundscape world that some Kaluli care little about, a world that other Kaluli momentarily choose to forget, a world that some Kaluli are increasingly nostalgic and uneasy about, a world that other Kaluli are still living and creating and listening to. It is a sound world that increasingly fewer Kaluli will actively know about and value, but one that increasingly more Kaluli will only hear on cassette and sentimentally wonder about. (Feld 1991, p. 137)

Despite these concerns, Feld was met with an overwhelmingly positive response when he returned to Papua-New Guinea in 1992 armed with a boombox and the recording. The Education Department has put copies of the recording into every high school library. The people of Bosavi also reacted very favorably. Not only did they appreciate the recording, they have also been able to build a much-needed community school with the *Voices of the Rainforest* royalties that have been donated to the Bosavi People's Fund.

Source: Based on Steven Feld, "Voices of the Rainforest," *Public Culture* 4(1): 131–140 (1991).

Native peoples, such as these Tanala ("Forest People") of eastern Madagascar, may be threatened by development plans that would destroy their homelands. Ironically, native groups may also be harmed by environmental plans that seek to save their homelands. Because environmental preservation depends on local cooperation, conservation schemes must be culturally appropriate.

Religious Domination

Religious proselytizing can promote ethnocide, as native beliefs and practices are replaced by Western ones. Sometimes a religion and associated customs are completely replaced by ideology and behavior more compatible with Western culture. One example is the Handsome Lake religion (as described in the chapter on religion), which led the Iroquois Indians to copy European farming techniques, stressing male rather than female labor. The Iroquois also gave up their communal longhouses and matrilineal descent groups for nuclear family households. The teachings of Handsome Lake led to a new church and religion. This revitalization movement helped the Iroquois survive in a drastically modified environment, but much ethnocide was involved.

Handsome Lake was a native who created a new religion, drawing on Western models. More commonly, missionaries and proselytizers representing the major world religions, especially Christianity and Islam, are the proponents of religious change. Protestant and Catholic missionization continues even in remote corners of the world. Evangelical Protestantism, for example, is advancing in Peru, Brazil, and other parts of Latin America. It challenges a jaded Catholicism that has too few priests and that is sometimes seen mainly as women's religion.

Sometimes the political ideology of a nation-state (for example, "godless communism") is pitted against traditional religion. Officials of the former Soviet empire discouraged Catholicism, Judaism, and Islam. In Central Asia, Soviet dominators destroyed Muslim mosques and discouraged religious practice. On the other hand, governments often use their power to advance a religion, such as Islam in Iran or Sudan. A military government seized power in Sudan in 1989. It immediately launched a campaign to change that country of 25 million people, where one-third are not Muslims, into an Islamic nation.

RESISTANCE AND SURVIVAL

Systems of domination—political, cultural, or religious—always have their more muted aspects along with their public dimensions. In studying apparent cultural domination, or actual political domination, we must pay careful attention to what lies beneath the surface of evident, public, behavior. In public the oppressed may seem to accept their own domination, but they always question it offstage. James Scott (1990) uses **"public transcript"** to describe the open, public interactions between dominators and oppressed—the outer shell of power relations. He uses **"hidden transcript"** to describe the critique of power that goes on offstage, where the power holders can't see it.

In public the oppressed and the elites observe the etiquette of power relations. The dominants act like haughty masters while their subordinates show humility and defer. Antonio Gramsci (1971) developed the concept of **hegemony** for a stratified social order in which subordinates comply with domination by internalizing its values and accepting its "naturalness" (this is the way things were meant to be). According to Pierre Bourdieu (1977, p. 164) every social order tries to make its own arbitrariness (including its oppression) seem natural. All hegemonic ideologies offer explanations about why the existing order is in everyone's interest. Often promises are made (things will get better if you're patient). Gramsci and others use the idea of hegemony to explain why people conform even without coercion, why they knuckle under when they don't really have to.

Hegemony, the internalization of a dominant ideology, is one way to curb resistance. Another way is to let subordinates know they will eventually gain power—as young people usually foresee when they let their elders dominate them. Another way of curbing resistance is to separate or isolate subordinates and supervise them closely. According to Michel Foucault (1979), describing control over prisoners, solitude (as in solitary confinement) is an effective way to induce submission. Subordinates may conclude that the severity of punishment makes open resistance too risky.

Weapons of the Weak

Often, situations that seem to be hegemonic do have active resistance, but it is individual and disguised rather than collective and defiant. Scott (1985) uses Malay peasants, among whom he did fieldwork, to illustrate small-scale acts of resistance—which he calls "weapons of the weak." The Malay peasants used an indirect strategy to resist a corrupt Islamic tithe (religious tax). The goods (usually rice) that peasants had to give went to the provincial capital. In theory, the tithe would come back as charity, but it never did. Peasants didn't resist the tithe by rioting, demonstrating, or protesting. Instead they used a "nibbling" strategy, based on small acts of resistance. For example, they failed to declare their land or lied about the amount they farmed. They underpaid or delivered rice paddy contaminated with water, rocks, or mud, to add weight. Because of this resistance, only 15 percent of what was due was actually paid (Scott 1990, p. 89).

Subordinates also use various strategies to resist *publicly*, but again, usually in disguised form. Discontent may be expressed in public rituals and language, including metaphors, euphemisms, and folktales. For example, trickster tales (like the Brer Rabbit stories told by slaves in the southern United States) celebrate the wiles of the weak as they triumph over the strong.

Resistance is most likely to be expressed openly when the oppressed are allowed to assemble. The hidden transcript may be publicly revealed on such occasions. People see their dreams and anger shared by others with whom they haven't been in direct contact. The oppressed may draw courage from the crowd, from its visual and emotional impact and its anonymity. Sensing danger, the elites discourage such public gatherings. They try to limit and control holidays, funerals, dances, festivals, and other occasions that might unite the oppressed. Thus in the southern United States gatherings of five or more slaves were forbidden unless a white person was present.

Factors that interfere with community formation—such as geographic, linguistic, and ethnic separation—also work to curb resistance. Consequently, southern U.S. plantation owners sought slaves with diverse cultural and linguistic backgrounds. But such divisive factors can be overcome. Despite the measures used to divide them, the slaves resisted, developing their own popular culture, linguistic codes, and religious vision. The masters taught portions of the Bible that stressed compliance, but the slaves seized on the story of Moses, the promised land, and deliverance. The cornerstone of slave religion became the idea of a reversal in the conditions of whites and blacks. Slaves also resisted directly, through sabotage and flight. In many New World areas slaves managed to establish free communities in the hills and other isolated areas (Price, ed. 1973).

Because of its costumed anonymity and its ritual structure (reversal), Carnival is an excellent arena for expressing normally suppressed speech. This is vividly symbolized by these Carnival headdresses in Trinidad.

Hidden transcripts tend to be publicly expressed at certain times (festivals and Carnivals) and in certain places (for example, markets). Because of its costumed anonymity and its ritual structure (reversal), Carnival is an excellent arena for expressing normally suppressed speech and aggression—antihegemonic discourse. (**Discourse** includes talk, speeches, gestures, and actions.) Carnivals, public rituals of reversal, celebrate freedom through immodesty, dancing, gluttony, and sexuality (DaMatta 1991). Carnival may begin as a playful outlet for frustrations built up during the year. Over time it may evolve into a powerful annual critique of domination and a threat to the established order (Gilmore 1987). (Recognizing that ceremonial license could turn into political defiance, the Spanish dictator Francisco Franco outlawed Carnival.)

Cultural Imperialism, Stimulus Diffusion, and Creative Opposition

Cultural imperialism refers to the rapid spread or advance of one culture at the expense of others, or its imposition on other cultures, which it modifies, replaces, or destroys—usually because of differential economic or political influence. Thus children in the French colonial empire learned French history, language, and culture from standard textbooks also used in France. Tahitians, Malagasy, Vietnamese, and

Senegalese learned the French language by reciting from books about "our ancestors the Gauls." Ironically, modern French intellectuals, seemingly forgetting France's colonialist past, are quick to complain about American cultural imperialism. Thus in 1992 French intellectuals protested the opening of Euro Disney as a threat to French (and European) culture. The French minister of culture Jack Lang lamented the extent to which American films and TV programs (purportedly) dominate popular culture in many countries.

The matter isn't as simple as the French intellectuals imagine. People aren't passive victims of cultural imperialism. Contemporary people—often with considerable creativity—constantly revise, rework, resist, and reject the messages they get from external systems.

Some critics worry that modern technology, including the mass media, is killing off traditional cultures by homogenizing products to reach more people. But others see an important role for modern technology in allowing social groups (local cultures) to express themselves and thus in disseminating particular subcultures (Marcus and Fisher 1986, p. 122). Modern radio and TV, for example, constantly bring local happenings (for example, a "chicken festival" in Iowa) to the attention of a larger public. The North American media play a role in stimulating local activities of many sorts. Similarly in Brazil, local practices, celebrations, and performances are changing in the context of outside forces, including the mass media and tourism.

In the town of Arembepe, TV coverage has stimulated participation in a traditional annual performance, the *Chegança*. This is a fishermen's dance-play that reenacts the Portuguese discovery of Brazil. Arembepeiros have traveled to the state capital to perform the *Chegança* before television cameras, for a TV program featuring traditional performances from many rural communities. Here one sees television's role in allowing social groups to express themselves and in disseminating local cultures.

One national Brazilian Sunday-night variety program (*Fantástico*) is especially popular in rural areas because it shows such local events. In several towns along the Amazon River, annual folk ceremonies are now staged more lavishly for TV cameras. In the Amazon town of Parantíns, for example, boatloads of tourists arriving any time of year are shown a videotape of the town's annual Bumba Meu Boi festival. This is a costumed performance mimicking bullfighting, parts of which have been shown on *Fantástico*. This pattern, in which communities preserve, revive, and intensify the scale of traditional ceremonies to perform for TV and tourists, is expanding.

However, Brazilian television has also played a "top-down" role, by spreading the popularity of national (and international) holidays like Carnival and Christmas (Kottak 1990b). TV has aided the national spread of Carnival beyond its traditional urban centers, especially Rio de Janeiro. Still, local reactions to the nationwide broadcasting of Carnival and its trappings (elaborate parades, costumes, and frenzied dancing) are not simple or uniform responses to external stimuli. These new forms of popular expression are cultural creations that develop from the interplay of local, regional, national, and international forces.

Rather than direct adoption of Carnival, or rote imitation of it, local Brazilians respond in various ways. These reactions include "stimulus diffusion" and "creative opposition." **Stimulus diffusion** describes the process by which a group modifies a custom by adopting images and behavior associated with an external practice, without borrowing the practice itself. We see stimulus diffusion when Brazilians don't take up Carnival itself but modify their local festivities to fit Carnival images. **Creative opposition** occurs when people change their behavior as they consciously and actively avoid or spurn an external image or practice. We see creative opposition when local Brazilians deliberately reject Carnival, sometimes by celebrating traditional local festivals on a previously unimagined scale, sometimes by rejecting certain local practices perceived as similar to the disdained external practice.

In Brazilian towns national Carnival coverage seems more often to inspire stimulus diffusion than direct borrowing through simple imitation. Local groups work hard not on Carnival per se but on incorporating its elements and themes in their own ceremonies. Some of these have grown in scale, in imitation of Carnival celebrations shown on national TV. But local reactions can also be negative, even hostile. One example is Arembepe, where Carnival has never been important, probably because of its calendrical closeness to the main local festival, which is held in February to honor Saint Francis of Assisi. In the past, villagers couldn't afford to celebrate both occasions. Now, not only do the people of Arembepe reject Carnival, they are also increasingly hostile to their own main festival. Arembepeiros resent the fact that Saint Francis has become "an outsiders' event," because it draws thousands of tourists to Arembepe each February. The villagers think that commercial interests and outsiders have appropriated Saint Francis.

In creative opposition, many Arembepeiros now say they like and participate more in the traditional June festivals honoring Saint John, Saint Peter, and Saint Anthony. In the past these were observed on a much smaller scale than was Saint Francis. Arembepeiros celebrate them now with a new vigor and enthusiasm, as they react to outsiders and their celebrations, real and televised.

MAKING AND REMAKING CULTURE

Any media-borne image, such as Carnival, can be considered a **text**—something that is creatively "read," interpreted, and assigned meaning by each person who receives it. Carnival images in Brazil illustrate some ways in which "readers" produce their own meanings from a text. Such meanings may be very different from what the creators of the text imagined. (The reading or meaning that the creators intended—or the one that the elites consider to be the intended or correct meaning—can be called the **hegemonic reading.**)

"Readers" of media messages constantly produce their own meanings. They may resist or creatively oppose the hegemonic meaning of a text, or they may seize on the antihegemonic aspects of a text. We saw this process when American slaves preferred the biblical story of Moses and deliverance to the hegemonic lessons of obedience that their masters taught.

Popular Culture

In his book *Understanding Popular Culture* (1989), John Fiske views each individual's use of popular culture as a creative act (an original "reading" of a text). (For example, Madonna, the Grateful Dead, and *Star Wars* mean something different to each of their fans.) As Fiske puts it, ". . . the meanings I make from a text are pleasurable when I feel that they are *my* meanings and that they relate to *my* everyday life in a practical, direct way" (1989, p. 57). All of us can creatively "read" magazines, books, music, television, films, celebrities, and other popular culture products.

Individuals also draw on popular culture to express resistance. Through their use of popular culture, people can symbolically resist the unequal power relations they face each day—in the family, at work, and in the classroom. Forms and readings of popular culture (from rap music to sitcoms) can express discontent and resistance by groups that are or feel oppressed.

Indigenizing Popular Culture

To understand culture change, it is important to recognize that meaning is not inherent or imposed but locally manufactured. People assign their own meanings and value to the texts, messages, and products they receive. Those meanings reflect their cultural backgrounds and experiences. When forces from world centers enter new societies, they are **indigenized**—modified to fit the local culture. This is true of cultural forces as different as fast food, music, housing styles, science, terrorism, celebrations, and political ideas and institutions (Appadurai 1990). Many new forms of popular expression have emerged from the interplay of local, regional, national, and international cultural forces. **Syncretisms,** for example, are cultural *blends* that emerge from acculturation. One example is the mixture of African, Native American, and Roman Catholic saints and deities in Caribbean vodun, or "voodoo," cults. This blend is also present in **candomblé,** an Afro-Brazilian cult.

The notion of cultural imperialism is flawed because it views people as victims rather than as creative agents in their own transformation. For example, Michaels (1986) found *Rambo* to be a popular movie among aborigines in the deserts of central Australia, who had manufactured their own meanings from the film. Their "reading" was very different from the one imagined by the movie's creators, and by most Americans. The Native Australians saw Rambo as a representative of the Third World battling the white officer class. This reading expressed their negative feelings

The notion of cultural imperialism is flawed because it
views people as victims rather than as creative agents in
their own transformation. Here, people in Tokyo
buy tickets to see *Beverly Hills Cop*, being advertised
by a poster with a distinctly Japanese rendering of
the film's star, Eddie Murphy.

about white paternalism and existing race relations. The Native Australians also created tribal ties and kin links between Rambo and the prisoners he was rescuing. All
this made sense, based on their experience. Native Australians are disproportion-
ately represented in Australian jails, and their most likely liberator would be someone with a personal link to them. These readings of *Rambo* were relevant meanings
produced *from* the text, not *by* it (Fiske 1989).

A World System of Images

All cultures express imagination—in dreams, songs, fantasies, myths, and stories.
Today, however, more people in many more places imagine "a wider set of 'possible'
lives than they ever did before. One important source of this change is the mass media, which present a rich, ever-changing store of possible lives" (Appadurai 1991,
p. 197). The United States as a media center has been joined by Canada, Japan,
Western Europe, Brazil, Mexico, Nigeria, Egypt, India, and Hong Kong.

As print has done for centuries (Anderson 1991), the electronic mass media can also spread, and even create, national and ethnic identities. Like print, television and radio can diffuse the cultures of different countries within their own boundaries, thus enhancing national cultural identity. For example, millions of Brazilians who were formerly cut off (by geographic isolation or illiteracy) from urban and national events and information now join in a national communication system, thanks to the national TV network called Globo. Through television modern Brazilians have a sense of regular participation in national events (Kottak 1990*b*).

Cross-cultural studies of television contradict a belief Americans ethnocentrically hold about televiewing in other countries. This misconception is that American programs inevitably triumph over local products. This doesn't happen when there is appealing local competition. In Brazil, for example, the most popular network (TV Globo) relies heavily on native productions. American imports like *Dallas* and *Dynasty* have drawn small audiences. TV Globo's most popular programs are *telenovelas*, locally made serials that are similar to American soap operas. Globo plays each night to the world's largest and most devoted audience (60 to 80 million viewers throughout the nation). The programs that attract this horde are made by Brazilians, for Brazilians. Thus it is not North American culture but a new pan-Brazilian national culture that Brazilian TV is propagating. Brazilian productions also compete internationally. They are exported to over 100 countries, spanning Latin America, Europe, Asia, and Africa.

We may generalize that American programming that is culturally alien won't do very well anywhere when a quality local choice is available. Confirmation comes from many countries. National productions are highly popular in Japan, Mexico, India, Egypt, and Nigeria. In a survey during the mid-1980s, 75 percent of Nigerian viewers preferred local productions. Only 10 percent favored imports, and the remaining 15 percent liked the two options equally. Local productions are successful in Nigeria because "they are filled with everyday moments that audiences can identify with. These shows are locally produced by Nigerians" (Gray 1986). Thirty million people watched one of the most popular series, *The Village Headmaster*, each week. That program brought rural values to the screens of urbanites who had lost touch with their rural roots (Gray 1986).

The electronic mass media also play a key role in preserving ethnic and national identities among people who lead transnational lives. As groups move, they stay linked to each other and to their homeland through the media. Diasporas have enlarged the markets for media and travel services targeted at specific ethnic, national, or religious audiences. In 1992, for a fee, a PBS station in Fairfax, Virginia, offered more than thirty hours a week to immigrant groups in the D.C. area, to make programs in their own languages. *Somali Television*, for instance, is a half-hour program with about 5,000 Somali viewers, who can see their flag and hear their language on TV each week. Starting the program is a reading from the Koran, with clips of mosques from around the world (thus contributing, too, to a transnational Islamic identity). Formerly, an entertainment segment featured folk dances and Somali music. As Somalia's civil war dragged on, the entertainment segment was replaced in 1992 by images of bony children and parched countryside. *Somali Television* also features obituaries, rallies, and a segment called "Somalia Today," which has interviews with diplomats, immigration lawyers, and travel agents discussing airfares. Guests represent various tribes and subclans. *Somali Television* became a vital link between emigrant Somalis and their homeland. This was particularly true before images of Somalia became widespread on network news in late 1992 and early 1993 (*New York Times*, December 18, 1992).

A Transnational Culture of Consumption

Another key transnational force is finance. Moneymakers look beyond national boundaries for places to invest. As Appadurai (1991, p. 194) puts it, "money, commodities, and persons unendingly chase each other around the world." Many Latin American communities have lost their autonomy because their residents now depend on cash derived from international labor migration. The United States also relies more on foreign cash. Long dominated by domestic capital, the economy of the United States is increasingly influenced by foreign investment, especially from Britain, Canada, Germany, the Netherlands, and Japan (Rouse 1991). The American economy has also increased its dependence on foreign labor—through both the immigration of laborers and the export of jobs.

Contemporary global culture is driven by flows of people, technology, finance, information, and ideology (Appadurai 1990). Business, technology, and the media have increased the craving for commodities and images throughout the world. This has forced nation-states, including "Iron Curtains," to open to a global culture of consumption. Almost everyone today participates in this culture. Few people have never seen a T-shirt advertising a Western product. Michael Jackson's *Beat It* blasts through the streets of Rio de Janeiro, while taxi drivers from Toronto to Madagascar play Brazilian *lambada* tapes. Peasants and tribal people participate in the modern world system not only because they (willingly or unwillingly) work for cash but also because their products and images are appropriated by world capitalism. They are commercialized by others (like the San in the movie *The Gods Must Be Crazy*). And, seizing their own destinies, often helped by outsiders, indigenous peoples also market their own images and products through outlets like the Body Shop and Cultural Survival. David Maybury-Lewis's ten-program 1992 TV series *Millennium (Tribal Wisdom and the Modern World)* was designed to remedy misconceptions about tribal people, to help ensure their autonomy and survival.

Some social commentators see contemporary flows of people, technology, finance, information, and ideology as a cultural imperialist steamroller. This view ignores the selective, synthesizing activity of human beings as they deal with external forces, images, and messages. Anthropological studies show that domination is usually met by resistance and that cultural diffusion is a creative process.

THE CONTINUANCE OF DIVERSITY

Anthropology has a crucial role to play in promoting a more humanistic vision of social change, one that respects the value of cultural diversity. The existence of anthropology is itself a tribute to the continuing need to understand social and cultural similarities and differences. Anthropology teaches us that the adaptive responses of humans can be more flexible than can those of other species because our main adaptive means are sociocultural. However, the cultural forms, institutions, values, and customs of the past always influence subsequent adaptation, producing continued diversity and giving a certain uniqueness to the actions and reactions of different groups.

Let us hope that vigorous cultural differences will continue to prevent what some social scientists see as a bland convergence in the future, so that free and open investigation of human diversity can continue. With our knowledge and our awareness of our professional responsibilities, let us work to keep anthropology, the study of humankind and mirror for humanity, the most humanistic of all the sciences.

SUMMARY

The linkages in the modern world system have both enlarged and erased old boundaries and distinctions. People travel more than ever, but migrants maintain their ties with home, so that they live multilocally. With so many people "in motion," the unit of anthropological study expands from the local community to the diaspora. *Postmodernity* describes this world in flux, these people on the move who have learned to manage multiple social identities depending on place and context. *Globalization* describes the accelerating links between nations and people in a world system connected economically, politically, and by modern media and transportation. New kinds of political and ethnic units are emerging as others break down or disappear.

Different degrees of destruction, domination, resistance, survival, adaptation, and modification of native cultures may follow interethnic contact. This may lead to the tribe's cultural collapse (*ethnocide*) or its physical extinction (*genocide*). The native landscape and its traditional management system may be attacked. Outsiders often attempt to remake native landscapes and cultures in their own image, a process called *terraforming*.

Multinational business corporations are a major force in the modern world system. Core nations continue to send predatory enterprises to noncore nations, where multinationals have fueled economic development and ecological devastation. Countries and cultures may resist interventionist philosophies aimed at either development or globally oriented environmentalism. The non-Western world tends to be cynical about Western ecological morality, seeing it as yet another imperialist message.

A clash of cultures related to environmental change may occur when development threatens indigenous peoples and their environments. Another clash may occur when external regulation threatens indigenous peoples. Native groups may be harmed by regional, national, and international environmental plans that seek to *save* their homelands. Like development projects, conservation schemes may ask people to change the way they have been doing things for generations to satisfy planners' goals rather than local goals. When people are asked to give up the basis of their livelihood, they usually resist.

Religious proselytizing can promote ethnocide, as native beliefs and practices are replaced by Western ones. Sometimes the political ideology of a nation-state is pitted against traditional religion. Governments often use their power to advance a religion, such as Islam in Iran or Sudan.

Systems of domination have their muted aspects along with their public dimensions. *Public transcript* describes the open, public interactions between dominators and oppressed. *Hidden transcript* describes the critique of power that goes on offstage, where the power holders can't see it. *Hegemony* describes a stratified social order in which subordinates comply with domination by internalizing its values and accepting its "naturalness."

Often, situations that appear hegemonic have active resistance, but it is individual and disguised rather than collective and defiant. Subordinates also use various strategies to resist publicly, but again, usually in disguised form. Discontent may be expressed in public rituals and language. Resistance is most likely to be expressed openly when the oppressed are allowed to assemble. Sensing danger, the elites discourage such public gatherings. Factors that interfere with community formation—such as geographic, linguistic, and ethnic separation—work to curb resistance. But such divisive factors can be overcome. Hidden transcripts tend to be publicly expressed at certain times (festivals and Carnivals) and in certain places (markets).

Cultural imperialism refers to the rapid spread or advance of one culture at the expense of others, or its imposition on other cultures, which it modifies, replaces, or destroys—usually because of differential economic or political influence. But people aren't passive victims of cultural imperialism. Contemporary people—often with considerable creativity—constantly revise, rework, resist, and reject the messages they get from external systems.

Some critics worry that modern technology, including the mass media, is killing off traditional cultures by homogenizing products to reach more people. But others see an important role for modern technology in allowing local cultures to express themselves. *Stimulus diffusion* describes the process by which a group modifies a custom by adopting images and behavior associated with an external practice, without borrowing the practice itself. *Creative opposition* occurs when people change their behavior as they consciously and actively avoid or spurn an external image or practice.

Any media-borne image can be considered a *text*—something that is creatively "read," interpreted, and assigned meaning by each person who receives it. People may resist or creatively oppose the hegemonic meaning of a text, or they may seize on the antihegemonic aspects of a text. Forms and readings of popular culture can express discontent and resistance by groups that are or feel oppressed. Meaning is not inherent or imposed but locally manufactured. When forces from world centers enter new societies, they are *indigenized*—modified to fit the local culture.

All cultures express imagination, but today, through the mass media, people imagine a wider set of possible lives than they ever did before. The electronic mass media can spread, even create, national and ethnic identities. Like print, television and radio can diffuse the cultures of different countries within their own boundaries, thus enhancing national cultural identity. The electronic mass media also play a key role in preserving ethnic and national identities among people who lead transnational lives.

Contemporary global culture is driven by flows of people, technology, finance, information, and ideology. Transnational finance and labor modify the economic control and the ethnic mix of local life. Business, technology, and the media have increased the craving for commodities and images throughout the world, creating a global culture of consumption. Anthropological studies show that domination is usually met by resistance and that cultural diffusion is a creative process.

Glossary

acculturation: The exchange of cultural features that results when groups come into continuous firsthand contact; the original cultural patterns of either or both groups may be altered, but the groups remain distinct.

achieved status: Social status that comes through talents, actions, efforts, activities, and accomplishments, rather than ascription.

adaptation: The process by which organisms cope with environmental stresses.

age set: Group uniting all men or women (usually men) born during a certain time span; this group controls property and often has political and military functions.

agnates: Members of the same patrilineal descent group.

agriculture: Nonindustrial system of plant cultivation characterized by continuous and intensive use of land and labor.

animism: Belief in souls or doubles.

anthropology and education: Anthropological research in classrooms, homes, and neighborhoods, viewing students as total cultural creatures whose enculturation and attitudes toward education belong to a larger context that includes family, peers, and society.

apical ancestor: In a descent group, the individual who stands at the apex, or top, of the common genealogy.

applied anthropology: The application of anthropological data, perspectives, theory, and methods to identify, assess, and solve contemporary social problems.

archaic state: Nonindustrial state.

ascribed status: Social status (e.g., race or gender) that people have little or no choice about occupying.

assimilation: The process of change that a minority group may experience when it moves to a country where another culture dominates; the minority is incorporated into the dominant culture to the point that it no longer exists as a separate cultural unit.

attitudinal discrimination: Discrimination against members of a group because of prejudice toward that group.

balanced reciprocity: See *generalized reciprocity.*

band: Basic unit of social organization among foragers. A band includes fewer than one hundred people; it often splits up seasonally.

berdaches: Among the Crow Indians, members of a third gender, for whom certain ritual duties were reserved.

big man: Figure often found among tribal horticulturalists and pastoralists. The big man occupies no office but creates his reputation through entrepreneurship and generosity to others. Neither his wealth nor his position passes to his heirs.

bilateral kinship calculation: A system in which kinship ties are calculated equally through both sexes: mother and father, sister and brother, daughter and son, and so on.

binary opposition: Pairs of opposites, such as good-evil and old-young, produced by converting differences of degree into qualitative distinctions; important in structuralism.

biological kin types: Actual genealogical relationships, designated by letters and symbols (e.g., FB), as opposed to the kin terms (e.g., uncle) used in a particular society.

biomedicine: Western medicine, which attributes illness to scientifically-demonstrated agents—biological organisms (e.g., bacteria, viruses, fungi, or parasites) or toxic materials.

biopsychological equality: The premise that although individuals differ in emotional and intellectual capacities, all human populations have equivalent capacities for culture.

blood feud: Feud between families, usually in a nonstate society.

bourgeoisie: One of Karl Marx's opposed classes; owners of the means of production (factories, mines, large farms, and other sources of subsistence).

brideprice: See *progeny price.*

bridewealth: See *progeny price.*

call systems: Vocal systems of communication used by nonhuman primates, composed of a limited number of sounds—calls—which are produced only when particular environmental stimuli are encountered.

candomblé: A syncretic "Afro-Brazilian" religion.

capital: Wealth or resources invested in business, with the intent of producing a profit.

ceremonial fund: Resources invested in ceremonial or ritual expenses or activity.

chiefdom: Form of sociopolitical organization intermediate between the tribe and the state; kin-based with differential access to resources and a permanent political structure.

clan: Unilineal descent group based on stipulated descent.

class consciousness: Recognition of collective interests and personal identification with one's economic group (particularly the proletariat); basic to Marx's view of class.

close-knit networks: Characteristic of rural communities and nonindustrial societies; many of one's friends, neighbors, and relatives know one another.

colonialism: The political, social, economic, and cultural domination of a territory and its people by a foreign power for an extended time.

communal religions: In Wallace's typology, these religions have—in addition to shamanic cults—communal cults in which people organize community rituals such as harvest ceremonies and rites of passage.

communitas: Intense community spirit, a feeling of great social solidarity, equality, and togetherness; characteristic of people experiencing liminality together.

community study: Anthropological method for studying complex societies. Small communities are studied ethnographically as being (partially) representative of regional culture or particular contrasts in national life.

competence: What native speakers must (and do) know about their language in order to speak and understand it.

complex societies: Nations; large and populous, with social stratification and central governments.

core: Dominant structural position in the world system; consists of the strongest and most powerful states with advanced systems of production.

core values: Key, basic, or central values that integrate a culture and help distinguish it from others.

correlation: An association between two or more variables such that when one changes (varies), the other(s) also change(s) (covaries); for example, temperature and sweating.

creative opposition: Process in which people change their behavior as they consciously and actively avoid or spurn an external image or practice.

cultivation continuum: A continuum based on the comparative study of nonindustrial cultivating societies in which labor intensity increases and fallowing decreases.

cultural convergence: Development of similar traits, institutions, or behavior patterns as a result of adaptation to similar environments; parallel development without contact or mutual influence.

cultural imperialism: The rapid spread or advance of one culture at the expense of others, or its imposition on other cultures, which it modifies, replaces, or destroys—usually because of differential economic or political influence.

cultural learning: Learning based on the human capacity to think symbolically.

cultural relativism: The position that the values and standards of cultures differ and deserve respect. Extreme relativism argues that cultures should be judged solely by their own standards.

culturally compatible economic development projects: Projects that harness traditional organizations and locally perceived needs for change and that have a culturally appropriate design and implementation strategy.

culture: Traditions and customs that govern behavior and beliefs; distinctly human; transmitted through learning.

Culture, general: Spelled with a capital C, culture in the general sense as a capacity and possession shared by hominids.

culture, specific: Spelled with a small c; culture in the specific sense, any one of the different and varied cultural traditions of specific societies.

curer: Specialized role acquired through a culturally appropriate process of selection, training, certification, and acquisition of a professional image; the curer is consulted by patients, who believe in his or her special powers, and receives some form of special consideration; a cultural universal.

daughter languages: Languages developing out of the same parent language; for example, French and Spanish are daughter languages of Latin.

deep structure: In transformational grammar, the mental level; a sentence is formed in the speaker's mind and then interpreted by the hearer.

demonstrated descent: Basis of the lineage; descent-group members cite the names of their forebears in each generation from the apical ancestor through the present.

descent: Rule assigning social identity on the basis of some aspect of one's ancestry.

descent group: A permanent social unit whose members claim common ancestry; fundamental to tribal society.

diaspora: The offspring of an area who have spread to many lands.

differential access: Unequal access to resources; basic attribute of chiefdoms and states. Superordinates have favored access to such resources, while the access of subordinates is limited by superordinates.

diffusion: Borrowing between cultures either directly or through intermediaries.

diglossia: The existence of "high" (formal) and "low" (familial) dialects of a single language, such as German.

discourse: Talk, speeches, gestures, and actions.

discrimination: Policies and practices that harm a group and its members.

disease: An etic or scientifically identified health threat caused by a bacterium, virus, fungus, parasite, or other pathogen.

displacement: A basic feature of language; the ability to speak of things and events that are not present.

domestic: Within or pertaining to the home.

domestic system (of manufacture): Also known as home handicraft production; preindustrial manufacturing system in which organizer-entrepreneurs supplied raw materials to people who worked at home and collected finished products from them.

domestic-public dichotomy: Contrast between women's role in the home and men's role in public life, with a corresponding social devaluation of women's work and worth.

dowry: A marital exchange in which the wife's group provides substantial gifts to the husband's family.

ecocide: Destruction of local ecosystems.

economic typology: Classification of societies based on their adaptive strategies, e.g., foraging, horticulture, pastoralism, agriculture.

economizing: The rational allocation of scarce means (or resources) to alternative ends (or uses); often considered the subject matter of economics.

economy: A population's system of production, distribution, and consumption of resources.

ego: Latin for I. In kinship charts, the point from which one views an egocentric genealogy.

emic: The research strategy that focuses on native explanations and criteria of significance.

emotionalistic disease theories: Theories that assume that illness is caused by intense emotional experiences.

enculturation: The social process by which culture is learned and transmitted across the generations.

endogamy: Marriage between people of the same social group.

environmental racism: The systematic use of institutionally-based power by a majority group to make policy decisions that create disproportionate environmental hazards in minority communities.

environmentalists: See *nurturists*.

equity, increased: A reduction in absolute poverty and a fairer (more even) distribution of wealth.

ethnic expulsion: A policy aimed at removing groups who are culturally different from a country.

ethnic group: Group distinguished by cultural similarities (shared among members of that group) and differences (between that group and others); ethnic group members share beliefs, values, habits, customs, and norms, and a common language, religion, history, geography, kinship, and/or race.

ethnic minorities: Indigenous peoples who have moved to urban areas.

ethnicity: Identification with, and feeling part of, an ethnic group, and exclusion from certain other groups because of this affiliation.

ethnocentrism: The tendency to view one's own culture as best and to judge the behavior and beliefs of culturally different people by own's own standards.

ethnocide: Destruction by a dominant group of the culture of an ethnic group.

ethnography: Field work in a particular culture.

ethnoscience: See *ethnosemantics*.

ethnosemantics: The study of lexical (vocabulary) contrasts and classifications in various languages.

etic: The research strategy that emphasizes the observer's rather than the natives' explanations, categories, and criteria of significance.

Etoro: Papua-New Guinea culture in which males are culturally trained to prefer homosexuality.

exogamy: Mating or marriage outside one's kin group; a cultural universal.

extradomestic: Outside the home; within or pertaining to the public domain.

family of orientation: Nuclear family in which one is born and grows up.

family of procreation: Nuclear family established when one marries and has children.

fictive kinship: Personal relationships modeled on kinship, such as that between godparents and godchildren.

First World: The "democratic west"—traditionally conceived in opposition to a "Second World" ruled by "communism."

fiscal: Pertaining to finances and taxation.

focal vocabulary: A set of words and distinctions that are particularly important to certain groups (those with particular foci of experience or activity), such as types of snow to Eskimos or skiers.

food production: Plant cultivation and animal domestication.

foraging: Hunting and gathering.

forced assimilation: Use of force by a dominant group to compel a minority to adopt the dominant culture—for example, penalizing or banning the language and customs of an ethnic group.

Fourth World: The very poorest of the "less-developed countries"—e.g., Madagascar, Bangladesh.

gender roles: The tasks and activities that a culture assigns to each sex.

gender stereotypes: Oversimplified but strongly held ideas about the characteristics of males and females.

gender stratification: Unequal distribution of rewards (socially valued resources, power, prestige, and personal freedom) between men and women, reflecting their different positions in a social hierarchy.

genealogical method: Procedures by which ethnographers discover and record connections of kinship, descent, and marriage, using diagrams and symbols.

general anthropology: The field of anthropology as a whole, consisting of cultural, archeological, biological, and linguistic anthropology.

generality: Culture pattern or trait that exists in some but not all societies.

generalized reciprocity: Principle that characterizes exchanges between closely related individuals: As social distance increases, reciprocity becomes balanced and finally negative.

genitor: Biological father of a child.

genocide: The deliberate elimination of a group, e.g., through mass murder, warfare, or introduced diseases.

globalization: The accelerating interdependence of nations in a world system linked economically and through mass media and modern transportation systems.

grammar: The formal organizing principles that link sound and meaning in a language; the set of abstract rules that makes up a language.

green revolution: Agricultural development based on chemical fertilizers, pesticides, twentieth-century cultivation techniques, and new crop varieties such as IR-8 ("miracle rice").

head, village: A local leader in a tribal society who has limited authority, leads by example and persuasion, and must be generous.

health care systems: Beliefs, customs, and specialists concerned with ensuring health and preventing and curing illness; a cultural universal.

hegemonic reading (of a "text"): The reading or meaning that the creators intended, or the one the elites consider to be the intended or correct meaning.

hegemony: As used by Antonio Gramsci, a stratified social order in which subordinates comply with domination by internalizing its values and accepting its "naturalness."

hidden transcript: As used by James Scott, the critique of power by the oppressed that goes on offstage—in private—where the power holders can't see it.

historical linguistics: Subdivision of linguistics that studies languages over time.

holistic: Interested in the whole of the human condition: past, present, and future; biology, society, language, and culture.

homeostasis: Equilibrium, or a stable relationship, between a population and its resource base.

hominids: Members of the zoological family (*Hominidae*) that includes fossil and living humans.

horticulture: Nonindustrial system of plant cultivation in which plots lie fallow for varying lengths of time.

hypodescent: A rule that automatically places the children of a union or mating between members of different socioeconomic groups in the less privileged group.

ideal types: Labels that make contrasts seem more extreme than they really are (e.g., big and little). Instead of discrete categories, there is actually a continuum from one type to the next.

illness: An emic condition of poor health felt by individual.

incest: Sexual relations with a close relative.

incest taboo: Universal prohibition against marrying or mating with a close relative.

income: Earnings from wages and salaries.

independent invention: Development of the same culture trait or pattern in separate cultures as a result of comparable needs and circumstances.

indigenized: Modified to fit the local culture.

indigenous peoples: The original inhabitants of particular territories; often descendants of tribespeople who live on as culturally distinct colonized peoples, many of whom aspire to autonomy.

individual situational learning: Type of learning in which animals learn from and base their future behavior on personal experience.

Industrial Revolution: The historical transformation (in Europe, after 1750) of "traditional" into "modern" societies through industrialization of the economy.

infanticide: Killing a baby; a form of population control in some societies.

informants: Subjects in ethnographic research; people the ethnographer gets to know in the field, who teach him or her about their culture.

institutional discrimination: Programs, policies, and arrangements that deny equal rights and opportunities to, or differentially harm, members of particular groups.

international culture: Cultural traditions that extend beyond national boundaries.

intervention philosophy: Guiding principle of colonialism, conquest, missionization, or development; an ideological justification for outsiders to guide native peoples in specific directions.

interview schedule: Ethnographic tool for structuring a formal interview. A prepared form (usually printed or mimeographed) that guides interviews with households or individuals being compared systematically. Contrasts with a questionnaire because the researcher has personal contact with the informants and records their answers.

Iroquois: Confederation of tribes in aboriginal New York State; matrilineal with communal longhouses and a prominent political, religious, and economic role for women.

kin terms: The words used for different relatives in a particular language, as opposed to actual genealogical relationships (biological kin types).

kin-based: Characteristic of many nonindustrial societies. People spend their lives almost exclusively with their relatives; principles of kinship, descent, and marriage organize social life.

kinship calculation: The system by which people in a particular society reckon kin relationships.

!Kung: Group of San (Bushmen) foragers of southern Africa; the exclamation point

indicates a click sound in the San language.

Kwakiutl: A potlatching society on the North Pacific Coast of North America.

lactation: Milk production.

language: Spoken (speech) and written (writing—which has existed for about 6,000 years); the primary human means of communication; key features of language include cultural transmission, displacement, and productivity.

law: A legal code, including trial and enforcement; characteristic of state-organized societies.

leveling mechanisms: Customs and social actions that operate to reduce differences in wealth and thus to bring standouts in line with community norms.

levirate: Custom by which a widow marries the brother of her deceased husband.

lexicon: Vocabulary; a dictionary containing all the morphemes in a language and their meaning.

life history: Of an informant; provides a personal cultural portrait of existence or change in a culture.

liminality: The critically important marginal or in-between phase of a rite of passage.

lineage: Unilineal descent group based on demonstrated descent.

linguistic relativity: Notion that all languages and dialects are equally effective as systems of communication.

linkages: Interconnections between small-scale and large-scale units and systems; political, economic, informational, and other cultural links between village, region, nation, and world.

liturgical order: A set sequence of words and actions invented prior to the current performance of the ritual in which it occurs.

local descent group: All the members of a particular descent group who live in the same place, such as the same village.

longitudinal research: Long-term study of a community, society, culture, or other unit, usually based on repeated visits.

loose-knit networks: Characteristic of

urban and complex societies; people who know each other often don't know each other's friends, neighbors, and relatives.

magic: Use of supernatural techniques to accomplish specific aims.

majority groups: Superordinate, dominant, or controlling groups in a social/political hierarchy.

maladaptive: Harmful to survival and reproduction.

mana: Sacred impersonal force in Melanesian and Polynesian religions.

manioc: Cassava, a tuber abundant in South American tropical forests. Along with maize and white potatoes, it is one of the three major caloric staples of the aboriginal New World.

market principle: Profit-oriented principle of exchange that dominates in states, particularly industrial states. Goods and services are bought and sold, and values are determined by supply and demand.

marriage: Socially approved relationship between a socially recognized male (the husband) and a socially recognized female (the wife) such that the children born to the wife are accepted as the offspring of both husband and wife.

matriarchy: A society ruled by women; unknown to ethnography.

matrifocal: Mother-centered; often refers to a household with no resident husband-father.

matrilateral skewing: A preference for relatives on the mother's side.

matrilineal descent: Unilineal descent rule in which people join the mother's group automatically at birth and stay members throughout life.

matrons: Senior women, as among the Iroquois.

means (or factors) of production: Land, labor, technology, and capital—major productive resources.

medical anthropology: Unites biological and cultural anthropologists in the study of disease, health problems, health care systems, and theories about illness in different cultures and ethnic groups.

mestizo: Mixed. In Latin America, having a combination of European, African, and Native American ancestors. Mestizos speak the national language.

microenculturation: The process by which people learn particular roles in a limited social system; creates microcultures.

minimal pairs: Words that resemble each other in all but one sound; used to discover phonemes.

minority groups: Subordinate groups in a social/political hierarchy, with inferior power and less secure access to resources than majority groups have.

mode of production: Way of organizing production—a set of social relations through which labor is deployed to wrest energy from nature by means of tools, skills, and knowledge.

monocrop production: System of production, often on plantations, based on the cultivation of a single cash crop.

monograph: A report based on ethnographic field work.

monotheism: Worship of an eternal, omniscient, omnipotent, and omnipresent supreme being.

morpheme: Minimal linguistic form (usually a word) with meaning.

morphology: The study of form; used in linguistics (the study of morphemes and word construction) and for form in general—for example, biomorphology relates to physical form.

multicentric exchange system: Economy organized into different categories or spheres.

multiculturalism: The view of cultural diversity in a country as something good and desirable; a multicultural society socializes individuals not only into the dominant (national) culture, but also into an ethnic culture.

namesakes: People who share the same name; a form of fictive kinship among the San, who have a limited number of personal names.

nation: Once a synonym for "ethnic group," designating a single culture sharing a language, religion, history, territory, ancestry, and kinship; now usually a synonym for "state" or "nation-state."

nation-state: An autonomous political entity, a country like the United States or Canada.

national culture: Cultural experiences, beliefs, learned behavior patterns, and values shared by citizens of the same nation.

nationalities: Ethnic groups that once had, or wish to have or regain, autonomous political status (their own country).

naturalistic disease theories: Includes scientific medicine; theories that explain illness in impersonal systemic terms.

naturists: Those who argue that human behavior and social organization are biologically determined.

negative reciprocity: See *generalized reciprocity*.

négritude: African identity—developed by African intellectuals in Francophone (French-speaking) West Africa.

neolocality: Postmarital residence pattern in which a couple establishes a new place of residence rather than living with or near either set of parents.

network analysis: Technique developed by anthropologists to adapt ethnographic procedures to modern cities and nations. Focuses on types of contacts (networks of relationships) between people.

NGOS: Nongovernmental organizations.

Nilotic populations: Populations, including the Nuer, that inhabit the Upper Nile region of eastern Africa.

nomadism, pastoral: Movement throughout the year by the whole pastoral group (men, women, and children) with their animals. More generally, such constant movement in pursuit of strategic resources.

nuclear family: Kinship group consisting of parents and children.

nurturists: Those who link behavior and social organization to environmental factors. Nurturists focus on variation rather than universals and stress learning and the role of culture in human adaptation.

office: Permanent political position.

Olympian religions: In Wallace's typol-

ogy, develop with state organization; have full-time religious specialists—professional priesthoods.

open, noncorporate peasant community: Located in the lowlands of Latin America; admixture of Indians, Europeans, and Africans. Noncorporate; members do not farm a joint estate. Not closed; flexible in admitting new members.

overinnovation: Characteristic of projects that require major changes in natives' daily lives, especially ones that interfere with customary subsistence pursuits.

pantheon: A collection of supernatural beings in a particular religion.

pantribal sodality: A non-kin-based group that exists throughout a tribe, spanning several villages.

participant observation: A characteristic ethnographic technique; taking part in the events one is observing, describing, and analyzing.

particularity: Distinctive or unique culture trait, pattern, or integration.

pastoralists: People who use a food-producing strategy of adaptation based on care of herds of domesticated animals.

pater: Socially recognized father of a child; not necessarily the genitor.

patrilineal descent: Unilineal descent rule in which people join the father's group automatically at birth and stay members throughout life.

patrilineal-virilocal complex: An interrelated constellation of patrilineality, virilocality, warfare, and male supremacy.

peasant: Small-scale agriculturist living in a state, with rent fund obligations.

performance: What people actually say; the use of speech in social situations.

periphery: Weakest structural position in the world system.

personal network: Each person's particular set of relationships (economic, social, political, religious) with all others.

personalistic disease theories: Theories that attribute illness to sorcerers, witches, ghosts, or ancestral spirits.

personalty: Items other than strategic resources that are indelibly associated with a particular person; contrasts with property.

phenotype: An organism's evident traits, its "manifest biology"—anatomy and physiology.

phone: Any speech sound.

phoneme: Significant sound contrast in a language that serves to distinguish meaning, as in minimal pairs.

phonemics: The study of the sound contrasts (phonemes) of a particular language.

phonetics: The study of speech sounds in general; what people actually say in various languages.

phonology: The study of sounds used in speech.

pidgins: Mixed languages that develop to ease communication between members of different cultures in contact, usually in situations of trade or colonial domination.

polity: The political order.

polyandry: Variety of plural marriage in which a woman has more than one husband.

polygyny: Variety of plural marriage in which a man has more than one wife.

polytheism: Belief in several deities who control aspects of nature.

postmodern: In its most general sense, describes the blurring and breakdown of established canons (rules, standards), categories, distinctions, and boundaries.

postmodernism: A style and movement in architecture that succeeded modernism. Compared with modernism, postmodernism is less geometric, less functional, less austere, more playful, and more willing to include elements from diverse times and cultures; *postmodern* now describes comparable developments in music, literature, and visual art.

postmodernity: Condition of a world in flux, with people on-the-move, in which established groups, boundaries, identities, contrasts, and standards are reaching out and breaking down.

potlatch: Competitive feast among Indians on the North Pacific Coast of North America.

power: The ability to exercise one's will over others—to do what one wants; the basis of political status.

prejudice: Devaluing (looking down on) a group because of its assumed behavior, values, capabilities, or attributes.

prestige: Esteem, respect, or approval for acts, deeds, or qualities considered exemplary.

primitive: Characterized by small size and technological and economic simplicity.

productivity: A basic feature of language; the ability to use the rules of one's language to create new expressions comprehensible to other native speakers.

progeny price: A gift from the husband and his kin to the wife and her kin before, at, or after marriage; legitimizes children born to the woman as members of the husband's descent group.

proletarianization: Separation of workers from the means of production through industrialism.

protolanguage: Language ancestral to several daughter languages.

public transcript: As used by James Scott, the open, public interactions between dominators and oppressed—the outer shell of power relations.

questionnaire: Form (usually printed) used by sociologists to obtain comparable information from respondents. Often mailed to and filled in by research subjects rather than by the researcher.

race: An ethnic group assumed to have a biological basis.

racism: Discrimination against an ethnic group assumed to have a biological basis.

random sample: A sample in which all members of the population have an equal statistical chance of being included.

reciprocity: One of the three principles of exchange. Governs exchange between social equals; major exchange mode in band and tribal societies.

redistribution: Major exchange mode of chiefdoms, many archaic states, and some states with managed economies.

refugees: People who have been forced (involuntary refugees) or who have chosen (voluntary refugees) to flee a country, to escape persecution or war.

regulation: The management of variables within a system of related and interacting variables. Regulation assures that variables stay within their normal ranges, corrects deviations from the norm, and thus maintains the system's integrity.

religion: Belief and ritual concerned with supernatural beings, powers, and forces.

rent fund: Scarce resources that a social inferior is required to render to an individual or agency that is superior politically or economically.

replacement fund: Scarce resources invested in technology and other items essential to production.

revitalization movements: Movements that occur in times of change, in which religious leaders emerge and undertake to alter or revitalize a society.

rites of passage: Culturally defined activities associated with the transition from one place or stage of life to another.

ritual: Behavior that is formal, stylized, repetitive, and stereotyped, performed earnestly as a social act; rituals are held at set times and places and have liturgical orders.

role: A set of expected (culturally "proper") behaviors, attitudes, rights, and obligations attached to a particular status.

Romer's rule: Evolutionary rule stating that an innovation that evolves to maintain an existing system can play a major role in changing that system.

sample: A smaller study group chosen to represent a larger population.

San: Foragers of southern Africa, also known as Bushmen; speakers of San languages.

Sapir-Whorf hypothesis: Theory that different languages produce different ways of thinking.

schistosomiasis: Disease caused by liver flukes transmitted by snails inhabiting ponds, lakes, and waterways, often created by irrigation projects.

scientific medicine: As distinguished from Western medicine, a health care system based on scientific knowledge and procedures, encompassing such fields as pathology, microbiology, biochemistry, surgery, diagnostic technology, and applications.

Second World: The Warsaw Pact nations, including the former Soviet Union, the Socialist and once-Socialist countries of eastern Europe and Asia.

secret societies: Sodalities, usually all-male or all-female, with secret initiation ceremonies.

sectorial fallowing: Intensive horticulture; plots are cultivated for two to three years, then fallowed for three to five, with a longer rest after several of these shorter cycles.

segmentary lineage organization (SLO): Political organization based on descent, usually patrilineal, with multiple descent segments that form at different genealogical levels and function in different contexts.

semantics: A language's meaning system.

semiperiphery: Structural position in the world system intermediate between core and periphery.

serial monogamy: Marriage of a given individual to several spouses, but not at the same time.

settlement hierarchy: A ranked series of communities differing in size, function, and type of building.

sexual dimorphism: Marked differences in male and female biology besides the contrasts in breasts and genitals.

shaman: A part-time religious practitioner who mediates between ordinary people and supernatural beings and forces.

slash and burn: Form of horticulture in which the forest cover of a plot is cut down and burned before planting to allow the ashes to fertilize the soil.

social fund: Scarce resources invested to assist friends, relatives, in-laws, and neighbors.

social race: A group assumed to have a biological basis but actually perceived and defined in a social context—by a particular culture rather than by scientific criteria.

social situational learning: Learning from other members of the social group, not necessarily through language.

society: Organized life in groups; typical of humans and other animals.

sociolinguistics: Study of relationships between social and linguistic variation; study of language (performance) in its social context.

sociopolitical typology: Classification scheme based on the scale and complexity of social organization and the effectiveness of political regulation; includes band, tribe, chiefdom, and state.

sodality: See *pantribal sodality.*

sororate: Custom by which a widower marries the sister of the deceased wife.

state (nation-state): Complex sociopolitical system that administers a territory and populace with substantial contrasts in occupation, wealth, prestige, and power. An independent, centrally-organized political unit, a government.

status: Any position that determines where someone fits in society, may be ascribed or achieved.

stereotypes: Fixed ideas—often unfavorable—about what members of a group are like.

stimulus diffusion: The process by which a group modifies a custom by adopting images and behavior associated with an external practice, without borrowing the practice itself.

stipulated descent: Basis of the clan; members merely say they descend from their apical ancestor; they don't trace the actual genealogical links between themselves and that ancestor.

strategic resources: Those necessary for life, such as food and space.

stratification: Characteristic of a system with socioeconomic strata; see also *stratum.*

stratified: Class-structured; stratified societies have marked differences in wealth, in prestige, and in power between social classes.

stratum: One of two or more groups that contrast in regard to social status and access to strategic resources. Each stratum includes people of both sexes and all ages.

structuralism: Structural analysis; technique developed by Lévi-Strauss not to explain sociocultural similarities and differences but to uncover themes, relations, and other cross-cultural connections.

style shifts: Variations in speech in different contexts.

subcultures: Different cultural symbol-based traditions associated with subgroups in the same complex society.

subgroups: Languages within a taxonomy of related languages that are most closely related.

subordinate: The lower, or underprivileged, group in a stratified system.

subsistence fund: Scarce resources invested to provide food in order to replace the calories expended in daily activity.

sumptuary goods: Items whose consumption is limited to the elite.

superordinate: The upper, or privileged, group in a stratified system.

supply and demand, law of: Economic rule that things cost more the scarcer they are and the more people want them.

surface structure: In transformational grammar, the message that passes from speaker to hearer; an actual speech event.

survey research: Characteristic research procedure among social scientists other than anthropologists. Studies society through sampling, statistical analysis, and impersonal data collection.

symbiosis: An obligatory interaction between groups that is beneficial to each.

symbol: Something, verbal or nonverbal, that arbitrarily and by convention stands for something else, with which it has no necessary or natural connection.

syncretisms: Cultural blends or mixtures that emerge from acculturation, particularly under colonialism, such as African, Native American, and Roman Catholic saints and deities in Caribbean vodun, or "voodoo," cults.

syntax: The arrangement and order of words in phrases and sentences.

systemic perspective: View that changes

have multiple consequences, some unforeseen.

taboo: Prohibition backed by supernatural sanctions.

terraforming: From science fiction, the use of technology to make other worlds as much like earth (*terra*) as possible; applied by analogy to results of political and economic domination on earth.

text: Something which is creatively "read," interpreted, and assigned meaning by each person who receives it; includes any media-borne image, such as Carnival.

Third World: The "less-developed countries" (LDCs); used in combination with "Fourth World," "Third World" refers to the better-off LDCs (e.g., Brazil, India) compared with poorer LDCs (Bangladesh, Madagascar).

totem: An animal or plant apical ancestor of a clan.

transformational-generative grammar: Approach associated with Noam Chomsky; views language as set of abstract rules with deep and surface structures.

transhumance: One of two variants of pastoralism; part of the population moves seasonally with the herds while the other part remains in home villages.

tribe: Form of sociopolitical organization usually based on horticulture or pastoralism. Socioeconomic stratification and centralized rule are absent in tribes, and there is no means of enforcing political decisions.

typology, economic: See *economic typology*.

typology, sociopolitical: See *sociopolitical typology*.

underdifferentiation: Planning fallacy of viewing less-developed countries as an undifferentiated group; ignoring cultural diversity and adopting a uniform approach (often ethnocentric) for very different types of project beneficiaries.

unilineal descent: Matrilineal or patrilineal descent.

unilocal: Either virilocal or uxorilocal postmarital residence; requires that a married couple reside with the relatives of either the husband (vir) or the wife (uxor), depending on the society.

universal: Something that exists in every culture.

universal grammar: According to Chomsky, a genetically transmitted blueprint for language, a basic linguistic plan in the human brain.

urban anthropology: The anthropological study of cities.

uxorilocality: Customary residence with the wife's relatives after marriage.

variables: Attributes (e.g., sex, age, height, weight) that differ from one person or case to the next.

vernacular: Ordinary, casual speech.

virilocality: Customary residence with the husband's relatives after marriage.

wealth: All a person's material assets, including income, land, and other types of property; the basis of economic status.

well-informed informant: Person who is an expert on a particular aspect of native life.

westernization: The acculturative influence of Western expansion on native cultures.

working class (or proletariat): Those who must sell their labor to survive; the antithesis of the bourgeoisie in Marx's class analysis.

world-system perspective: Recognition that we live in a single world system, based on a capitalist world economy, which emerged in the sixteenth century, committed to production for sale, with the object of maximizing profits rather than supplying domestic needs.

Bibliography

AHMED, A. S.
  1992 *Postmodernism and Islam: Predicament and Promise.* New York: Routledge.

AMADIUME, I.
  1987 *Male Daughters, Female Husbands.* Atlantic Highlands, NJ: Zed.

AMERICAN ALMANAC 1994–1995
  1994 *(Statistical Abstract of the United States,* 114th ed.) Austin, TX: Reference Press.

AMERICAN ANTHROPOLOGICAL ASSOCIATION
  Anthropology Newsletter. Published nine times annually by the American Anthropological Association, Washington, DC.

ANDERSON, B.
  1991 *Imagined Communities: Reflections on the Origin and Spread of Nationalism,* rev. ed. London: Verso.

AOKI, M. Y., AND M. B. DARDESS, EDS.
  1981 *As the Japanese See It: Past and Present.* Honolulu: The University Press of Hawaii.

APPADURAI, A.
  1990 Disjuncture and Difference in the Global Cultural Economy. *Public Culture* 2(2):1–24.
  1991 Global Ethnoscapes: Notes and Queries for a Transnational Anthropology. In *Recapturing Anthropology: Working in the Present,* ed. R. G. Fox, pp. 191–210. Santa Fe: School of American Research Advanced Seminar Series.

APPIAH, K. A.
  1990 Racisms. In *Anatomy of Racism,*
  ed. David Theo Goldberg, pp. 3–17. Minneapolis: University of Minnesota Press.

BAILY, R. C.
  1990 *The Behavioral Ecology of Efe Pygmy Men in the Ituri Forest, Zaire.* Ann Arbor: Anthropological Papers, Museum of Anthropology, University of Michigan, no. 86.

BAILEY, R. C., G. HEAD, M. JENIKE, B. OWEN, R. RECHTMAN, AND E. ZECHENTER
  1989 Hunting and Gathering in Tropical Rain Forests: Is It Possible? *American Anthropologist* 91:59–82.

BANTON, M.
  1957 *West African City. A Study in Tribal Life in Freetown.* London: Oxford University Press.

BARNABY, F., ED.
  1984 *Future War: Armed Conflict in the Next Decade.* London: M. Joseph.

BARNARD, A.
  1979 Kalahari Settlement Patterns. In *Social and Ecological Systems,* eds. P. Burnham and R. Ellen. New York: Academic Press.

BARRINGER, F.
  1989 32 Million Lived in Poverty in '88, a Figure Unchanged. *The New York Times,* October 19, p. 18.
  1992 New Census Data Show More Children Living in Poverty. *The New York Times,* May 29, pp. A1, A12, A13.

BARTH, F.
  1968 (orig. 1958). Ecological Rela-

tions of Ethnic Groups in Swat, North Pakistan. In *Man in Adaptation: The Cultural Present*, ed. Yehudi Cohen, pp. 324–331. Chicago: Aldine.

1969   *Ethnic Groups and Boundaries: The Social Organization of Cultural Difference.* London: Allen and Unwin.

BEEMAN, W.
1986   *Language, Status, and Power in Iran.* Bloomington: Indiana University Press.

BENNETT, J. W.
1969   *Northern Plainsmen: Adaptive Strategy and Agrarian Life.* Chicago: Aldine.

BERLIN, B. D., E. BREEDLOVE, AND P. H. RAVEN
1974   *Principles of Tzeltal Plant Classification: An Introduction to the Botanical Ethnography of a Mayan-Speaking People of Highland Chiapas.* New York: Academic Press.

BERLIN, B., AND P. KAY
1992   *Basic Color Terms: Their Universality and Evolution*, 2d ed. Berkeley: University of California Press.

BERNARD, H. R.
1994   *Research Methods in Cultural Anthropology, Qualitative and Quantitative Approaches*, 2d ed. Thousand Oaks, CA: Sage.

BERREMAN, G. D.
1962   Pahari Polyandry: A Comparison. *American Anthropologist* 64:60–75.

1975   Himalayan Polyandry and the Domestic Cycle. *American Ethnologist* 2:127–138.

BETTELHEIM, B.
1975   *The Uses of Enchantment: The Meaning and Importance of Fairy Tales.* New York: Vintage.

BIRD-DAVID, N.
1992   Beyond "The Original Affluent Society": A Culturalist Reformulation. *Current Anthropology* 33(1): 25–47.

BLOCH, M., ED.
1975   *Political Language and Oratory in Traditional Societies.* London: Academic.

BOAS, F.
1966   (orig. 1940). *Race, Language, and Culture.* New York: Free Press.

BODLEY, J. H.
1985   *Anthropology and Contemporary Human Problems*, 2d ed. Palo Alto, CA: Mayfield.

BODLEY, J. H., ED.
1988   *Tribal Peoples and Development Issues: A Global Overview:* Palo Alto, CA: Mayfield.

BOGORAS, W.
1904   The Chukchee. In *The Jesup North Pacific Expedition*, ed. F. Boas. New York: Memoir of the American Museum of Natural History.

BOLLINGER, D.
1976   *Aspects of Language*, 2d ed. New York: Harcourt Brace Jovanovich.

BOLTON, R.
1981   Susto, Hostility, and Hypoglycemia. *Ethnology* 20(4)227–258.

BOSERUP, E.
1970   *Women's Role in Economic Development.* London: Allen and Unwin.

BOURDIEU, P.
1977   *Outline of a Theory of Practice.* R. Nice (trans.). Cambridge, England: Cambridge University Press.

1982   *Ce Que Parler Veut Dire.* Paris: Fayard.

1984   *Distinction: A Social Critique of the Judgment of Taste.* R. Nice (trans.). Cambridge, MA: Harvard University Press.

BOURQUE, S. C., AND K. B. WARREN
1981   *Women of the Andes: Patriarchy and Social Change in Two Peruvian Villages.* Ann Arbor: University of Michigan Press.

1987   Technology, Gender and Development. *Daedalus* 116(4): 173–197.

BRAUDEL, F.
1973 *Capitalism and Material Life, 1400–1800*. M. Kochan (trans.). London: Weidenfeld and Nicolson.
1981 *Civilization and Capitalism, 15th–18th Century, Volume I: The Structure of Everyday Life: The Limits*. S. Reynolds (trans.). New York: Harper & Row.
1982 *Civilization and Capitalism, 15th–18th Century, Volume II: The Wheels of Commerce*. New York: Harper & Row.
1984 *Civilization and Capitalism 15th–18th Century, Volume III: The Perspective of the World*. New York: Harper & Row.

BRENNEIS, D.
1988 Language and Disputing. *Annual Review of Anthropology* 17:221–237.

BRONFENBRENNER, U.
1975 Nature with Nurture: A Reinterpretation of the Evidence. In *Race and IQ*, ed. A. Montagu, pp. 114–144. New York: Oxford University Press.

BROOKE, J.
1992 Rio's New Day in Sun Leaves Laplander Limp. *The New York Times*, June 1, p. A7

BROWN, D.
1991 *Human Universals*. New York: McGraw-Hill.

BROWN, J. K.
1975 Iroquois Women: An Ethnohistoric Note. In *Toward an Anthropology of Women*, ed. R. Reiter, pp. 235–251. New York: Monthly Review Press.

BROWN, R. W.
1958 *Words and Things*. Glencoe, IL: Free Press.

BRYANT, B., AND P. MOHAI, EDS.
1991 Race, Class, and Environmental Quality in the Detroit Area. In *Environmental Racism: Issues and Dilemmas*. Ann Arbor: The University of Michigan Office of Minority Affairs.

BURLING, R.
1970 *Man's Many Voices: Language in Its Cultural Context*. New York: Holt, Rinehart & Winston.

CARNEIRO, R. L.
1956 Slash-and-Burn Agriculture: A Closer Look at Its Implications for Settlement Patterns. In *Men and Cultures*, Selected Papers of the Fifth International Congress of Anthropological and Ethnological Sciences, pp. 229–234. Philadelphia: University of Pennsylvania Press.
1968 (orig. 1961). Slash-and-Burn Cultivation among the Kuikuru and Its Implications for Cultural Development in the Amazon Basin. In *Man in Adaptation: The Cultural Present*, ed. Y. A. Cohen, pp. 131–145. Chicago: Aldine.
1970 A Theory of the Origin of the State. *Science* 69:733–738.

CHAGNON, N.
1992 *Yanomamo: The Fierce People*, 4th ed. New York: Harcourt Brace.

CHOMSKY, N.
1957 *Syntactic Structures*. The Hague: Mouton.

CLIFFORD, J.
1982 *Person and Myth: Maurice Leenhardt in the Melanesian World*. Berkeley: University of California Press.
1988 *The Predicament of Culture: Twentieth-Century Ethnography, Literature and Art*. Cambridge, MA: Harvard University Press.

COHEN, R.
1967 *The Kanuri of Bornu*. New York: Holt, Rinehart & Winston.

COHEN, Y.
1974 *Man in Adaptation: The Cultural Present*. 2d ed. Chicago: Aldine.

COHEN, Y., ED.
1974 Culture as Adaptation. In *Man in Adaptation: The Cultural Present*, 2d ed., pp. 45–68. Chicago: Aldine.

COHEN, M. N., AND G. ARMELAGOS, EDS.
1984 *Paleopathology at the Origins of*

Agriculture. New York: Academic Press.

COLLINS, T. W.
1989 Rural Economic Development in Two Tennessee Counties: A Racial Dimension. Paper presented at the annual meetings of the American Anthropological Association, Washington, D.C.

COLSON, E., AND T. SCUDDER
1975 New Economic Relationships between the Gwembe Valley and the Line of Rail. In *Town and Country in Central and Eastern Africa,* ed. David Parkin, pp. 190–210. London: Oxford University Press.

CONKLIN, H. C.
1954 *The Relation of Hanunóo Culture to the Plant World.* Unpublished Ph.D. dissertation, Yale University.

CONNOR, W.
1972 Nation-building or Nation destroying. *World Politics* 24(3).

CROSBY, A. W., JR.
1972 *The Columbian Exchange: Biological and Cultural Consequences of 1492.* Westport, CT: Greenwood Press.
1986 *Ecological Imperialism: The Biological Expansion of Europe 900–1900.* New York: Cambridge University Press.

CULTURAL SURVIVAL QUARTERLY
Quarterly journal. Cambridge, MA: Cultural Survival, Inc.

DALTON, G., ED.
1967 *Tribal and Peasant Economies.* Garden City, NY: The Natural History Press.

DAMATTA, R.
1991 *Carnivals, Rogues, and Heroes: An Interpretation of the Brazilian Dilemma.* Translated from the Portuguese by John Drury. Notre Dame, IN: University of Notre Dame Press.

D'ANDRADE, R.
1984 Cultural Meaning Systems. In *Culture Theory: Essays on Mind, Self, and Emotion,* eds. R. A. Shweder and R. A. Levine, pp. 88–119. Cambridge, England: Cambridge University Press.

DAVIS, D. L., AND R. G. WHITTEN
1987 The Cross-Cultural Study of Human Sexuality. *Annual Review of Anthropology* 16:69–98.

DEGLER, C.
1970 *Neither Black nor White: Slavery and Race Relations in Brazil and the United States.* New York: Macmillan.

DENTAN, R. K.
1979 *The Semai: A Nonviolent People of Malaya.* Fieldwork edition. New York: Harcourt Brace.

DEVOS, G. A., AND H. WAGATSUMA
1966 *Japan's Invisible Race: Caste in Culture and Personality.* Berkeley: University of California Press.

DEVOS, G. A., W. O. WETHERALL, AND K. STEARMAN
1983 *Japan's Minorities: Burakumin, Koreans, Ainu and Okinawans.* Report no. 3. London: Minority Rights Group.

DI LEONARDO, M., ED.
1990 *Toward an New Anthropology of Gender.* Berkeley: University of California Press.

DIVALE, W. T., AND M. HARRIS
1976 Population, Warfare, and the Male Supremacist Complex. *American Anthropologist* 78: 521–538.

DRAPER, P.
1975 !Kung Women: Contrasts in Sexual Egalitarianism in Foraging and Sedentary Contexts. In *Toward an Anthropology of Women,* ed. R. Reiter, pp. 77–109. New York: Monthly Review Press.

DURKHEIM, E.
1951 (orig. 1897). *Suicide: A Study in Sociology.* Glencoe, IL: Free Press.
1961 (orig. 1912). *The Elementary*

Forms of the Religious Life. New York: Collier Books.

DWYER, K.
1982 *Moroccan Dialogues: Anthropology in Question.* Baltimore: Johns Hopkins University Press.

EAGLETON, T.
1983 *Literary Theory: An Introduction.* Minneapolis: University of Minnesota Press.

EARLE, T.
1987 Chiefdoms in Archaeological and Ethnohistorical Perspective. *Annual Review of Anthropology* 16:279–308.

EASTMAN, C. M.
1975 *Aspects of Language and Culture.* San Francisco: Chandler and Sharp.

ECKERT, P.
1989 *Jocks and Burnouts: Social Categories and Identity in the High School.* New York: Teachers College Press, Columbia University.

ERLANGER, S.
1992 An Islamic Awakening in Central Asian Lands. *The New York Times* June 9, Section pp. A1, A7.

ERRINGTON, F., AND D. GEWERTZ
1987 *Cultural Alternatives and a Feminist Anthropology: An Analysis of Culturally Constructed Gender Interests in Papua New Guinea.* New York: Cambridge University Press.

ESCOBAR, A.
1991 Anthropology and the Development Encounter: The Making and Marketing of Development Anthropology. *American Ethnologist* 18:658–682.

EVANS-PRITCHARD, E. E.
1940 *The Nuer: A Description of the Modes of Livelihood and Political Institutions of a Nilotic People.* Oxford: Clarendon Press.
1970 Sexual Inversion among the Azande. *American Anthropologist* 72:1428–1433.

FAROOQ, M.
1966 Importance of Determining Transmission Sites in Planning Bilharziasis Control: Field Observations from the Egypt-49 Project Area. *American Journal of Epidemiology* 83:603–612.

FASOLD, R. W.
1990 *The Sociolinguistics of Language.* Oxford: Basil Blackwell.

FELD, S.
1991 Voices of the Rainforest. *Public Culture* 4(1):131–140.

FINKLER, K.
1985 *Spiritualist Healers in Mexico: Successes and Failures of Alternative Therapeutics.* South Hadley, MA: Bergin and Garvey.

FISKE, J.
1989 *Understanding Popular Culture.* Boston: Unwin Hyman.

FORD, C. S., AND F. A. BEACH
1951 *Patterns of Sexual Behavior.* New York: Harper Torchbooks.

FOSTER, G. M.
1965 Peasant Society and the Image of Limited Good. *American Anthropologist* 67:293–315.

FOSTER, G. M., AND B. G. ANDERSON
1978 *Medical Anthropology.* New York: McGraw-Hill.

FOUCAULT, M.
1979 *Discipline and Punish: The Birth of the Prison.* A. Sheridan (trans.). New York: Vintage Books.

FRAKE, C. O.
1961 The Diagnosis of Disease among the Subanun of Mindanao. *American Anthropologist* 63:113–132.

FRANKE, R.
1977 Miracle Seeds and Shattered Dreams in Java. In *Readings in Anthropology,* pp. 197–201. Guilford, CT: Dushkin.

FRICKE, T.
1994 *Himalayan Households: Tamang Demography and Domestic Processes,* 2d ed. New York: Columbia University Press.

FRIED, M. H.
1967   The Evolution of Political Society: An Essay in Political Anthropology. New York: McGraw-Hill.

FRIEDL, E.
1975   Women and Men: An Anthropologist's View. New York: Holt, Rinehart & Winston.

GAL, S.
1989   Language and Political Economy. Annual Review of Anthropology 18: 345–367.

GEERTZ, C.
1973   The Interpretation of Cultures. New York: Basic Books.

GEIS, M. L.
1987   The Language of Politics. New York: Springer-Verlag.

GIDDENS, A.
1973   The Class Structure of the Advanced Societies. New York: Cambridge University Press.

GILMORE, D.
1987   Aggression and Community: Paradoxes of Andalusian Culture. New Haven, CT: Yale University Press.

GOODENOUGH, W. H.
1953   Native Astronomy in the Central Carolines. Philadelphia: University of Pennsylvania Press.

GRAMSCI, A.
1971   Selections from the Prison Notebooks. Edited and translated by Quenten Hoare and Geoffrey Nowell Smith. London: Wishart.

GRASMUCK, S., AND P. PESSAR
1991   Between Two Islands: Dominican International Migration. Berkeley: University of California Press.

GRAY, J.
1986   With a Few Exceptions, Television in Africa Fails to Educate and Enlighten. Ann Arbor News, December 8.

GREEN, E. C.
1992   (orig. 1987) The Integration of Modern and Traditional Health Sectors in Swaziland. In Applying Anthropology, eds. A. Podolefsky and P. J. Brown, pp. 246–251. Mountain View, CA: Mayfield.

HARDING, S.
1975   Women and Words in a Spanish Village. In Toward an Anthropology of Women, ed. R. Reiter, pp. 283–308. New York: Monthly Review Press.

HARRIS, M.
1964   Patterns of Race in the Americas. New York: Walker.
1970   Referential Ambiguity in the Calculus of Brazilian Racial Identity. Southwestern Journal of Anthropology 26(1):1–14.
1974   Cows, Pigs, Wars, and Witches: The Riddles of Culture. New York: Random House.

HARRIS, M., AND C. P. KOTTAK
1963   The Structural Significance of Brazilian Racial Categories. Sociologia 25:203–209.

HART, C. W. M., AND A. R. PILLING
1960   The Tiwi of North Australia. New York: Holt, Rinehart & Winston.

HAWKES, K., J. O'CONNELL, AND K. HILL
1982   Why Hunters Gather: Optimal Foraging and the Aché of Eastern Paraguay. American Ethnologist 9:379–398.

HEADLAND, T. N., ED.
1992   The Tasaday Controversy: Assessing the Evidence. Washington, D.C.: American Anthropological Association.

HEADLAND, T. N., AND L. A. REID
1989   Hunter-Gatherers and Their Neighbors from Prehistory to the Present. Current Anthropology 30:43–66.

HENRY, J.
1955   Docility, or Giving Teacher What She Wants. Journal of Social Issues 2:33–41.

HERDT, G.
1981   Guardians of the Flutes. New York: McGraw-Hill.

1987   *Sambia: Ritual and Gender in New Guinea*. New York: Harcourt Brace.

HERRNSTEIN, R. J.
1971   I.Q. *The Atlantic* 228(3):43–64.

HERRNSTEIN, R. J., AND C. MURRAY
1994   *The Bell Curve: Intelligence and Class Structure in American Life*. New York: The Free Press.

HEYNEMAN, D.
1984   Development and Disease: A Dual Dilemma. *Journal of Parasitology* 70:3–17.

HILL, K., H. KAPLAN, K. HAWKES, AND A. HURTADO
1987   Foraging Decisions among Aché Hunter-gatherers: New Data and Implications for Optimal Foraging Models. *Ethology and Sociobiology* 8:1–36.

HILL-BURNETT, J.
1978   Developing Anthropological Knowledge through Application. In *Applied Anthropology in America*, eds. E. M. Eddy and W. L. Partridge, pp. 112–128. New York: Columbia University Press.

HOEBEL, E. A.
1954   *The Law of Primitive Man*. Cambridge, MA: Harvard University Press.
1968   (orig. 1954). The Eskimo: Rudimentary Law in a Primitive Anarchy. In *Studies in Social and Cultural Anthropology*, ed. J. Middleton, pp. 93–127. New York: Crowell.

HOPKINS, T., AND I. WALLERSTEIN
1982   Patterns of Development of the Modern World System. In *World System Analysis: Theory and Methodology*, by T. Hopkins, I. Wallerstein, R. Bach, C. Chase-Dunn, and R. Mukherjee, pp. 121–141. Thousand Oaks, CA: Sage.

INHORN, M. C., AND P. J. BROWN
1990   The Anthropology of Infectious Disease. *Annual Review of Anthropology* 19:89–117.

JENSEN, A.
1969   How Much Can We Boost I.Q. and Scholastic Achievement? *Harvard Educational Review* 29:1–123.

JOHNSON, A. W.
1978   *Quantification in Cultural Anthropology: An Introduction to Research Design*. Stanford, CA: Stanford University Press.

JOHNSON, A. W., AND T. EARLE
1987   *The Evolution of Human Societies: From Foraging Group to Agrarian State*. Stanford, CA: Stanford University Press.

KAN, S.
1986   The 19th-Century Tlingit Potlatch: A New Perspective. *American Ethnologist* 13:191–212.
1989   *Symbolic Immortality: The Tlingit Potlatch of the Nineteenth Century*. Washington, D.C.: Smithsonian Institution Press.

KELLY, R. C.
1976   Witchcraft and Sexual Relations: An Exploration in the Social and Semantic Implications of the Structure of Belief. In *Man and Woman in the New Guinea Highlands*, eds. P. Brown and G. Buchbinder, pp. 36–53. Special Publication, no. 8. Washington, D.C.: American Anthropological Association.

KENT, S.
1992   The Current Forager Controversy: Real Versus Ideal Views of Hunter-Gatherers. *Man* 27:45–70.

KENT, S., AND H. VIERICH
1989   The Myth of Ecological Determinism: Anticipated Mobility and Site Organization of Space. In *Farmers as Hunters: The Implications of Sedentism*, ed. S. Kent, pp. 96–130. New York: Cambridge University Press.

KINSEY, A. C., W. B. POMEROY, AND C. E. MARTIN
1948   *Sexual Behavior in the Human*

Male. Philadelphia: W. B. Saunders.

KLEINFELD, J.
1975   Positive Stereotyping: The Cultural Relativist in the Classroom. *Human Organization* 34: 269–274.

KLINEBERG, O.
1951   Race and Psychology. In *The Race Question in Modern Science.* Paris: UNESCO.

KOTTAK, C. P.
1980   *The Past in the Present: History, Ecology, and Social Organization in Highland Madagascar.* Ann Arbor: University of Michigan Press.
1990a   Culture and "Economic Development." *American Anthropologist* 93(3):723–731.
1990b   *Prime-Time Society: An Anthropological Analysis of Television and Culture.* Belmont, CA: Wadsworth.
1992   *Assault on Paradise: Social Change in a Brazilian Village,* 2d ed. New York: McGraw-Hill.

LABOV, W.
1972a   *Language in the Inner City: Studies in the Black English Vernacular.* Philadelphia: University of Pennsylvania Press.
1972b   *Sociolinguistic Patterns.* Philadelphia: University of Pennsylvania Press.

LAGUERRE, M.
1984   *American Odyssey: Haitians in New York.* Ithaca, NY: Cornell University Press.

LAKOFF, R.
1975   *Language and Woman's Place.* New York: Harper & Row.

LANCE, L. M., AND E. E. MCKENNA
1975   Analysis of Cases Pertaining to the Impact of Western Technology on the Non-Western World. *Human Organization* 34:87–94.

LARSON, A
1989   Social Context of Human Immunodeficiency Virus Transmission in Africa: Historical and Cultural Bases of East and Central African Sexual Relations. *Review of Infectious Diseases* 11: 716–731.

LEACH, E. R.
1955   Polyandry, Inheritance and the Definition of Marriage. *Man* 55:182–186.
1961   *Rethinking Anthropology.* London: Athlone Press.

LEE, R. B.
1974   (orig. 1968). What Hunters Do for a Living, or, How to Make Out on Scarce Resources. In *Man in Adaption: The Cultural Present,* 2d ed., ed. Y. A. Cohen, pp. 87–100. Chicago: Aldine.
1979   *The !Kung San: Men, Women, and Work in a Foraging Society.* New York: Cambridge University Press.
1984   *The Dobe !Kung.* New York: Harcourt Brace.

LEE, R. B., AND I. DEVORE, EDS.
1977   *Kalahari Hunter-Gatherers: Studies of the !Kung San and Their Neighbors.* Cambridge, MA: Harvard University Press.

LENSKI, G.
1966   *Power and Privilege: A Theory of Social Stratification.* New York: McGraw-Hill.

LÉVI-STRAUSS, C.
1963   *Totemism,* R. Needham (trans.). Boston: Beacon Press.
1967   *Structural Anthropology.* New York: Doubleday.
1969   (orig. 1949). *The Elementary Structures of Kinship.* Boston: Beacon Press.

LEWIS, P.
1992   U.N. Sees a Crisis in Overpopulation. *The New York Times,* p. A6.

LIEBAN, R. W.
1977   The Field of Medical Anthropology. In *Culture, Disease, and Healing: Studies in Medical An-*

thropology, ed. D. Landy, pp. 13–31. New York: Macmillan.

LIGHT, D., S. KELLER, AND C. CALHOUN
1994   Sociology, 6th ed. New York: McGraw-Hill.

LINDENBAUM, S.
1972   Sorcerers, Ghosts, and Polluting Women: An Analysis of Religious Belief and Population Control. Ethnology 11:241–253.

LINTON, R.
1943   Nativistic Movements. American Anthropologist 45:230–240.

LITTLE, K.
1965   West African Urbanization: A Study of Voluntary Associations in Social Change. Cambridge, England: Cambridge University Press.
1971   Some Aspects of African Urbanization South of the Sahara. Reading, MA: Addison-Wesley, McCaleb Modules in Anthropology.

LOWIE, R. H.
1935   The Crow Indians. New York: Farrar and Rinehart.

MALINOWSKI, B.
1961   (orig. 1922). Argonauts of the Western Pacific. New York: Dutton.
1978   (orig. 1931). The Role of Magic and Religion. In Reader in Comparative Religion: An Anthropological Approach, 4th ed., eds. W. A. Lessa and E. Z. Vogt, pp. 37–46. New York: Harper & Row.

MANNERS, R.
1973   (orig. 1956). Functionalism, Realpolitik and Anthropology in Underdeveloped Areas. American Indigena 16 (also in T. Weaver, gen. ed., pp. 113–126).

MARCUS, G. E., AND D. CUSHMAN.
1982   Ethnographies as Texts. Annual Review of Anthropology 11:25–69.

MARCUS, G. E., AND M. M. J. FISCHER.
1986   Anthropology as Cultural Critique: An Experimental Moment in the Human Sciences. Chicago: University of Chicago Press.

MARGOLIS, M.
1984   Mothers and Such: American Views of Women and How They Changed. Berkeley: University of California Press.
1994   Little Brazil: An Ethnography of Brazilian Immigrants in New York City. Princeton, NJ: Princeton University Press.

MARTIN, E.
1987   The Woman in the Body: A Cultural Analysis of Reproduction. Boston: Beacon Press.
1992   The End of the Body? American Ethnologist 19:121–140.

MARTIN, K., AND B. VOORHIES
1975   Female of the Species. New York: Columbia University Press.

MARTIN, P., AND E. MIDGLEY
1994   Immigration to the United States: Journey to an Uncertain Destination. Population Bulletin: 49(3): 1–47.

MARX, K., AND F. ENGELS
1976   (orig. 1948). Communist Manifesto. New York: Pantheon.

McDONALD, G.
1984   Carioca Fletch. New York: Warner Books.

MEAD, M.
1950   (orig. 1935). Sex and Temperament in Three Primitive Societies. New York: New American Library.

MICHAELS, E.
1986   Aboriginal Content. Paper presented at the meeting of the Australian Screen Studies Association. Sydney, December.

MILLER, N., AND R. C. ROCKWELL, EDS.
1988   AIDS in Africa: The Social and Policy Impact. Lewiston, NY: Edwin Mellen.

MINTZ, S.
1985   Sweetness and Power: The Place of Sugar in Modern History. New York: Viking Penguin.

MITCHELL, J. C.
  1966 Theoretical Orientations in African Urban Studies. In *The Social Anthropology of Complex Societies,* ed. M. Banton, pp. 37–68. London: Tavistock.

MOERMAN, M.
  1965 Ethnic Identification in a Complex Civilization: Who Are the Lue? *American Anthropologist* 67(5 Part I): 1215–1230.

MORGEN, S., ED.
  1989 *Gender and Anthropology: Critical Reviews for Research and Teaching.* Washington, D.C.: American Anthropological Association.

MUKHOPADHYAY, C., AND P. HIGGINS
  1988 Anthropological Studies of Women's Status Revisited: 1977–1987. *Annual Review of Anthropology* 17: 461–495.

MULLINGS, L., ED.
  1987 *Cities of the United States: Studies in Urban Anthropology.* New York: Columbia University Press.

MURDOCK, G. P.
  1934 *Our Primitive Contemporaries.* New York: Macmillan.
  1949 *Social Structure.* New York: Macmillan.
  1957 World Ethnographic Sample. *American Anthropologist* 59:664–687.

MURPHY, R. F., AND L. KASDAN
  1959 The Structure of Parallel Cousin Marriage. *American Anthropologist* 61:17–29.

MYDANS, S.
  1992*a* Criticism Grows over Aliens Seized during Riots. *The New York Times,* May 29, p. A8.
  1992*b* Judge Dismisses Case in Shooting by Officer. *The New York Times,* June 4, p. A8.

NASH, J., AND H. SAFA, EDS.
  1986 *Women and Change in Latin America.* South Hadley, MA: Bergin and Garvey.

NEW YORK TIMES
  1992 Alexandria Journal: TV Program for Somalis Is a Rare Unifying Force. 12/18/92.

NEWMAN, M.
  1992 Riots Bring Attention to Growing Hispanic Presence in South-Central Area. *The New York Times,* May 11, p. A10.

NIELSSON, G. P.
  1985 States and Nation-Groups: A Global Taxonomy. In *New Nationalisms of the Developed West,* ed. E. A. Tiryakian and R. Rogowski, pp. 27–56. Boston: G. Allen and Unwin.

ONG, A.
  1987 *Spirits of Resistance and Capitalist Discipline: Factory Women in Malaysia.* Albany: State University of New York Press.
  1989 Center, Periphery, and Hierarchy: Gender in Southeast Asia. In *Gender and Anthropology: Critical Reviews for Research and Teaching,* ed. S. Morgen, pp. 294–312. Washington, D.C.: American Anthropological Association.

PELETZ, M.
  1988 *A Share of the Harvest: Kinship, Property, and Social History among the Malays of Rembau.* Berkeley: University of California Press.

PELTO, P.
  1973 *The Snowmobile Revolution: Technology and Social Change in the Arctic.* Menlo Park, CA: Cummings.

PIDDOCKE, S.
  1969 The Potlatch System of the Southern Kwakiutl: A New Perspective. In *Environment and Cultural Behavior,* ed. A. P. Vayda, pp. 130–156. Garden City, N.Y.: Natural History Press.

POLANYI, K.
  1968 *Primitive, Archaic and Modern*

Economies: Essays of Karl Polanyi, ed. G. Dalton. Garden City, NY: Anchor Books.

POSPISIL, L.
1963 *The Kapauku Papuans of West New Guinea*. New York: Holt, Rinehart & Winston.

POTASH, B., ED.
1986 *Widows in African Societies: Choices and Constraints*. Stanford, CA: Stanford University Press.

PRICE, R., ED.
1973 *Maroon Societies*. New York: Anchor Press/Doubleday.

RADCLIFFE-BROWN, A. R.
1965 (orig. 1962). *Structure and Function in Primitive Society*. New York: Free Press.

RAPPAPORT, R. A.
1974 Obvious Aspects of Ritual. *Cambridge Anthropology* 2:2–60.

REDFIELD, R.
1941 *The Folk Culture of Yucatan*. Chicago: University of Chicago Press.

REDFIELD, R., R. LINTON, AND M. HERSKOVITS
1936 Memorandum on the Study of Acculturation. *American Anthropologist* 38:149–152.

REITER, R.
1975 Men and Women in the South of France: Public and Private Domains. In *Toward an Anthropology of Women*, ed. R. Reiter, pp. 252–282. New York: Monthly Review Press.

ROBERTSON, J.
1992 Koreans in Japan. Paper presented at the University of Michigan Department of Anthropology, Martin Luther King Jr. Day Panel, January 1992. Ann Arbor: University of Michigan Department of Anthropology (unpublished).

ROMER, A. S.
1960 *Man and the Vertebrates*, 3d ed., vol. 1. Harmondsworth, England: Penguin, 1960.

ROSALDO, M. Z.
1980a *Knowledge and Passion: Notions of Self and Social Life*. Stanford: Stanford University Press.
1980b The Use and Abuse of Anthropology: Reflections on Feminism and Cross-Cultural Understanding. *Signs* 5(3):389–417.

ROUSE, R.
1991 Mexican Migration and the Social Space of Postmodernism. *Diaspora* 1(1):8–23.

ROYAL ANTHROPOLOGICAL INSTITUTE
1951 *Notes and Queries on Anthropology*, 6th ed. London: Rutledge and Kegan Paul.

RYAN, S.
1990 *Ethnic Conflict and International Relations* (1990) Brookfield, MA: Dartmouth.

SAHLINS, M. D.
1961 The Segmentary Lineage: An Organization of Predatory Expansion. *American Anthropologist* 63:322–345.
1968 *Tribesmen*. Englewood Cliffs, NJ: Prentice-Hall.
1972 *Stone Age Economics*. Chicago: Aldine.

SANDAY, P. R.
1974 Female Status in the Public Domain. In *Woman, Culture, and Society*, ed. M. Z. Rosaldo and L. Lamphere, pp. 189–206. Stanford, CA: Stanford University Press.

SANTINO, J.
1983 Night of the Wandering Souls, *Natural History*, vol. 92, no. 10.

SAPIR, E.
1931 Conceptual Categories in Primitive Languages. *Science* 74:578–584.

SCHAEFER, R., AND R. P. LAMM
1992 *Sociology*, 4th ed. New York: McGraw-Hill.

SCHIEFFELIN, E.
1976 *The Sorrow of the Lonely and the Burning of the Dancers*. New York: St. Martin's.

SCOTT, J. C.
1985 *Weapons of the Weak.* New Haven, CT: Yale University Press.
1990 *Domination and the Arts of Resistance.* New Haven, CT: Yale University Press.

SCUDDER, T., AND E. COLSON
1980 *Secondary Education and the Formation of an Elite: The Impact of Education on Gwembe District, Zambia.* London: Academic Press.

SERVICE, E. R.
1962 *Primitive Social Organization: An Evolutionary Perspective.* New York: McGraw-Hill.
1966 *The Hunters.* Englewood Cliffs, NJ: Prentice-Hall.

SHANNON, T. R.
1989 *An Introduction to the World System Perspective.* Boulder, CO: Westview.

SHOSTAK, M.
1981 *Nisa: The Life and Words of a !Kung Woman.* Cambridge, MA: Harvard University Press.

SILBERBAUER, G.
1981 *Hunter and Habitat in the Central Kalahari Desert.* New York: Cambridge University Press.

SLADE, M.
1984 Displaying Affection in Public. *New York Times,* December 17.

SOLWAY, J., AND R. LEE
1990 Foragers, Genuine and Spurious: Situating the Kalahari San in History (with CA treatment). *Current Anthropology* 31(2): 109–146.

STATISTICAL ABSTRACT OF THE UNITED STATES
1991 111th ed. Washington, D.C.: U.S. Bureau of the Census, U.S. Government Printing Office.

STEVENS, W. K.
1992 Humanity Confronts Its Handiwork: An Altered Planet. *The New York Times,* May 5, pp. B5–B7.

STEWARD, J. H.
1955 *Theory of Culture Change.* Urbana: University of Illinois Press.

STOLER, A.
1977 Class Structure and Female Autonomy in Rural Java. *Signs* 3:74–89.

STRATHERN, M.
1988 *The Gender of the Gift: Problems with Women and Problems with Society in Melanesia.* Berkeley: University of California Press.

SWIFT, M.
1963 Men and Women in Malay Society. In *Women in the New Asia,* ed. B. Ward, pp. 268–286. Paris: UNESCO.

TANAKA, J.
1980 *The San Hunter-Gatherers of the Kalahari.* Tokyo: University of Tokyo Press.

TANNER, N.
1974 Matrifocality in Indonesia and Africa and among Black Americans. In *Women, Culture, and Society,* eds. M. Z. Rosaldo and L. Lamphere, pp. 129–156. Stanford, CA: Stanford University Press.

THOMPSON, W.
1983 Introduction: World System with and without the Hyphen. In *Contending Approaches to World System Analysis,* ed. W. Thompson, pp. 7–26. Thousand Oaks, CA: Sage.

TOFFLER, A.
1980 *The Third Wave.* New York: William Morrow.

TONER, R.
1992 Los Angeles Riots Are a Warning, Americans Fear. *The New York Times,* May 11, pp. A1, A11.

TURNBULL, C.
1965 *Wayward Servants: The Two Worlds of the African Pygmies.* Garden City, NY: Natural History Press.

TURNER, V. W.
1974 (orig. 1969). *The Ritual Process.* Harmondsworth, England: Penguin.

TYLOR, E. B.
1889 On a Method of Investigating the Development of Institutions: Applied to Laws of Marriage and Descent. *Journal of the Royal Anthropological Institute* 18:245–269.
1958 (orig. 1871). *Primitive Culture.* New York: Harper Torchbooks.

VIOLA, H. J., AND C. MARGOLIS
1991 *Seeds of Change: Five Hundred Years since Columbus, a Quincentennial Commemoration.* Washington, D.C.: Smithsonian Institution Press.

WAGLEY, C. W.
1968 (orig. 1959). The Concept of Social Race in the Americas. In C. Wagley, *The Latin American Tradition,* pp. 155–174. New York: Columbia University Press.

WALLACE, A. F. C.
1956 Revitalization Movements. *American Anthropologist* 58:264–281.
1966 *Religion: An Anthropological View.* New York: McGraw-Hill.
1970 *The Death and Rebirth of the Seneca.* New York: Knopf.

WALLERSTEIN, I.
1982 The Rise and Future Demise of the World Capitalist System: Concepts for Comparative Analysis. In *Introduction to the Sociology of "Developing Societies,"* eds. H. Alavi and T. Shanin, pp. 29–53. New York: Monthly Review Press.

WATSON, P.
1972 Can Racial Discrimination Affect IQ? In *Race and Intelligence; The Fallacies Behind the Race-IQ Controversy,* eds. K. Richardson and D. Spears, pp. 56–67. Baltimore: Penguin.

WEBER, M.
1958 (orig. 1904). *The Protestant Ethic and the Spirit of Capitalism.* New York: Scribner's.
1968 (orig. 1922). *Economy and Society.* E. Fischoff et al. (trans.). New York: Bedminster Press.

WHITE, L. A.
1959 *The Evolution of Culture: The Development of Civilization to the Fall of Rome.* New York: McGraw-Hill.

WHORF, B. L.
1956 A Linguistic Consideration of Thinking in Primitive Communities. In *Language, Thought, and Reality: Selected Writings of Benjamin Lee Whorf,* ed. J. B. Carroll, pp. 65–86. Cambridge, MA: MIT Press.

WILLIAMS, B.
1989 A CLASS ACT: Anthropology and the Race to Nation across Ethnic Terrain. *Annual Review of Anthropology* 18:401–444.

WILMSEN, E.
1989 *Land Filled with Flies: A Political Economy of the Kalahari.* Chicago: University of Chicago Press.

WOLF, E. R.
1966 *Peasants.* Englewood Cliffs, NJ: Prentice-Hall.
1982 *Europe and the People without History.* Berkeley: University of California Press.

WORLD ALMANAC & BOOK OF FACTS
1992 New York: Newspaper Enterprise Association.

YETMAN, N.
1991 *Majority and Minority: The Dynamics of Race and Ethnicity in American Life,* 5th ed. Boston: Allyn and Bacon.

Acknowledgments

Photo Credits

4: Robert Phillips/Image Bank. **7:** Yoram Kahana/Peter Arnold. **13:** American Folkline Center/Library of Congress. **16:** John Coletti/Picture Cube. **23:** (left) Howard Dratch/Image Works; (right) Jeffrey L. Rotman/Peter Arnold. **29:** (top) H. Armstrong Roberts; (bottom) Rick Reinhard/Impact Visuals. **40:** Abbas/Magnum. **44:** Alain Buu/Gamma-Liaison. **53:** Alexandra Avakian/Woodfin Camp. **59:** Donna Binder/Impact Visuals. **63:** P. J. Griffiths/Magnum. **69:** David Madison/Duomo. **78:** Bruno Barbey/Magnum. **81:** David Hiser. **83:** Burt Glinn/Magnum. **84:** Spencer Grant/Picture Cube. **93:** David Alan Harvey/Woodfin Camp. **96:** Sylvain Grandadam/Photo Researchers. **99:** (top) Thierry Secretan/Cosmos/Woodfin Camp; (bottom) Michael J. Minardi/Peter Arnold. **110:** Steve McCurry/Magnum. **114:** Victor Englebert. **115:** Martha Cooper/Peter Arnold. **119:** (top) Victor Englebert; (bottom) Bill Gillette/Stock, Boston. **143:** Burt Glinn/Magnum. **147:** Dr. J. F. E. Bloss/Anthro-Photo. **150:** Douglas Kirkland/Image Bank. **153:** Photo by R. H. Beck. Courtesy Department of Library Services, American Museum of Natural History. **173:** Terry Gydesen/Impact Visuals. **176:** Lila Abu-Lughod/Anthro-Photo. **182:** Thomas L. Kelly. **188:** *Amiga TV Tudo* magazine, Rio de Janiero, Brazil, 1/26/90. **191:** Michael Peletz, Hamilton, NY. **195:** George Holton/Photo Researchers. **199:** Martha Cooper/Peter Arnold. **212:** Picture Collection, New York Public Library. **213:** Culver Pictures. **226:** Robert Caputo/Stock, Boston. **227:** Peter Frey/Image Bank. **232:** Peggy/Yoram Kahana/Peter Arnold. **240:** Andrea Brizzi/Stock Market. **244:** John Moss/Photo Researchers. **246:** Dr. Steven Lansing. **255:** M. Gunther/BIOS/Peter Arnold. **261:** Rob Crandall/Stock, Boston. **265:** Eli Reed/Magnum.

Illustration Credits

Figure 3-2: Figure 3 from Philip Martin and Elizabeth Midgley, "Immigration to the United States: Journey to an Uncertain Destination," *Population Bulletin*, vol. 49, no. 2 (Washington, D.C.: Population Reference Bureau, September 1994), p. 9. Reprinted by permission. **Table 4-1:** Table from Felicity Barringer, "New Census Data Show More Children Living in Poverty," *The New York Times*, May 29, 1992, p. A12. Copyright © 1992 by The New York Times Company. Reprinted by permission. **Figure 5-1:** Figure 3-1 (p. 44) and excerpt (p. 42) from Dwight Bolinger, *Aspects of Language*, Second Edition (Harcourt Brace, 1975). Copyright © 1975 by Harcourt Brace & Company. Reproduced by permission of the publisher. **Table 6-1:** Table adapted from Victor W. Turner, *The Ritual Process* (Aldine de Gruyter, 1969). Copyright © 1969 by Victor W. Turner. Reprinted by permission of Aldine de Gruyter, New York. **Figure 8-3:** Two figures from E. E. Evans-Pritchard, *The Nuer: A Description of the Modes of Livelihood and Political Institutions of a Nilotic People* (Oxford: Clarendon Press, 1940). Reprinted by permission of Oxford University Press. **Table 10-1:** Table 13-1 from K. Martin and B. Voorhies, *Female of the Species* (Columbia University Press, 1975), p. 283. Copyright © 1975 by Columbia University Press. Reprinted with permission of the publisher. **Table 11-1:** Table from Thomas Richard Shannon, *An Introduction to the World-System Perspective* (Westview Press, 1989), p. 130. Reprinted by permission of Westview Press, Boulder, Colorado. **Figure 11-1:** Two maps from Thomas Richard Shannon, *An Introduction to the World-System Perspective* (Westview Press, 1989), pp. 84, 100. Reprinted by permission of Westview Press, Boulder, Colorado. **Table 11-2:** Table from John H. Bodley, *Anthropology and Contemporary Human Problems* (Mayfield Publishing, 1985). Reprinted by permission of the publisher.

INDEX